GLOBAL
GENDER ISSUES

DILEMMAS IN WORLD POLITICS

Series Editor
George A. Lopez, University of Notre Dame

Dilemmas in World Politics offers teachers and students of international relations a series of quality books on critical issues, trends, and regions in international politics. Each text examines a "real world" dilemma and is structured to cover the historical, theoretical, practical, and projected dimensions of its subject.

EDITORIAL BOARD

FORTHCOMING TITLES

Sarah Tisch and Michael Wallace
**Dilemmas of Development Assistance:
The What, Why, and Who of Foreign Aid**

□ □ □

Bruce E. Moon
International Trade in the 1990s

□ □ □

Ted Robert Gurr and Barbara Harff
Ethnic Conflict in World Politics

□ □ □

Frederic S. Pearson
The Spread of Arms in the International System

GLOBAL
GENDER ISSUES

■ ■ ■

V. Spike Peterson
UNIVERSITY OF ARIZONA

Anne Sisson Runyan
STATE UNIVERSITY OF NEW YORK–POTSDAM

Westview Press
BOULDER □ SAN FRANCISCO □ OXFORD

To our sisters,
for all that we share

Dilemmas in World Politics Series

Cover photos: (*left*) UNHCR/S. Errington; (*center top*) Anne Sisson Runyan; (*center bottom*) Gary Massoni/AFSC; (*right*) Amnesty International

Published in 1993 in the United States of America by Westview Press, Inc., 5500 Central Avenue, Boulder, Colorado 80301-2877, and in the United Kingdom by Westview Press, 36 Lonsdale Road, Summertown, Oxford OX2 7EW

Library of Congress Cataloging-in-Publication Data
Peterson, V. Spike.
Global gender issues / V. Spike Peterson, Anne Sisson Runyan.
      p.   cm.—(Dilemmas in world politics)
   Includes bibliographical references (p.   ) and index.
   ISBN 0-8133-1309-0. — ISBN 0-8133-1310-4 (pbk)
   1. Women in politics.   2. World politics—20th century.
I. Runyan, Anne Sisson.   II. Title.   III. Series.
HQ1236.P45   1993
305.42—dc20   93-24881
                                                                                    CIP

Printed and bound in the United States of America

      The paper used in this publication meets the requirements
(∞) of the American National Standard for Permanence of Paper
      for Printed Library Materials Z39.48-1984.

10   9   8   7   6   5   4   3

Contents

□ □ □   **1 Introduction:**
      The Gender of World Politics   **1**

How Lenses Work, 1
Why Global? 3
Why Gender? 5
Why Issues? 10
The Immediacy and Import of Global
   Gender Issues, 11
Notes About This Text, 13
Mapping the Book, 14

□ □ □   **2 Gender as a Lens on World Politics**   **17**

The Social Construction of Gender
   and Gender Hierarchy, 19
The Gendered Who, What, and How
   of World Politics, 29
Gendered Divisions of World Politics, 33
Conclusion, 40

□ □ □   **3 Gendered Divisions of Power**   **45**

Women as State Actors, 46
How and Why Are These Women Rendered
   Invisible? 51
Why So Few? 58
How Do Women Get to the Top? 68
What Are the Gender Consequences of
   Women in Power? 69

□ □ □

Tables and Illustrations

Tables

Boxes

Figures

Cartoons

□ □ □

Acknowledgments

Venturing into new terrain requires vision as well as commitment. Our thanks go first to George Lopez, the series editor, for recognizing the importance of gender as a dilemma in world politics. Jennifer Knerr's professional guidance and personal warmth were invaluable for keeping not only our efforts but also our enthusiasm on track. Of the many other people at Westview who eased our task, and editorial board members who supported our project, we thank especially Marian Safran, Libby Barstow, Deborah Gerner, and Karen Mingst. From start to finish, the farsightedness and expertise of Lev Gonick and Mary Ann Tetreault have enhanced this project and its product.

Exploring new terrain requires bold spirits and reliable support systems. Among the bold spirits, we thank our foremothers, who took great risks to clear new paths, and our feminist colleagues, who also take risks in order to pursue and expand those paths. Our support system is the global community of feminists who refuse to separate theory and practice. Of the countless women and men who make up this community, we thank especially our friends in the Feminist Theory and Gender Studies section of the International Studies Association, who have given us invaluable support, encouragement—and permission to party. In particular, because the integrity of their energy makes such an important difference, we acknowledge our appreciation of Simona Sharoni, Theresa Scionti, and Judy Logan.

More personally, Anne thanks her secretary, Jackie Brisson, and her student assistants, Michele Sylvestri and Mary Burns, for their tremendous assistance with research, photocopying, mailings, and tracking down addresses and phone numbers (mostly of illustration copyright holders, many of whom were very gracious and helpful). It was, indeed, an all-women struggle at SUNY–Potsdam that brought Anne's part of the book to fruition. She also thanks her husband, Al Kanters, who, as always, lovingly cared for her basic needs throughout this project. It is the reproductive work of men like him that makes the productive work of women possible. She is also grateful to family members, friends, and colleagues, close by and far away, who have so strongly supported her feminist ideals and her feminist work. Finally, she offers her heartfelt appreciation to

xii □ Acknowledgments

Spike, who has been not only an intellectual partner but a dear friend and true "sister."

Spike leaned heavily on the research assistance and emotional support so effectively rendered by graduate students Stacey Mayhall, Jacqui True, and Anwara Begum. Words only begin to convey how the community generated during the states seminar has enhanced Spike's quality of life. She is indebted to this group especially—and students more generally— because they not only make the hard work worthwhile but also keep her mentally and physically dancing. "It doesn't get any better than this." Her deepest thanks, as ever, go to family and friends whose love, affirmation, and inspiration keep her going—and growing; to those whose ways of being, loving, and knowing offer a lighted path: thanks especially to beryl, eva, rosie, and ozone. Finally, she wants to let Anne know that the best part of this project, like their friendship, was/is learning to love better, for which Anne gets the credit.

V. Spike Peterson
Anne Sisson Runyan

□ □ □

Acronyms

AAWORD	African Association of Women for Research and Development
AMNLAE	Luisa Amanda Espinosa Nicaraguan Women's Association
AMPRONAC	Association of Nicaraguan Women Confronting the Nation's Problems
B-WAC	Brooklyn Welfare Action Council
CDS	Sandinista Defense Committees
CEDAW	Convention on the Elimination of All Forms of Discrimination Against Women
CEO	chief executive officer
DAWN	Development Alternatives with Women for a New Era
EPS	Sandinista People's Army
EPZ	export-processing zone
FLS	Forward-Looking Strategies for the Advancement of Women
FSLN	Sandinista National Liberation Front
GDP	gross domestic product
IFAD	International Fund for Agricultural Development
IGO	intergovernmental organization
IMF	International Monetary Fund
IR	international relations
ISIS/WICCE	Women's International Information and Communication Service
MNC	multinational corporation
MPS	Sandinista Popular Militias
NAFTA	North American Free Trade Agreement
NGO	nongovernmental organization
OPEC	Organization of Petroleum Exporting Countries
PR	proportional representation
SEWA	Self-Employed Women's Association
TNC	transnational corporation
UK	United Kingdom
UN	United Nations

UNCED	United Nations Conference on Environment and Development
UNDP	United Nations Development Programme
UNFPA	United Nations Fund for Population Activities
UNIFEM	United Nations Development Fund for Women
UNSNA	United Nations System of National Accounts
USAID	U.S. Agency for International Development
WAND	Women and Development Unit
WID	Women in Development
WPP	Woman's Peace Party

ONE

□ □ □

Introduction: The Gender of World Politics

In this text, we explore how world politics looks when viewed through a **gender-sensitive lens.** The latter enables us to "see" how the world is shaped by gendered concepts, practices, and institutions. To introduce the text—and establish its significance to international relations—we first consider the metaphor of lenses: How do lenses focus our vision and filter what we "know"? How does this focusing and filtering shape our lived experience—what we think of as "reality"—and our understanding of it? We then take each of the terms in our title, *Global Gender Issues,* and answer the questions: Why global? Why gender? Why issues? We also clarify why global gender issues, which have not traditionally been a focus of analysis, are important to the study of world politics *now.* Finally, we identify some assumptions made in this text and outline the chapters to follow.

HOW LENSES WORK

Whenever we study a topic, we do so through a lens that necessarily focuses our attention in particular ways. By "ordering" what we look at, each lens enables us to see some things in greater detail or more accurately or in better relation to certain other things. But this is unavoidably at the expense of seeing other things that are rendered out of focus—filtered out—by each particular lens.

According to Paul Viotti and Mark Kauppi, "images" of international politics contain certain assumptions and lead us "to ask certain questions, seek certain types of answers, and use certain methodological tools."[1] For

1

example, different images act as lenses and shape our assumptions about who are the significant actors (individuals? states? multinational corporations?), what are their attributes (rationality? self-interest? power?), how are social processes categorized (politics? cooperation? dependence?), and what outcomes are desirable (peace? national security? global equity?).

The images or lenses we use have important consequences because they structure what we look for and are able to "see." In Patrick Morgan's words, "our conception of [IR acts as a] map for directing our attention and distributing our efforts, and using the wrong map can lead us into a swamp instead of taking us to higher ground."[2]

What we look for depends a great deal on how we make sense of, or "order," our experience. We learn our ordering systems in a variety of contexts. From early childhood on, we are taught to make distinctions enabling us to perform appropriately within a particular culture. As college students, we are taught the distinctions appropriate to particular disciplines (psychology, anthropology, political science) and particular schools of thought within them (realism, behavioralism, structuralism). No matter in which context we learned them, the categories and ordering frameworks shape the lens through which we look at, think about, and make sense of the world around us. At the same time, the lens we adopt shapes our experience of the world itself because it shapes what we do and how and why we do it. For example, a political science lens focuses our attention on particular categories and events (the meaning of power, democracy, or elections) in ways that variously influence our behavior (questioning authority, protesting abuse of power, or participating in electoral campaigns).

By filtering our ways of thinking about and ordering experience, the categories and images we rely on shape how we behave and thus the world we live in: They have concrete consequences. We observe this readily in the case of self-fulfilling prophecies: If we *expect* hostility, our own behavior (acting superior, displaying power) may elicit responses (defensive posturing, aggression) that we then interpret as "confirming" our expectations.

In general, as long as our lens and images seem to "work," we keep them and build on them. Lenses simplify our thinking. Like maps, they "frame" our choices and exploration, enabling us to take advantage of knowledge already gained and to move more effectively toward our objectives. The more useful they appear to be, the more we are inclined to take them for granted and to resist making major changes in them. We forget that our particular ordering or meaning system is a choice among many alternatives. Instead, we tend to believe we are seeing "reality" as it "*is*" rather than as our culture or discipline interprets or "maps" reality. It is difficult and sometimes unpleasant to reflect critically on our assumptions, to question their accuracy or desirability, and to explore the implications of adopting a different lens.

Of course, the world we live in and therefore our experiences are constantly changing; we have to continuously modify our images, mental maps, and ordering systems as well. The required shift in lens may be minor: from liking one type of music to liking another, from being a high school student in a small town to being a college student in an urban environment. Or the shift may be more pronounced: from casual dating to parenting, from the freedom of student life-styles to the assumption of full-time job responsibilities, from Newtonian to quantum mechanics, from East-West rivalry to post–cold war complexities. More dramatic shifts occur as we experience and respond to radical or systemic transformations, such as economic recession, environmental degradation, or the effects of war.

To function effectively as students and scholars of world politics, we must modify our thinking in line with historical developments. That is, as "reality" changes, our ways of understanding or ordering need to change as well. This is especially the case to the extent that outdated worldviews or lenses place us in danger, distort our understanding, or lead us away from our objectives.

WHY GLOBAL?

In textbooks on world politics, the history of international relations (IR) has two interrelated dimensions. On the one hand, actual world events are identified as the "substance"—the *what*—of IR. Examples include: the formation of European states since the Peace of Westphalia, the wars between nation-states that shift boundaries and shape international power dynamics, and the economic and technological developments that affect interactions between states. On the other hand, the history of IR refers to the development of the academic discipline itself, that is, *how* we study or think about the "what" of IR. This second dimension is about what framework, image, or lens is used to make sense of the events and institutions that we are studying. Typically, textbooks present images of IR or schools of thought as they have appeared in the historical development of the discipline (e.g., idealism, realism, pluralism). It is important to remember that the "what" and the "how" of IR are not separable but rather two interacting dimensions of what we call IR. We use the word *interacting* to mean not only that concrete events shape how we think but also that our frameworks—how we think about the real world—shape our behaviors, with concrete consequences for the real world of actors and events.

Developments in the discipline of IR exemplify this interaction of changing events and frameworks. The "what" of IR after World War II included East-West blocs, bipolar economic and military rivalry, expanded militarization, and a U.S.-based capitalist world economy. The dominant IR lens, realism, made sense of these events by identifying states, acting as unitary and rational decision-makers in pursuit of the national interest, as the primary units of analysis. The national interest was defined as national security (maintaining state sovereignty), which could be achieved most effectively by manipulations of power (understood as material attributes enabling military success).

In contrast, the "what" of IR in the 1970s included increasingly powerful multinational, or transnational, corporations (MNCs, or TNCs), many new Third World states, a U.S. defeat in Vietnam, energy issues raised by the Organization of Petroleum Exporting Countries (OPEC) power, and transformations in the global economic system. As international relations responded to and shaped these historical developments, the images of IR were altered and expanded. International relations analysts increasingly recognized the significance of nonstate and interstate actors as well as the complexity of states as actors. They asked new questions about whether states were unitary decision-makers and focused more on the multiple actors and agencies determining foreign policy. The U.S. defeat in Vietnam confirmed that military power alone could not determine victory. Analysts questioned existing categories and frameworks as they sought more accurate descriptions and more useful explanations. Previous images were adjusted and new images emerged to make better sense of changes taking place on the stage of world politics.

As images and frameworks were adjusted, different issues, actors, and processes gained visibility. Domestic bureaucratic politics were revealed as significant factors in foreign policy decision-making. The role of misperceptions in decision-making by national leaders became a focus of inquiry. Increased Third World voices in the General Assembly of the United Nations (UN) focused attention on the relationships between prosperity of the North and underdevelopment of the South. Regimes analysis explored how states in fact cooperate even without reference to governmental structures.

The world of the 1990s confirms the need to rethink categories and frameworks as we pursue new understandings that "match" new world politics. For example, both decentralization—marked by subnationalist movements—and centralization processes—exemplified by the European Economic Community—challenge conventional accounts of sovereign states. The demise of the former Soviet Union disrupts decades of East-West analysis. Global crises of nuclearism, economic maldevelopment, and environmental degradation cannot be addressed by state-centric decision-making. And in response to global crises, social movements around the world demand more than the absence of war: People are raising deeper questions about the nature of power, the abuse of human rights, the human costs of global inequities, and the meaning of a just world order.

Consistent with trends in IR thinking that recognize the limitations of state-centric analyses, the reference to global in our title points not simply to the actions of states or between states but to how those actions are embedded in *global* processes. The global focus does not exclude states or minimize their political power but includes more than interstate actions. As current events suggest, it is not only state power but also *global* political, military, economic, and social processes that are the "what" of today's "real world." To study this "what" effectively requires a global lens.

WHY GENDER?

The data regarding how men and women are situated differently within global processes reveals, starkly, the extent of gender inequality. Women compose one-half of the world's population and perform two-thirds of the world's work hours, yet are everywhere poorer in resources and poorly represented in positions of decision-making power (see Figure 1.1). Although systematic inequalities between men and women are made vividly clear through these statistics, the important question in this text is how this inequality is relevant to the study of world politics.

Unlike **sex** (the biological distinction between males and females), **gender** refers to socially learned behavior and expectations that distinguish between masculinity and femininity. Whereas biological sex identity is determined by reference to genetic and anatomical characteristics, socially learned gender is an acquired identity. We *learn*, through culturally specific socialization, how to be masculine and feminine and to assume the identities of men and women. In fact, the socialization dimension is so powerful that apparently unequivocal gender identities are formed even when biological sex is unclear (hermaphroditism) or mistaken (when the absence of a penis on a genetically male infant leads to a false identification as female).[3]

The extent of inequality between men and women and the specific attributes of masculinity and femininity vary dramatically over time and across cultures. Men are not exclusively leaders and warriors, and women are not exclusively in charge of maintaining the home and caring for children. What appears fairly constant throughout the historical record,[4] however, is the relationship between masculinity and femininity. Two points are important in regard to this relationship (we explore gender as a lens more thoroughly in Chapter 2). First, masculinity and femininity are

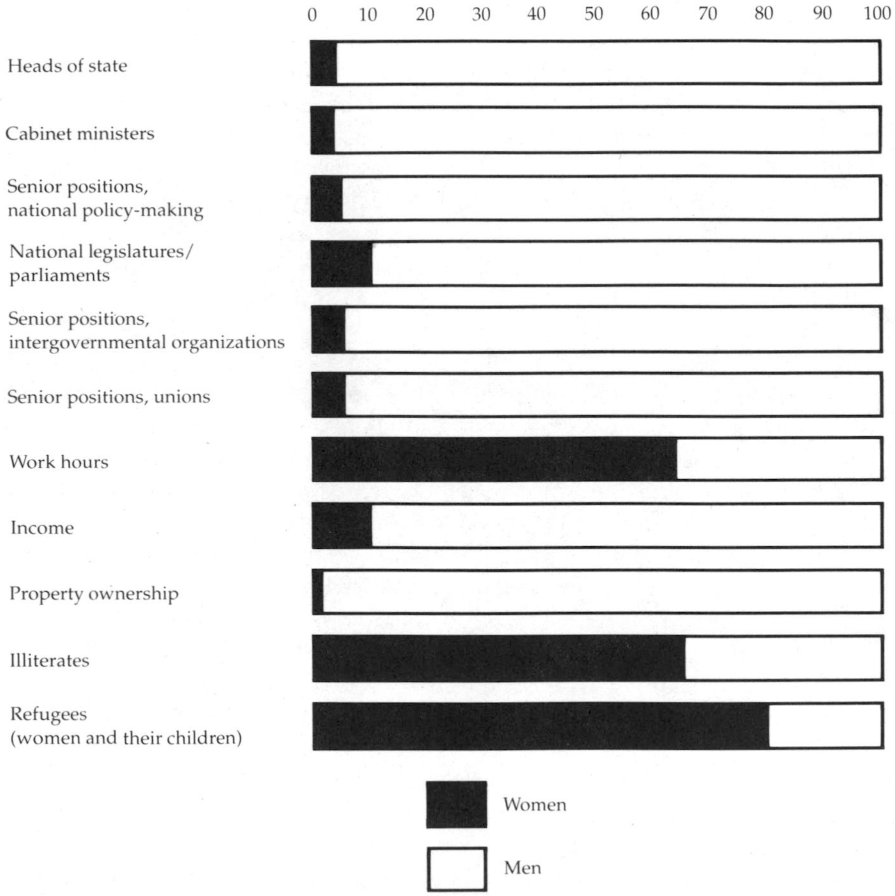

6

	0	10	20	30	40	50	60	70	80	90	100

Heads of state

Cabinet ministers

Senior positions,
national policy-making

National legislatures/
parliaments

Senior positions,
intergovernmental organizations

Senior positions, unions

Work hours

Income

Property ownership

Illiterates

Refugees
(women and their children)

■ Women

□ Men

FIGURE 1.1   Global gender inequality. Percentages respectively women and men in various important categories. *Sources:* Data from United Nations, *The World's Women: 1970–1990 Trends and Statistics* (New York, 1991); Ruth Leger Sivard, *Women ... A World Survey* (Washington, D.C.: World Priorities, 1985); United Nations, Division for the Advancement of Women, "Women and Decision-Making," EGM/EPPDM/1989/WP.1/Rev.1 (Vienna: United Nations, 1989); Joni Seager and Ann Olson, *Women in the World: An International Atlas* (New York: Simon & Schuster, 1986).

not independent categories, such as fruit, children, labor, but are defined in oppositional relation to each other: more of one is less of the other—as in ripe versus unripe fruit, active versus passive children, mental versus manual labor. Specifically, the dominant masculinity in Western culture is associated with qualities of rationality, "hardheadedness," ambition, and strength. To the extent that a man displays emotionality, "softheadedness," passivity, and weakness, he is likely to be identified as non-masculine, which is to say, feminine. Similarly, women who appear hard-headed and ambitious are often described as masculine.

Second, the relationship between masculinity and femininity shows constancy in assigning greater value to that which is associated with masculinity and lesser value to that which is associated with femininity. Again, the terms are not independent but form a hierarchical (unequal) relation that we refer to as a dichotomy (we clarify this term in Chapter 2). Thus, in most situations rationality, hardheadedness, ambition, and strength are perceived as positive and admired traits that are in contrast to less desirable feminine qualities. This hierarchy is readily observed. Consider (in the United States) how differently we respond to women wearing pants and even business suits compared to our response to men wearing dresses, ruffles, or flowery prints. Similarly, girls can be tomboys and adopt boyish names but boys avoid behaving in ways that might result in their being called sissies or girlish names. And we applaud women who achieve success in previously male-dominated activities (climbing mountains, becoming astronauts, presiding over colleges), but men who enter traditionally female arenas (water ballet, child care, nursing) are rarely applauded and often treated with suspicion. Females dressing or acting like males appear to be copying or aiming for something valued—they are attempting to improve their status by "moving up." Because feminine characteristics are less valued, boys and men who adopt feminine dress or undertake female roles are more likely to be perceived as "failing" in their manhood or, in fact, "moving down."

Because of the interdependent nature of this relationship, when we study gender we learn about both men *and* women. When we look at activities associated with masculinity (e.g., team sports, politics, military), it appears simply that men are present and women are absent. Moreover, it appears that we can explain what is going on simply by attending to the men engaging in these activities. Gender analysis helps us understand how this presence-absence dynamic occurs and offers a more comprehensive explanation; it enables us to "see" how women are in fact an important part of the picture even though they are obscured when we focus on the men. Through a gender-sensitive lens, we see how constructions of masculinity are not independent of, but dependent upon, opposing constructions of femininity. In a sense, the presence of men depends on the absence of women. Because of this interdependence, a gender analysis of women's lives and experiences does not simply "add something" about women but *transforms* what we know about *men* and the activities they undertake.

Gender shapes not only how we identify ourselves but also how others identify and relate to us and how we are positioned within social structures. For now, we will look at gender divisions of labor as exemplifying this either-or construction, the dichotomy, of masculine and feminine. Consider that women are traditionally associated with childbearing, child rearing, emotional caretaking, and responsibility for the physical maintenance of the household. In contrast, men are associated with the activities of wage labor, physical prowess, intellectual achievements, and political agency. This gender labeling is so strong that even though women increasingly participate in the paid labor force, they tend to do so in areas regarded as "women's work": taking care of others and providing emotional and maintenance services (counseling, welfare services, clerical support, cleaning).

Labor markets are thus segregated horizontally by gender, with women and men clustered in different occupational roles, as well as vertically: Women are concentrated in the lowest paid, least protected, and least powerful positions. And individual women who begin to move up corporate ladders run into a "glass ceiling" that obstructs their access to the most powerful positions. This horizontal and vertical gender segregation accounts in part for the fact that women—about 40 percent of the paid work force worldwide—earn approximately 70 cents for every dollar earned by men.[5]

The point is that divisions of gender identity (masculinity and femininity) have consequences for the difference between men's and women's experience, for example, in earning money and exercising public power. Around the world, women are relatively absent from the top decision-making positions of political, economic, and ideological power: Consider the leadership of nations, corporations, churches, and media. And women are absent in part because gender stereotypes establish leadership as a masculine activity and because gender structures discriminate against women seeking positions of power (we illustrate these points in the text). It is in this sense that we assert that where women (or men) are absent, principles of gender are at work. That is, the absence or invisibility of women does not suggest gender neutrality but in fact demonstrates the personal, political, systemic, and structural effects of gender differentiation. The latter involves defining different qualities, roles, and activities for men and women and ensuring the reproduction of these discriminating structures.

Gender is not a traditional category of analysis in IR, either in terms of "what" we study or "how" we study it. Nor has gender been raised very often as an issue in IR policy-making. In today's world, however, this lack of attention to gender is neither possible nor defensible. As this text illustrates, gender is salient both as a substantive topic and as a dimension of how we study world politics. The former we characterize as the effects of IR on gender or "the presence of women": where and how women are situated differently than men as a consequence of the practices, processes, and institutions we identify as world politics. We deal with gender as a dimension of the way world politics is studied by referring to the effects of gender on IR or "the power of gender": how gender is a category of our mental ordering (a filter or lens) that has consequences for practices, processes, and institutions we think of as world politics. The presence of women and the power of gender are two interacting themes that frame the material presented in this text.

The Presence of Women in World Politics

We can observe historical changes in men's and women's lives that are elements of world politics and (like developments in state interactions) require alterations in our analytical frameworks if we are to accurately and effectively make sense of our world.

Although the influence of gender is not new (any more than global processes are), our awareness of and ability to analyze gender has grown in the past three decades. The roles of women and the gender issues they raise are particularly obvious in the following developments: the impact of women's liberation movements (especially in the industrialized First World) and the role of women in revolutionary movements; the shifting international division of labor as women around the world enter the paid labor force; the significance of gender in designing and implementing Third World economic development policies; the urgency of reproductive issues and population-planning policies; and, in general, small but steady improvements in percentages of women engaged in formal politics. The UN Decade for Women (1976–1985) not only marked the convergence of these issues and movements but also generated—for the first time— worldwide data on the actual conditions of women. In addition, activities of the United Nations itself—especially the declarations of women's equal rights and the convention to eliminate sex discrimination—focused attention on the specific conditions of women and on global commitments to gender equality.

The confluence of these and other developments has enabled us to assess "the presence of women": We now have extensive data documenting how women and men are affected differently by global processes. More specifically, we can identify how gendered divisions of power, violence, labor, and resources have concrete consequences that differ for men and women—how they, in fact, constitute a systemic condition of gender inequality. To make sense of these effects requires that we take gender seriously in our ways of thinking about or understanding world politics.

The Power of Gender in World Politics

In the past several decades, the study of gender has grown considerably, as women's studies programs have expanded and individual scholars have explored the meaning and significance of gender in all disciplines. Perhaps the most profound insight to emerge from this scholarship was the recognition of how pervasive a filtering category gender is (we elaborate on gender in the next chapter). In fact, the studies did more than document the pattern of excluding or trivializing women and their experiences. Studies also documented how gender influences the very categories and frameworks within which scholars work.

In sum, how we care about, perceive, understand, analyze, and critique the world we live in is profoundly shaped by gender. Gender thus influences not only who we are, how we live, and what we have but also "how" we think, order reality, claim to know what is true, and, therefore, how we understand and explain the social world. As subsequent chapters illustrate, gender shapes our identification of global actors, characterization of state and nonstate actions, framing of global problems, and consideration of possible alternatives.

These interacting phenomena—the presence of women in world politics and the power of gender as a lens on the world—indicate that gender is important for contemporary understanding of world politics. It is no longer adequate—and never was accurate—to treat gender as irrelevant to our knowledge of world politics. For these reasons, we offer in this text a *gender*-sensitive lens on global processes. Through this lens, not only the "what" of world politics but also "how" we view—and therefore understand—world politics is different. We see the extent and structure of gender inequality, the role of gender in structuring the experience of women *and* men worldwide, the significance of gender in shaping how we think about world politics, and how world politics itself is shaped by gendered thought. A text on global gender issues affords more accurate and comprehensive understanding of world politics than approaches that ignore the effect of world politics on gender relations and the effect of gender on world politics.

WHY ISSUES?

In this book, we examine the "dilemma" of global gender inequality as a central, not peripheral, dimension of world politics. Designed for courses in world politics, this text introduces gender as a lens through which to examine traditional IR categories and makes gender *visible* in additional ways that inform our understanding. We organize the text around central themes of IR inquiry: politics, security, economics, equity, and ecology. We present and analyze these topics by examining the gendered divisions of power (politics), violence (security), labor (economics), and resources (equity and ecology). These gendered divisions become the issues in this text. Questions we raise in regard to these issues include: How do we understand power and politics? Who gets to participate in politics and who is accountable for what? How do we understand security and who is it for? How do we understand work and who gets paid for what? How are resources distributed and controlled? How do we understand our relationship to nature and what are the consequences of that understanding?

We cannot address all the concerns raised by a critique of global gender inequality. Nor can we explore how IR theories might be transformed by an awareness of gender bias.[6] Our presentation of global gender issues is suggestive, not definitive: We attempt to suggest to what extent and in what ways gender is at work in—and a consequence of—world politics. This includes exploring how gender shapes traditional categories and frameworks—thus making gender visible—and asking how gender sensitivity enables new insights to emerge—thus making transformation possible. By restating old and/or raising new questions, we reveal how current approaches are selective and omit important dimensions of world politics. We also open up new ways of seeing, and therefore understanding, issues that confront all students of world politics.

THE IMMEDIACY AND IMPORT OF GLOBAL GENDER ISSUES

As ways of being and knowing become institutionalized, we begin to see them as "natural" rather than socially constructed. Hilary Lips argued that "this apparent naturalness is a source of power for those who would maintain things as they are . . . because they help to make the system [of power relations] invisible, like water to a fish."[7]

Real world developments force us to revise our categories and frameworks to make better sense of those developments. In IR, notions of security have been revised in light of the spiraling costs of militarization and transformations in East-West rivalries, and the meaning of development has been reexamined in the face of deepening Third World poverty. Similarly, recognition of global gender inequality and the power of gender to order our thinking and shape our reality forces us to acknowledge and make sense of the role of gender in world politics.

Gender issues surface *now* because new questions have been raised that cannot be addressed within traditional frameworks. The amassing of global data reveals the extent and pattern of gender inequality: Women everywhere have less access to political power and economic resources and less control over processes that reproduce this systemic inequality. Moreover, our knowledge of the world of men and the politics they create is incomplete and inaccurate without knowing how men's activities, including their politics, are related to, even dependent upon, what women are doing—and why.

Additionally, our recognizing the power of gender forces us to reevaluate traditional explanations, to ask how they are biased and hence render inaccurate accounts. As in other disciplines, the study of world politics is enriched by acknowledging and systematically examining how gender shapes categories and frameworks that we take for granted. This is necessary for answering the new questions raised and for generating fresh insights—about the world as we currently "know" it and how it might be otherwise.

Finally, gender-sensitive studies improve our understanding of global crises, their interaction, and possibilities of moving beyond them. These include crises of political legitimacy and security as states are increasingly unable to protect their citizens against nuclear, economic, or ecological threats; crises of maldevelopment as the dynamics of our global economic system enrich a few and impoverish most; and crises of environmental degradation as the exploitation of natural resources continues in nonsustainable fashion.

These global crises cannot be understood or addressed without acknowledging the structural inequalities of the current world system. These inequalities extend well beyond gender issues: They are embodied in interacting hierarchies of race, class, ethnicity, nationality, and religious identification. Examining gender, as this text does, permits us to see how *this* particular structural inequality works in the world: how it is institutionalized, legitimated, and reproduced. We also begin to see how gender hierarchy interacts with other structural inequalities. Gender shapes, and is shaped by, all of us. We daily reproduce its dynamics—and suffer its costs—in multiple ways. By learning how gender works, we learn a great deal about structures of inequality and how they are intentionally and *unintentionally* reproduced. We can then use this knowledge in our struggles to transform not only global gender inequality but also other oppressive hierarchies at work in the world.

In short, *Global Gender Issues* addresses traditional IR concerns and also expands our understanding of global processes. By examining how men and women are differently affected by these global processes and how gender shapes the way we think about—and in part "create"—the world we live in, this text reframes and expands our knowledge of world politics. By including women's experience—of politics, security, economics, ecology, and equity—the book generates understanding that is more comprehensive and accurate because it is less partial and distorted than conventional accounts.

NOTES ABOUT THIS TEXT

Some final clarifications are in order. First, there is considerable diversity even within mainstream approaches to world politics. It is therefore inappropriate to characterize IR as one school of thought with a set of basic and unchanging principles. However, because of space constraints and the orientation of this text, we tend to present traditional approaches as having a variety of features in common that generally differ from the gender-sensitive approach we undertake here.

Second, we assume that readers are relatively unfamiliar with gender analyses. In a text of this size, we cannot address all the relevant issues or do more than introduce the scholarship on gender that underpins our arguments: The text makes no pretense of surveying the issues completely. We focus, instead, on providing data and analyses that introduce students to the significance of gender generally and its role in shaping world politics specifically. We hope that students will gain a broader and deeper understanding of these new subjects of study and debate and perhaps pursue them further.

Because we recognize that a gender-sensitive approach is unfamiliar, we have presented what is now a rich and sophisticated literature in extremely simplified form. This simplification imposes its own distortions. We wish especially to point out that our attention to gender, which distinguishes primarily between masculine and feminine as identities associated with men and women, tends to underplay the considerable differences *among* men and *among* women. We remind students that men, women, masculine, feminine, masculinist, and feminist are not homogeneous or unchanging categories. Like references to racism, developed countries, or the Third World, our references to these general and familiar categories always risk obscuring differences *within* the categories. We try throughout the text to note and analyze how women and men are in reality divided along multiple dimensions: class, race, physical abilities, age, ethnicity, sexual orientation, nationality. Nevertheless, the demands of introducing unfamiliar material have prompted our use of many generalizations. In reality, as well as in our own thinking, things are always more complex.

Third, we acknowledge our political commitments. Every lens is shaped by historical context and has normative and political implications. Diverse approaches, though they offer alternative perspectives, cannot simply be "added up" to gain a greater understanding of a static world. Rather, how we think about the world affects the world we think about: Different approaches have different concrete effects.

Just as realism makes conflict more visible and idealism makes cooperation more visible, this text makes gender more visible. In the process, it exposes distortions and limitations of conventional accounts. Existing frameworks do not adequately explain the nature, sources, and levels of conflict and cooperation in world politics. In fact, one begins to see that traditional IR accounts can misread situations of conflict and cooperation by failing to analyze the difference that gender makes.

We acknowledge that our gender-sensitive lens affords often critical accounts of both the "what" and "how" of contemporary world politics. Our perspective challenges a variety of institutions and practices in world politics because we are concerned with changing the negative conditions experienced by a majority of women, men, girls, and boys in our world. Many perspectives, in addition to gender-sensitive ones, are legitimate and necessary for understanding world politics and its current inequalities. We attempt to build upon and engage with these. In sum, we examine world politics through a gender-sensitive lens to enable a broader and deeper understanding of how the world works—or does not work—for all of us.

MAPPING THE BOOK

The focus of Chapter 2 is on "the power of gender," elaborating on the meaning of a gender-sensitive lens, how such a lens works in shaping our lives, and how it filters our understanding. We examine how the interaction of stereotypes, dichotomies, and ideology obscures the power of gender in shaping our world. We conclude by introducing the issue areas: gendered divisions of power, violence, labor, and resources.

In Chapter 3 we begin to examine "the presence of women"—how and where women and men are differently situated—in relation to the gendered division of power. We present data and analyses of women as political actors in state structures. Then we examine how and why the presence of these powerful women is rendered invisible by asking: Why so few? How do the few succeed? What effect do they have? What makes actors powerful?

Chapter 4 contains our examination of how women and men are differently situated in relation to gendered divisions of violence (security issues), labor (economic issues), and resources (equity and ecology issues). Within each issue area, we ask what dichotomies are at work, how they differently affect men and women, and what their consequences are, especially in relation to global processes and crises.

In Chapter 5 we explore the politics of resistance by surveying and analyzing gender as a dimension of nonstate, antistate, and transstate movements. After identifying four feminist orientations and distinguishing between practical and strategic interests, we examine gender at work in revolutionary movements, in activities promoting peace, antimilitarization and antiviolence, and in movements for economic justice and sustainable ecology.

In our conclusion, Chapter 6, we review the main points of the foregoing chapters and their implications for studying world politics. We then take a final, integrative look at the gender divisions of power, violence, labor, and resources. We ask how a gender-sensitive lens informs the objectives of participatory politics, security based on the minimization of indirect as well as direct violence, equitable economic systems, and sustainable ecology. We close with policy recommendations, suggesting how individuals, as well as institutional actors, can promote a world less burdened by the dilemma of gender—and other—inequalities.

"It's a man's world." Cartoon suggesting that when men rule the world, they leave destruction in their wake. Reprinted with special permission of King Features Syndicates.

TWO

□ □ □

Gender as a Lens
on World Politics

Too typically, and quite erroneously, gender is understood as inter-
changeable with sex, which refers to the biological basis for distinguishing male and female. Instead, gender should be understood as a social, not physiological, construction: *"Femininity* and *masculinity,* the
terms that denote one's gender, refer to a complex set of characteristics
and behaviors prescribed for a particular sex by society and learned
through the socialization experience."[1]

The particular characteristics associated with femininity and masculinity vary across cultures, races, classes, and even age groups. "Acting like a
man" means different things to different groups of people (e.g., hetero-
sexual Catholics, Native Americans, British colonials) and to the same
group of people at different points in time (e.g., nineteenth- versus
twentieth-century Europeans, prepuberty versus elderly age sets, women
in the labor force during versus after World War II). Because models of appropriate gender behavior vary, we know that femininity and masculinity
are not timeless or separable from the contexts in which they are observed. This suggests that gender rests not on biological sex differences
but on *interpretations* of behavior that are culturally associated with sex
differences.

In other words, although biology is ostensibly the basis for establishing
gender models, it plays an ambiguous and often purely symbolic role in
our actual use of gendered concepts. Consider that a man (e.g., Mahatma
Gandhi) may be characterized as "feminine" and a woman (e.g., Margaret
Thatcher) as "masculine." Even activities and institutions are characterized in gender terms, regardless of whether they are associated mainly

with men or women. For example, computer programming and government bureaucracies are often described as "masculine."

Recognizing the complexity in our use of gender is important for clarifying distinctions between the *biological* categories of male and female, the *socially constructed* models of masculine and feminine, and the *political* positions of **masculinist** and **feminist.** Our discussion in this section explicates the meaning of masculinist and feminist. Although the specific traits that mark gender-appropriate behavior vary cross-culturally, males are expected to conform to models of masculinity and females to models of femininity. The construction of gender identities is closely related to how cultures organize work, power, and pleasure along gender-differentiated lines. That is, the way we think about who people are (images and identities) is inextricable from what we expect people to do (roles and activities).

Because masculine activities are more highly valued or privileged than feminine activities in most of the world, the identities and activities associated with men and women are typically unequal. Thus, the social construction of gender is actually a system of power that not only divides men and women as masculine and feminine but typically also places men and masculinity above women and femininity and operates to value more highly those institutions and practices that are male dominated and/or representative of masculine traits and style.

Because masculine and feminine are constructed oppositionally, when we favor or privilege that which is associated with masculinity we tend to do so at the expense of that which is associated with femininity. Politics in a broad sense is about differential access to power—about who gets what and how. Therefore, the privileging of masculinity is political insofar as relations of inequality, manifested in this case as gender inequality, represent men's and women's differential access to power. In this text, the term *masculinist* refers to individuals, perspectives, practices, and institutions that are masculine in orientation (embodying and privileging the traits of masculinity) and, thus, engaged in producing and sustaining relations of gender inequality.

Like other social hierarchies, gender inequality is maintained by various means ranging from direct violence (rape, domestic battering) and structural discrimination (job segregation, inadequate health care) to psychological mechanisms (**sexist** humor, blaming the victim, internalization of oppressive stereotypes). And like many social hierarchies, gender inequality is "justified" by focusing on physical differences and exaggerating their significance as determinants of what are in fact social, *learned*, behaviors. Thus, Arthur Brittan argued that by denying the social construction of gender, **masculinism** serves to justify and "naturalize" (depoliticize) male domination because "it takes for granted that there is a fundamental difference between men and women, it assumes that heterosexuality is normal, it accepts without question the sexual division of labour, and it sanctions the political and dominant role of men in the public and private spheres."[2]

Feminism, in contrast, is a more complicated and contested term. There are, in fact, many forms of feminism that we will discuss. Here we suggest that the common thread among feminisms is an orientation valuing women's diverse experiences and taking seriously women's interests in and capacities for bringing about social and political change. It is our position that feminists do not want a simplistic role reversal in which women gain power over men. Rather, feminists seek an end to social constructions of gender inequality. We also note that masculinist perspectives can be held by women and feminist perspectives can be held by men because those perspectives are politically, not biologically, grounded. As we illustrate in this text, many of the most serious global issues facing humankind and the planet today are caused, in part, by the practices, processes, and structures of **gender hierarchy** (the power system that privileges maleness over femaleness). Thus, it is no longer possible or advisable to ignore this feature of the international system.

Through a gender-sensitive lens, not only the "what" of world politics but also "how" we think about it looks different. In the chapters to follow we demonstrate how IR affects gender: As a consequence of gendered divisions of power, violence, labor, and resources, women and men are positioned differently. In the remainder of this chapter, we focus on how gender affects IR. Specifically, we consider the power of gender to shape our thinking, our ordering of reality, our claims of knowing what is true, and, therefore, our understanding and explanation of the social world. Because a gender-sensitive lens is unfamiliar to most students of IR, this chapter focuses on such a lens and its implications for the study of world politics.

THE SOCIAL CONSTRUCTION OF GENDER AND GENDER HIERARCHY

To understand how gender works, we examine two interacting dimensions of social systems: the formation of gendered identities and the reproduction of gendered social structures. The first is about **socialization:** how individuals are taught culturally appropriate attitudes and behaviors. Families, schools, religious institutions, and media are important sources of this socialization. The second dimension is about systemic, or structural, control: how practices and institutions keep gender hierarchy in place by generating conformity and compliance. Moral and intellectual control is effected through privileging certain belief systems (e.g., myth,

Changing lenses. A graphic depiction of how lenses affect fields of vision and how women at the bottom of the world politics hierarchy are struggling to make elite men see the world more clearly. Courtesy of the United Nations "The State of the World's Women 1985." Illustrator: Wendy Hoile.

religion, and even science). More direct social control is effected through job markets, laws, governance, and physical coercion.

From birth on, the way we are treated depends on our gender assignment, and we learn in multiple ways how to adopt gender-appropriate behaviors. There are few occasions or interactions where our gender is truly irrelevant; our names, clothes, games, rewards and punishments; the attention we get, the subjects we study, the knowledge claims we make, the jobs we work at, and the power we have are all profoundly shaped by gender expectations. As individuals, we differ considerably in the extent to which we conform to cultural expectations. But none of us escapes gender socialization or the systemic effects of gender inequality. Most significant, it is not only females but males as well who suffer from rigid gender roles.

> Everyone is born into a *culture*—a *set of shared ideas* about the nature of reality, the nature of right and wrong, *evaluation of what is good and desirable,* and the nature of the good and desirable versus the bad and nondesirable. ... As totally dependent infants we are *socialized*—taught the rules, roles and relationships of the social world. ... [I]n the process we learn to think, act, and feel as we are "supposed to."[3]

More than two thousand years ago, Plato recognized that the most effective way to maintain systems of rule was not through direct violence but by persuading those who are subordinated that social hierarchy is natural, therefore inevitable, and even desirable. When people believe that differences in status and wealth are part of the "natural order of things," they are less likely to challenge how society is organized to benefit some more than others. Such people do not require constant external policing because they have internalized their own policing in terms of selective perceptions and lowered expectations. As a consequence, they internalize an acceptance of their own, and others', inequality.

In the next two sections we examine how gender inequality is produced, reinforced, and reproduced through gender stereotypes, dichotomies, and masculinist ideology. (In subsequent chapters we focus on the gender-differentiated consequences of social control: how divisions of power, violence, labor, and resources affect women and men differently.)

Gender Stereotypes and Dichotomies

Stereotypes are pictures in our heads that filter how we "see." They are composite images that attribute—often incorrectly and always too generally—certain characteristics to whole groups of people. Thus groups are seen as others want or expect to see them, not necessarily as they are. The oversimplification in stereotypes encourages us to ignore complexity and contradictions that might prompt us to challenge the status quo. The use of stereotypes suggests that particular behaviors are timeless and inevitable.

By providing unquestioned categories and connections, stereotypes can mask actual relationships and in effect "excuse" discrimination. For example, the underrepresentation of women in political office is often "explained" by the stereotype of their being uninterested in power and politics. Similarly, high unemployment among African-Americans is often "explained" by the stereotype of their being lazy and irresponsible.

Stereotypes, because they oversimplify, overgeneralize, are resistant to change, and promote inaccurate images, significantly affect how we see ourselves, others, and social organization generally. Stereotypes are political because they both reproduce and naturalize (depoliticize) unequal power relations. They reproduce inequalities by being self-fulfilling: If we *expect* certain behaviors, we may act in ways that in fact create and reinforce such behaviors. (Expecting girls to hate mechanics and math affects how much encouragement we give them; without expectations of success or encouragement, girls may avoid or do poorly in these activities.) And stereotypes naturalize inequalities by presenting subordinated groups negatively. When members of such groups internalize oppressive stereotypes, they may hold themselves—rather than social structures—responsible for undesirable outcomes. (Females are more likely to blame themselves for ineptness or poor grades rather than ask how social structures discourage girls from exploring mechanics and discriminate educationally in favor of boys.) Those who believe they are acting out the inevitable are, in effect, reconciled to discriminatory treatment.

In the United States, dominant gender stereotypes depict men/masculinity as "strong, independent, worldly, aggressive, ambitious, logical, and rough" and women/femininity as the opposite: "weak, dependent, passive, naive, not ambitious, illogical, and gentle."[4] This exemplifies the binary nature of models of gender, constructing man/masculinity and woman/femininity as two poles of a **dichotomy**—oppositions—that define each other. Through this either-or lens women are not simply different from men: "Woman" is defined by what is "not man," and characteristics of femininity are those that are inappropriate to or contradict masculinity.

In every aspect of our lives, we are bombarded with gender stereotypes. Consider the depiction of men and women on television and in musical lyrics: How often is there a politically powerful or physically "rough" woman, especially one that is likable? Or a man who is nurturing and sensual as a way of being all the time, not just in certain circumstances? And most telling, why are there so few images of gender-free individuals—people whose gender status is not immediately and unequivocally apparent? Why are we so uncomfortable with gender ambiguities, virtually insisting that individuals be patently *either* men/masculine *or* women/feminine?

These questions bring into focus how gender stereotypes interact with Western patterns of thinking to institutionalize acritical and typically conservative patterns in how we think about, act upon, and therefore shape reality. In Cynthia Epstein's words, "No aspect of social life—whether the gathering of crops, the ritual of religion, the formal dinner party, or the organization of government—is free from the dichotomous thinking that casts the world in categories of 'male' and 'female.'"[5] Our argument here expands on the work of contemporary nonfeminist scholars who are critical of dichotomies for their role in sustaining status quo inequalities (elaborated below). But we go beyond their general critique to argue that dichotomized (either-or) thought cannot be adequately understood and therefore effectively transformed without attention to gender. In brief, dichotomies acquire the status and authority of givens in part because they so readily "map onto" the dichotomy of gender. And the gender dichotomy gains its "givenness" by (mistaken) association with biological ("natural") sex difference. Because of this interaction, gender stereotypes have political significance far beyond their role in male-female relations: They not only reproduce *gender* hierarchy but also sustain other relations of domination by promoting and naturalizing the practice of thinking in hierarchical dichotomies. We clarify these claims by examining how the structure, status, and androcentrism (use of male as norm) of dichotomies interact to (re)produce and legitimate social inequalities.

The structure of dichotomies severely constrains our thought and therefore action. The image of only two, mutually exclusive, choices keeps us locked into those, and only those, choices. Polarities (right versus wrong, rational versus emotional) forestall our consideration of non-oppositional constructions (right in relation to plausible, persuasive, misleading; rational in relation to consistent, intellectual, ardent). The meanings of the polar terms also appear fixed, as if they are givens of logic and language rather than social conventions.[6] In this sense, polarities resist critical reflection by presenting what appear to be inevitable categories. However, social reality is complex and conditioned by multiple variables. Categorical oppositions misrepresent (distort) *social* relations by eliminating this complexity and interdependence of terms. For example, in IR, we posit state sovereignty as independence and autonomy, the opposite of dependence and constraints. Until recently, this dichotomy prevented our seeing *interdependence* as a third option and, for many, a more accurate picture of actual relationships between states. Similarly, when we define the field's theoretical debates as "idealism versus realism," we make it impossible to address how virtually all theorists in fact adopt a mixture of idealist and realist positions.

In addition, the oppositional form of dichotomies denies any overlap or commonalities between terms: It puts difference in focus at the expense of viewing terms *relationally*. As humans, men and women exhibit more commonalities than differences. But the male-female dichotomy highlights differences, not shared characteristics, as primary. In reality, not all females bear children and no female bears them throughout her lifetime. But the dichotomy pitting men as performing **productive labor** (working for wages, creating ideas and products) against women as performing **reproductive labor** (maintaining the household, bearing and caring for children) masks this variation among females and commonality between males and many females. The dichotomies of sovereignty-anarchy, politics-economics, realism-idealism, and center-periphery similarly structure how we think about and therefore act in the world. They emphasize hierarchical difference rather than how states, transnational processes, and people are embedded in complex and ever-changing relationships. In sum, the structure of dichotomies promotes patterns of thought and action that are static (unable to acknowledge or address change), stunted (unable to envision alternatives), and dangerously oversimplified (unable to accommodate the complexities of social reality).

Whereas the *structure* of dichotomies makes gender stereotypes harder to "see," critique, and alter, the *status* of dichotomies in Western thought poses additional problems. Although all cultures employ categories of comparison, Western thought is singular in the extent to which binarism (thinking in either-or oppositions) is privileged. This is in large part due to the prominence of science in Western culture. Science takes two dichotomies as givens: the categorical separation of fact from value and of knower (subject) from that which is known (object). Deeply embedded in Western thought, these dualisms are accorded particular status because of their association with science and with claims to "objective knowledge." But they are not gender-neutral categories. On the contrary, the knowing subject, rationality, and objectivity are gendered in meaning and practice.[7] Take a moment to consider how the dichotomies in Table 2.1 are linked both to gender stereotypes and the stereotype of scientific knowledge claims.

Dichotomies are so pervasive and privileged in Western culture that they lend authority to the particular dichotomy of gender. And the dichotomy of gender is so taken as given that it lends authority to the "natural" separation of other categories into dualistic form. To the extent that other dichotomies have gendered connotations (culture-nature, reason-emotion, autonomy-dependency, realism-idealism), when they are repro-

TABLE 2.1   Gender and Science Dichotomies

Masculine/Subject	Feminine/Object
Knower/self/autonomy/agency	Known/other/dependence/passivity
Objective/rational/fact/logical/hard	Subjective/emotional/value/illogical/soft
Order/certainty/predictability/control over	Anarchy/uncertainty/unpredictability/ subject to control
Mind/abstract/transcendence/freedom/ intellectual	Body/concrete/contingency/necessity/ manual
Culture/civilized/exploiter/production/ public	Nature/primitive/exploited/ reproduction/private

duced they buttress the stereotypes of masculine and feminine. Such reciprocal interaction will be elaborated throughout this text, as gender dichotomies create social effects and these effects in turn reproduce gendered thought and practice.

Finally, these dichotomies are not only hierarchical (privileging the first term over the second) but also **androcentric:** The first term is associated with masculinity or assumes a male-as-norm point of view. This androcentrism has three interacting effects. First, because the primary term is androcentric and privileged, it effectively elevates the values of the primary term over those of the "other" term. Thus, reason, order, culture, and action are associated with maleness and are privileged over emotion, uncertainty, nature, and passivity. Second and closely related, characteristics and activities associated with femaleness are deemed not only less important but also unworthy or undesirable because they appear to threaten the values represented by the primary term. Thus, attitudes and activities associated with women (emotion, dependence, reproduction, caretaking) are given less attention and often disparaged.[8]

Androcentrism has a third effect: It assumes that men are the most important actors and the substance of their lives the most important topic to know about. As long as the realities of women, nonelite men, and children are treated as secondary to the "main story"—as the "background" that is never important enough to warrant being spotlighted—we in fact are unaware of what the background actually is and what relationship it actually has to the main story. What we are unaware of we cannot understand or analyze. Nor can we understand to what extent and in what ways the main story depends on background that is "hidden"—forced into darkness or silence by focusing illumination and attention elsewhere. Rendering the experience or realities of "others"—of those not privileged—"invisible" tends to present that which we do "know about" as real and authoritative, as if it were "natural" and knowing about it were all we needed to understand the story.

In sum, an interaction of gender stereotypes, dichotomies, hierarchies, and masculinism/androcentrism powerfully filters our understanding of social reality. Because we rarely question the dualism of male-female, we fail to see how the male-dominated hierarchy of masculine-feminine is socially constructed rather than natural. Recognizing the power of these filtering devices is an important first step toward analyzing their effects accurately and improving our knowledge of the world we both produce and are produced by.

Gender Ideology

As used, in this text, **ideology** refers to systems of belief—including notions of human nature and social life—that distort reality while they maintain it by justifying status quo social, economic, and political arrangements. In Margaret Andersen's words: "Ideologies serve the powerful by presenting us with a definition of reality that is false and yet orders our comprehension of the surrounding world. When ideas emerge from ideology, they operate as a form of social control by defining the status quo to be the proper state of affairs."[9]

Ideologies are thus political: They order how we "see" and in turn "create" differential access to power. Whereas stereotypes are expectations about certain groups of people, ideologies are beliefs about the nature of social systems and the relationships among groups of people within them. They buttress the effects of stereotyping by further filtering our perceptions and actions in ways that reproduce discrimination by "naturalizing" social hierarchies.

For example, social Darwinism is a belief that only the fittest survive and rise to the top. It emerged in the context of European capitalist and colonial expansion. As an ideology, social Darwinism justified the accumulation of wealth by powerful men while fostering a racist belief that biological inferiority—rather than European imperialism—explained the subordinated status of people of color.[10]

The dominant gender ideology in the United States fuses gender stereotypes with masculinist beliefs about families, sexuality, divisions of labor, and constructions of power and authority. The belief that men are by nature aggressive and sexually demanding and women are naturally passive and sexually submissive encourages other beliefs ("men can't help it," "women actually want it") that legitimate systemic sexual abuse. It "excuses" the pattern of male rape behavior and controls the behavior of girls and women, who attempt to avoid or diminish the effects of this violence. Although some males are targets of assault because of their cultural choices, class, or ethnicity, *all* females are threatened and therefore socially controlled by virtue of simply being female in a masculinist world.

The world on women's backs. Cartoon emphasizing women's enormous responsibilities but minimal power in the world. From the book *I'm Training to Be Tall and Blond* by Nicole Hollander. Copyright © 1979. Reprinted with permission from St. Martin's Press, Inc., New York, NY.

At the same time, beliefs that "women are mothers by nature" and that "a woman's place is in the home" legitimate society's holding women disproportionately responsible for child care, maintenance of family relations, and household tasks while denying that this is socially necessary *work*.

Ideologies, although they appear timeless, are context dependent and alterable to suit the interests of those with power. Depending on what the situation calls for, gender ideology may promote women as physically strong and capable of backbreaking work (e.g., slave women, frontier women), as competent to do men's work (e.g., Rosie the Riveter in World War II), as dexterous and immune to boredom (e.g., electronics assembly industries), or as full-time housewives and devoted mothers (e.g., postwar demands that women vacate jobs in favor of returning soldiers and repopulate the nation). Ideologies are reconfigured to suit the changing interests of those in power, not those whose lives are most controlled by them.

Ideologies are often couched in terms of biological determinism, positing narrow genetic or biological causes for complex social behaviors. In the real world, human behavior is always mediated by culture—by systems of meaning and the values they incorporate. The role that biology actually plays varies dramatically and can never be determined without reference to cultural context. Ideological beliefs may exaggerate the role of biological factors (arguing that men's testosterone explains male homicide rates) or posit biological factors where none need be involved (arguing that because some women during part of their life bear children, all women should *care* for children and are unfit for political power). Reliance on biological determinism means that ideologies tend to flourish in periods of disruption or transition, when political conservatism serves to buttress traditional power wielders.[11] When traditional power wielders are threatened by change, it is easy and often effective for them to repeat ideological claims that emphasize how natural and therefore unchanging inequality is.

Finally, ideologies are most effective when most taken for granted. They resist correction and critique by making the status quo appear natural, "the way things are," not the result of human intervention and practice. Like stereotypes, ideologies depoliticize what are in fact differences in power that serve some more than others. Religion, myths, educational systems, advertising, and the media are involved in reproducing stereotypes and ideologies that make the world we live in seem inevitable and, for some, even desirable. The point is not that the world is as bad as it could be but that ideologies prevent us from seeing the world as it really is.

Our final point is that much of our behavior *unintentionally* reproduces status quo inequalities. We cannot simply locate an "enemy" to blame for institutional discrimination and its many consequences. Although there are no doubt individuals who actively pursue discriminatory policies and the perpetuation of injustice, few of us would identify with such a characterization. Most of us believe in the possibilities of a better world and variously engage in working toward it. But stereotypes and ideologies play a particular role in shaping our expectations and behaviors. We begin to be socialized into these belief systems early in life, well before we have the capacity to reflect critically on their implications for our own or others' lives. Because ideologies are supported and sustained by those with power in our societies, there are powerful incentives for subscribing to these belief systems—and negative consequences of not doing so. Unless something or someone prompts us to "see things differently," these belief systems become unconscious assumptions. They serve to reinforce the status quo and blunt criticism of it. As such, they involve all of us in the often unintentional reproduction of social hierarchies that are not in fact inevitable but transformable. If we are to change the world, we have to change structures as well as how we think about them. Understanding the role of stereotypes and ideologies is crucial for both (see Box 2.1).

THE GENDERED WHO, WHAT, AND HOW OF WORLD POLITICS

A resurgence of women's movements has raised popular consciousness about the politics of gender relations, and three decades of feminist scholarship have placed gender on the agenda of most academic disciplines. In the humanities, history, anthropology, and even in sociology and political science, feminist critiques have altered disciplinary givens, challenged conventional explanations, and expanded the reach of intellectual inquiry. But, as Fred Halliday noted in 1988, "there has been one outstanding exception to this growing awareness of gender issues, namely international relations."[12] We shall look at *who* does IR, *what* it is about, and *how* it is studied and practiced in order to see how international relations scholars and practitioners do—and do not—address gender issues.

International relations has been and continues to be male dominated. The preponderance of male scholars and practitioners explains in part the silence on gender: Men checked with each other about what men were doing that was considered relevant to other men and was written by men for primarily male audiences! Though important, the absence of women from these activities is insufficient to explain why these men failed, until very recently, even to comment on this gender imbalance. Other reasons include IR's relative insulation as a discipline, which has distanced it from developments in those disciplines where feminist theories and research have been most influential.

But it is also the particular nature of IR inquiry—what it is about—that produces resistance to taking gender seriously. International relations distinguishes itself from political science generally by valuing matters of foreign policy over matters of domestic policy: Relations between but not within states define its focus. Whereas domestic political observers and policymakers have had to grapple with voting behavior, welfare state issues, domestic public interest groups, and social movements—areas in which gender issues figure prominently—IR practitioners have focused on national security (defined most often in terms of military might), economic power (defined typically by gross national product indicators), and international organizations and regimes (made up of government and financial elites). Not only are women infrequent actors in these matters of state, but also IR orthodoxy sees no place for women in these high-stakes games.

Box 2.1   Selected Quotations

On Sexism

Sexism is a many-headed, ubiquitous monster that has manifested itself in different ways in different historical periods and in different cultures. It is a belief system based on the assumption that the physical differences between males and females are so significant that they should determine virtually all social and economic roles of men and women. It holds that not just their reproductive functions are determined by sex, but that sex is the factor that rules their entire lives, all their functions in society and the economy, and their relation to the state and all public institutions and especially to each other. Sexism is manifest in all forms of behavior from subtle gestures and language to exploitation and oppression, and in all human institutions from the family to the multinational corporation.

—Betty A. Reardon, *Sexism and the War System,* p. 16.

On Oppression

Consider a birdcage. If you look very closely at just one wire in the cage, you cannot see the other wires. If your conception of what is before you is determined by this myopic focus, you could look at that one wire, up and down the length of it, and be unable to see why a bird would not just fly around the wire. … Furthermore, even if, one day at a time, you myopically inspected each wire, you still could not see why a bird would have trouble going past the wires to get anywhere. … It is only when you step back, stop looking at the wires one by one, microscopically, and take a macroscopic view of the whole cage, that you can see why the bird does not go anywhere; and then you will see it in a moment. … It is perfectly *obvious* that the bird is surrounded by a network of systematically related barriers, no one of which would be the least hindrance to its flight, but which, by their relations to each other, are as confining as the solid walls of a dungeon.

—Marilyn Frye, *The Politics of Reality,* pp. 4–5.

On Masculinism as Objectification

Objectification involves more than the subjection of the female body. Fundamentally, it is rooted in the human assertion of power over nature. It is men who, for a variety of reasons, come to see themselves as being the tamers of nature, as the vanguard fighting scarcity. In their subjection of nature they simultaneously begin to subjugate other human beings. The masculine ideology is the ideology of objectification. As such, it naturalizes the distinction between subject and object. In so doing, it distinguishes between the agency of man the maker, and the passivity of nature. The pacification of nature involves the pacification of women, as well as the subordination of other men perceived as potential rivals. Hence … masculinity as an ideology elevates the primacy of technique, rationality, and power. In objectifying nature, men lay the foundation for the objectification of all social and personal relationships.

—Arthur Brittan and Mary Maynard, *Sexism, Racism, and Oppression,*
pp. 201–202.

On Power and Responsibility
The penalties for inequality between women and men are very severe. And they are not borne by women alone. They are borne by the whole world.

Power, tempered by the wisdom and restraint of responsibility, is the foundation of a just society. But with too little responsibility, power turns to tyranny. And with too little power, responsibility becomes exploitation. Yet in every country in the world power and responsibility have become unbalanced and unhitched, distributed unequally between men and women. ... The penalties of women's too-great burden of responsibility and their too-small slice of power ... are hardship, sickness, hunger, even famine. But the penalties of man's disproportionate share of the world's power (without the intimate day-to-day knowledge of the effects of that power, or the responsibility for ensuring that the basic needs of the household are met) are just as great.

Of course, not all men are tyrants or despots and not all women are martyrs to duty and hard work. But *masculine* and *feminine* social roles have tilted the majority of men and women in those directions.
—Debbie Taylor, *Women: A World Report*, p. 87.

Yet the "what" of IR is changing. For instance, peace studies and development studies have challenged conventional definitions of security and economic growth. Proponents of these studies argue that militarized national security, particularly in a nuclear age, and economic development strategies, which put profits before the needs of people and a sustainable ecology, compromise both individual and global security. By focusing on the security needs of people and the planet, these approaches open the field to gender issues. They permit the articulation of demands for peace, economic justice, and global equality, and they permit work in defense of the environment, on which women and all other living things ultimately depend.

In addition to rethinking the meaning of security, IR analysts have shifted from viewing states as the dominant actors toward the study of transnational institutions, organizations, and social movements. Although barely present at the top, women are active members of local, national, and transnational organizations. Issues that transcend national borders are becoming increasingly important today, making **nongovernmental organizations** (NGOs), composed of private individuals and groups, significant actors in world politics.

Finally, recent developments point to the growing impact of "people power." Although armed struggles grab most of the headlines, nonviolent revolutions are also prominent in today's world politics. Women have always participated in all types of revolutionary struggle; however, they play a particularly central role in nonviolent insurgencies, which require mass mobilization to induce the populace to cease cooperation with, and, thereby, delegitimize regimes. Both women's activism in nongovernmental organizations and their traditional roles in sustaining families and communities uniquely position them to mobilize people at the grass-roots level and to devise alternative networks for food, clothing, shelter, and health services. In addition, women have taken great risks to protest governmental crimes and bear witness to human rights violations. These actions have not in themselves toppled governments, but they have been significant factors in bringing about political change.

Politics itself has to be redefined in view of the wide range of political activities in which women are highly involved. No longer can politics be defined narrowly as an activity of governmental officials and elite influence peddlers, or popular participation be reduced to voting and membership in political parties. Instead, politics is about differential access to resources—both material and symbolic—and how such power relations and structures are created, sustained, and reconfigured. According to this broader definition, politics operates at all levels, ranging from the family and community to the state and the international sphere. All people act politically in their everyday lives. When feminists claim that the "personal is political," they mean that all of us are embedded in various kinds of power relationships and structures that affect our choices and aspirations on a daily basis and that, most important, are not natural (apolitical) but are subject to change.

Recognition of gender inequality as a global phenomenon with global implications challenges traditional definitions of IR. Sarah Brown argued that "the proper object and purpose of the study of international relations is the identification and explanation of social stratification and of inequality as structured at the level of global relations."[13] Compared to a standard definition, Brown's draws greater attention to political, economic, and social forces below and above the level of the state, thereby revealing the greater complexity of international politics, which cannot be reduced to the actions of state leaders and their international organizations. It also highlights inequality as a significant source of conflict in international relations in addition to, but also in tension with, notions about the inevitable clash of states with differing ideologies and interests. Finally, it speaks to global patterns of inequality operating across states, creating divisions among people along not just national lines but also gender, race, class, and culture lines. The corollary of this is that people are finding common cause with each other across national boundaries and, thus, creating a different kind of international relations, or world politics, from that of elite policymakers.

While world leaders and those who study them concentrate on sustaining the balance of power among the most powerful—in the interests of stability—nonelites around the world and those who study them focus on the imbalances of power that are created in the name of stability and that compromise the security of the majority of the world's people. People around the world struggling against the tyrannies of sexism, racism, classism, militarism, and/or imperialism seek justice, which requires upsetting the status quo. An IR lens focused exclusively on elite interstate actors and narrow definitions of security keeps us from seeing many other important realities.

In recent years, IR scholars and practitioners have become more sensitive to a variety of forces that divide and bind in the international system. They pay more attention to power struggles going on within and across states over land, religion, language, race, class, and general access to resources. They also study the historical processes that created the inequalities that have erupted into conflict. And even though much IR literature continues to speak of states and their leaders as unitary actors in world affairs, IR observers are becoming less likely to assume that the interests of a political leader are necessarily shared by the people whom he or she rules, even in so-called democratic countries. What most IR scholars and practitioners continue to avoid dealing with in any depth is gender inequality, despite evidence that it is integrally tied into all other inequalities and many global problems.

GENDERED DIVISIONS
OF WORLD POLITICS

In this section we introduce the issue areas examined in the following chapters and begin to expose the "hidden" gender at work in conventional accounts of IR.

Politics and Power

Masculinism pervades politics. Wendy Brown wrote: "More than any other kind of human activity, *politics* has historically borne an explicitly masculine identity. It has been more exclusively limited to men than any other realm of endeavor and has been more intensely, self-consciously masculine than most other social practices."[14]

In IR, as in political science, power is usually defined as "power-over," specifically, the ability to get someone to do what you want. It is usually measured by control of resources, especially those supporting physical coercion. This definition emphasizes separation and competition: Those who have power use it (or its threat) to keep others from securing enough to threaten them. The emphasis on material resources and coercive ability obscures the fact that power reckoning is embedded in sociocultural dynamics and value systems. Also obscured is the way that power presupposes relationships—among actors, resources, meaning, situation—and its inability to be accurately understood when separated from these relationships.

In IR the concept of "political actor"—the legitimate wielder of society's power—is derived from classical political theory. Common to constructions of "political man"—from Plato and Aristotle to Hobbes, Locke, and Rousseau—is the privileging of man's capacity for reason. This unique ability distinguishes man from other animals and explains his pursuit of freedom—from nature as well as from tyranny. Feminists argue that the models of human nature underpinning constructions of "political man" are not in fact gender neutral but are models of "male nature, " generated by exclusively male experience. They are not universal claims about humankind but masculinist claims about gendered divisions of labor and identity that effectively and sometimes explicitly exclude women from definitions of "human," "moral agent," "rational actor," and "political man."

Conceptually, "woman" is excluded primarily by denying her the rationality that marks "man" as the highest animal. Concretely, women have historically been excluded from political power by states' limiting citizenship to those who perform military duty and/or are property owners. Under these conditions, most women are structurally excluded from formal politics, even though individual women, in exceptional circumstances, have wielded considerable political power. In this century, women have largely won the battle for the vote, though definitions of citizenship continue to limit women's access to public power, and their political power is circumscribed by a variety of indirect means (discussed elsewhere in this text). Most obvious are the continued effects of the dichotomy of **public-private** that separates men's productive and "political" activities from women's reproductive and "personal" activities.

These constructions—of power, "political man, " citizenship, public-private, and so on—reproduce, often unconsciously, masculinist and androcentric assumptions. Sovereign man and sovereign states are defined not by connection or relationships but by autonomy in decision-making and freedom from the power of others. Security is understood not in terms of celebrating and sustaining life but as the capacity to be indifferent to "others" and, if necessary, to harm them. Hobbes's androcentrism is revealed simply when we ask how helpless infants ever become adults if human nature is universally competitive and hostile. From the perspective of child-rearing practices, it makes more sense to argue that humans are naturally cooperative: Without the cooperation that is required to nurture children, there would be no men or women. And although Aristotle acknowledged that the public sphere depends upon the production of life's necessities in the private sphere, he denied the power relations or politics that this implies.

Gender is most apparent in these constructions when we examine the dichotomies they (re)produce: political-apolitical, reason-emotion, public-private, leaders-followers, active-passive, freedom-necessity. As with other dichotomies, difference and opposition are privileged and context and ambiguity are ignored. The web of meaning and human interaction within which political man acts and politics takes place remains hidden, as if irrelevant. The point is not that power-over, aggressive behavior, and life-threatening conflicts are not "real" but that they are only a part of a more complicated story. Focusing on them misrepresents our reality even as it (to some extent unnecessarily) reproduces power-over, aggressive behavior, and life-threatening conflicts.

Security and Violence

Claims about men's superior strength are favored justifications for gender hierarchy. But such claims are misleading. On the one hand, men's strength varies cross-culturally and within cultures, and a considerable number of women are in fact stronger than men. On the other hand, what do we mean by strength? Anyone who has observed women of Africa on lengthy treks carrying heavy loads of firewood and water cannot help seeing how arbitrary our indicators of strength are. Why do we consider men's upper-body muscular strength more significant than women's burden-carrying strength and greater endurance? On what basis do we assume that bigger is better? (Consider the plight of dinosaurs!) Ashley Montagu undertook a comprehensive review of scientific literature and concluded that only androcentric lenses prevent our acknowledging the "natural superiority of women." Specifically, "the female is *constitutionally* stronger than the male": She has greater stamina, lives longer, fights disease better, and endures "all sorts of devitalizing conditions better than men: starvation, exposure, fatigue, shock, illness and the like."[15] Superiority is often defined in terms of the most effective survival traits— but not when women's abilities are assessed.

Historically, the greater muscular strength of (some) males has been a crucial factor when the outcome of conflicts depended on this particular strength. Today's technology dramatically alters the relationship of muscular strength to success in battle or in the workplace. But there continues to be a preoccupation with power and strength defined in masculine terms—upper-body strength as well as access to and use of weapons. And there is no denying that men, worldwide, engage in violent behaviors more frequently and with greater negative effect than do women. Males are encouraged to act aggressively in more situations than females and are systematically placed in situations where proving their manhood requires aggressive behavior. In fact, most models of masculinity include elements of courage and ambition that are difficult to disassociate from physical aggression and even violence. Ancient, classical, and modern depictions of warriors and political actors typically identify risking life—one's own and that of others—as the surest mark of a free man: "A real man lays his life on the line. For what is death risked? For honor, for glory, for a value greater than life, for freedom from enslavement by life, for immortality, or for the 'ultimate value' of the state."[16]

A willingness to engage in violence is built into our constructions of masculinity and is exacerbated by **militarization**—the extension of military practices into civilian life. And to the extent that we define national security as the defense and protection of sovereignty, militarization becomes hard to avoid. Believing that peace requires preparation for war, we become locked into arms races and other self-perpetuating cycles. These involve sacrificing social welfare objectives in favor of defense spending and training young people—men and women—to risk lives and practice violence in the name of putatively higher objectives.

There are no simple formulas for determining appropriate trade-offs between "butter" and "guns," and we are not suggesting that security concerns are illusory or easily resolved. But in a climate of militarization, we must be careful to assess the ostensible gains from encouraging violence because the actual costs are very great.

Moreover, the construction of security in military terms—understood as direct violence—often masks the systemic insecurity of indirect or **structural violence**.[17] The latter refers to reduced life expectancy as a consequence of oppressive political and economic structures (e.g., greater infant mortality among poor women who are denied access to health-care services). Structural violence especially affects the lives of women and other subordinated groups. When we ignore this fact we ignore the security of the majority of the planet's occupants. Finally, because violence is gendered, militarization has a reciprocal relationship to masculinist ideologies: The macho effects of military activities, the objectifying effects of military technologies, and the violent effects of military spending *interact*, escalating not only arms races but also sexual violence.

What the gendered division of violence constructs is a world shaped by hostile forces. In a self-repeating cycle, threats (real or fictive) increase preparations for defense and/or retaliation that are inextricable from conditions of structural violence. An oppositional lens magnifies and legitimates self-other, us-them, friend-enemy, aggressive-passive, soldier-victim, and protector-protected dichotomies. The latter dichotomy is institutionalized in protection rackets: creating a threat and then charging for protection against it. Some theorists argue that nation-states engage in such rackets by creating a system of mutually threatening centralized governments and charging citizens taxes and military service to support effective defense of state boundaries.[18] Feminists have similarly identified marriage as a protection racket. Under conditions of systemic male violence, women are forced to seek protection by entering into disadvantageous marriages to individual men.[19] People often fail to see the repetition of the same pattern in different situations, recognize the self-perpetuating and costly nature of this violence, and seek a way to break these self-destructive cycles.

Economics and Labor

The division of gender and identities is nowhere clearer than in the ways we define "work" and in which kinds of work are most valued, who does what, and how much they are paid. The stereotypes of women and femininity here interact powerfully with the ideology of public-private to generate quite rigid patterns in what men and women do. Just as the public is seen as more important than the private, women's jobs and the status and pay they are accorded tend to be seen as "secondary," as providing the support system for "more important"—the "primary"—work that men, especially elite men, do. Thus we find that women's work is largely of a servicing nature: taking care of the emotional (e.g., counseling, nursing), "entertainment" (e.g., performing arts, sex industries), production (e.g., word processing, assembly-line jobs), and maintenance (e.g., cleaning, clerical, child care, teaching) needs of men as individuals and the masculinist social system generally.

Treated as secondary, these jobs are not assigned high status and are not well paid. And women who earn a paycheck rarely do less unpaid work at home. Instead, women worldwide have a "double workday": earning money for the family while also being held responsible for child care and household maintenance. It seems that women are expected, consistent with the stereotype of femininity, to labor both at home and in the workplace, not for status or income as we expect men to do, but purely for the joy of serving others. Whereas men may be asked to volunteer their time and energy for a special cause or specific occasion, women are expected to volunteer their entire lives in the service of male needs and masculinist social orders. Of course women are not entirely without benefits in these societies. Nor do *all* men benefit equally from the exploitation of women's labor. But as a generalization, all men do benefit in various ways from the systemic masculinism that treats women's energies, lives, intellects, demands, and needs as secondary.

Economic relations are addressed in IR almost exclusively through the lens of neoclassical economics. The ostensible "free market" of capitalist global relations is assumed to be the most efficient and therefore most desirable approach to national and international economic relations.

Through this lens, an expanding world economy provides an ever-larger pie and, through a process of "trickle down," ever-bigger pies translate into larger slices, theoretically, even for those with few initial resources. Economic-development policies promote growth as the way to provide more goods and services to the world's rapidly increasing population. And capitalism is identified as the most effective system for securing growth.

In addition, formal modeling of exchange relations and market systems are popular in IR. These models appear to provide analytically powerful tools for understanding human decision-making and its cumulative consequences. On the basis of a rational actor's ("his") utilitarian assessment of market trade-offs, projections of other decision-making activities and their consequences are mapped. Thus game theory models are said to illuminate a wide range of human behaviors, such as responding to deprivation, making threats, risk-taking, and developing nuclear strategies. All such models leave out the complexity of human behaviors in real life because to make models workable, the variables they include must be reduced to a very few. The complex, ambiguous, and nuanced *context* of decision-making must be sacrificed to generate clear patterns that accommodate quantifiable analysis.

Left out are the hard-to-quantify dimensions of social reality, such as culture, emotional investments, and normative commitments. And once preference formation, prior conditions, and the context are considered irrelevant, it becomes hard to say what the relevance of the actual findings is. What does the study of behavior in poorly modeled situations tell us about behavior in the real world, in real-life decision-making? We do not argue that rational-actor modeling is useless. Rather, we ask and attempt to evaluate whether, in a context of scarce research resources, different approaches to IR would not contribute more to our ability to resolve global crises and reduce global inequality.

On the face of it, advocates of traditional approaches tend to reproduce rather than challenge the status quo because the questions they frame result in answers that confirm the assumptions upon which the questions are based. Gender dichotomies are built into the dualities favored by economic analysis: paid-unpaid work, providers-dependents, production-reproduction, and independence in the marketplace versus dependence. Just as women are deemed feminine by their dependence within the family, the Third World is "unmanned" by its position of dependence in the global economy. Finally, "trickle down" theories tend to benefit those who control the most resources by promoting the continued growth that delivers the biggest pieces of pie to those in power. Many argue that not only do the poorest never see the benefits of "trickle down" but even if they get marginally larger pieces, today's ecological crises (which hurt the poorest most) challenge the entire premise of ever-expanding growth.

Equity, Ecology, and Resources

Traditional texts in world politics often contrast "high" and "low" politics. High politics are state-centric security and military affairs; low politics, economic relations. Even more removed from the traditional core of IR concerns are matters of ecology, which are often called "soft politics." Once again, a hierarchy is at work, pitting high over low and hard over soft politics. In recent years, the seriousness of environmental degradation and the dependence of *all* of us on sustainable ecology have prompted much greater attention to environmental issues. When we begin to take the environment seriously, we are forced to examine how resources are distributed and who controls them. It is not simply an increasing population but also the disproportionate and to a large extent irresponsible consumption of resources on the part of industrialized nations that exacerbate resource depletion.

What are the causes of ecological irresponsibility? We observe first that numerous variables interact in sometimes unpredictable ways to shape environmental use. Industrialization promotes resource consumption because it accelerates the consumption of fuels and other raw materials and fosters a growth mentality that condones environmental destruction and the waste of material and human resources. Tragically, the "success" of industrialization and expansion leads to many failures. For example, in the United States the apparent wealth of resources contributes to wasteful attitudes like "bigger is better" and "growth is the answer," which dull environmental sensibilities, discourage recycling, and ignore the need to reduce consumption. We put short-term profit and convenience ahead of long-term security.

Nonindustrialized peoples rarely have the luxury of a throw-away mentality. Without the illusion of constant growth, many live in a symbiotic relationship with their environment. There is neither need nor advantage in wasteful or unnecessary consumption. However, the presence of growing populations in resource-poor environments also creates environmental degradation. People are forced to secure their everyday subsistence by depleting the very resources they depend upon. Water, food, and fuel for domestic use are essential for life, but the acquisition and consumption of these goods in much of the Third World conflict with long-term ecological planning and resources. At the macrosocietal level, development policies—whether securing foreign currency through the sale of timber or building an industrial base with fossil-fuel-driven factories—often have costly ecological consequences. The choices are not easy.

Gender divisions are played out in terms of who has access to what resources, who controls resources and to what ends, who suffers most from environmental degradation, and how gender stereotypes relate to irresponsible resource use. At core, the characteristically Western ideology of limitless growth presupposes a belief in "man's" dominion over nature (promoted, for example, in Christian and capitalist belief systems) and the desirability of "man's" exploiting nature to further his own ends. Conquering nature, digging out her treasure and secrets, proving man's superiority through manipulation of nature—these are familiar and currently deadly refrains. The identification of nature as female is not an accident but a historical development that is visible in justifications by elites for territorial and intellectual expansion. Exploitation is most readily legitimated by "objectifying"—treating something or someone to be exploited as an "object" devoid of intelligence or feelings. Thus, "natural resources" are deemed exploitable by right, no questions asked, "there for the taking." Historically, women, colonies, and the earth's bounty have all been treated as such natural resources. The gendered dichotomies of culture-nature, subject-object, exploiter-exploited, agency-passivity, and leader-follower are reproduced in the process and justification of exploiting human mothers and "mother nature."

Sustainable ecology and the equity it entails is gendered. Worldwide, females are more dramatically affected by environmental degradation than males. As food providers, the work load of women increases when water, food, and fuel resources deteriorate; as caretakers, they have to work harder when family and community members are victims of environmental disasters; as last and least fed, they suffer most from starvation and malnutrition; as poorest, they are least able to quit jobs, acquire adequate health care, purchase safer products, or move away from immediate environmental threats. As we illustrate in this text, women have long been active in ecological movements. But it is no longer "just women" who are systemically threatened by environmental crises.

CONCLUSION

We conclude this chapter by looking at gender in world politics along three dimensions: normatively (how we evaluate), conceptually (how we categorize and think), and organizationally (how we act). In contrast to our approach in this text, writers of conventional accounts tend to deny the importance of gender, its relation to social inequalities, and, therefore, the moral costs imposed by gender hierarchy. In regard to the *normative dimension*, blindness to gender inequality is a consequence of reigning ideologies—religious and secular—that naturalize status quo masculinism. A paradox operates here because the exaggeration of gender

differences both confirms the existence of gender inequality and depoliti-
cizes that inequality by reducing it to "natural" gender difference.

Some writers "ignore" the politics (and costs) of gender hierarchy by
claiming that gender is irrelevant to topics such as presidential politics or
national security. Therefore, they "avoid" acknowledging gender inequality and the moral issues it raises. In this case, the moral costs of
masculinism remain invisible on the false assumption that unless women
are explicitly part of the picture or sexuality is central to the topic, gender
is irrelevant. In contrast, stereotypical differences between men and
women and the lives they lead are not only acknowledged by some
writers—they are celebrated. In those accounts, the moral costs of
masculinism remain invisible on the false assumption that gender differences are not *political*—and bear moral costs—but are natural, the inevitable consequence of biological difference. In both cases, denying the pervasive effects of gender has the consequence of obscuring gender inequality
and the moral issues it raises.

Not only difference but also the privileging of men and masculinity
over women and femininity are "justified" by the assumption that male
being and knowing is the norm and is more valuable than female being
and knowing. Androcentric moralities thus do not take into account how
men's and women's lives differ and that such differences limit the appli-
cability of evaluations based on male experience only. The problem is
twofold: Androcentric moralities exclude or silence women's experience
and moral orientations and also fail—normatively—to be critical of gender inequality and injustice.[20] In sum, gender remains normatively invisible as long as we do not see how extensively it operates and as long as we
take the differences we see for granted, as givens rather than as political
problems.

In world politics, the inequalities of power, the effects of direct and indirect violence, the disparities between rich and poor, and the unequally
distributed costs of environmental degradation are most often deemed
the regrettable but unavoidable price of "progress." Through a gender-
sensitive lens we begin to ask how the highly acclaimed benefits of progress are distributed and who pays the greatest costs for them. We also
ask what kind of morality operates to keep current inequities and their individual and systemic costs from becoming daily matters of public out-
rage.

We observe that progress looks most acceptable, even desirable, to
those most advantaged by the status quo. If system transformations had
only win-lose ramifications, these people would have the most to lose.
Those who benefit the most are seldom aware of the extent of their privilege or its relation to the poverty of others (as most residents of the First
World remain ignorant of Third World poverty and its relation to First

World abundance). Of course, some of those who benefit endorse improvements for "others" who are "less fortunate" (trickle down). The point is that no conspiracy of greed or malintent need be posited. And although we can identify particular groups as generally benefiting more than others from systemic inequities, it is neither adequate nor accurate to hold any particular group solely responsible for structural effects. What we want to emphasize is that, however they originated in historical time, systemic or structural inequities are reproduced through the interaction of multiple variables, including the internalization of oppression by subordinated individuals, the abuse of power by those who wield it, the unaccountability of the marketplace, the institutional structures of racism, classism, ageism, and heterosexism, and it is these we must become aware of and transform.

It is in this sense that masculinism is key to understanding how we normatively accept rather than struggle against systemic inequities. As we argue in this text, masculinism and its twin, androcentrism, are ideologies that pervade our thinking, doing, and evaluating. They are ubiquitous and largely unquestioned. They not only institutionalize the particular hierarchy of masculine over feminine but also perpetuate belief in the inevitability of hierarchies in general. They emphasize abstract reason, objectification, and instrumentalism too often at the expense of attention to context and normative consequences. Their codification of oppositional, nonrelational categories promotes a silence on responsibility: By denying the *relationship of (inter)dependence* between fact and value, subject and object, exploiter and victim, and culture and nature, they obscure who has the greatest power—and therefore responsibility. Finally, these ideologies, to the considerable extent that they inform other normative orientations, blind us to how gender both creates and reproduces a world of multiple inequities that today threatens all of us.

The *conceptual dimension* refers to how patterns of thought make gender invisible. This includes the forms our thought takes (e.g, categories, dichotomies, stereotypes) and more encompassing or more structured systems of thinking (e.g., ideologies, theoretical frameworks, religion, science). Language is extremely important for patterning our thought; a vast literature now documents how gender—and the hierarchy it constructs—is built into the English language. As Laurel Richardson and Verta Taylor noted:

> Embedded in the language are such ideas as "women are adjuncts to men" (e.g., the use of the generic "man" or "he"); women's aspirations are and should be different than men's (e.g., "The secretary ... *she*," "the pilot ... *he*"); women remain immature and incompetent throughout adult life (e.g., "The girls—office staff—have gone to lunch"); women are defined in terms

of their sexual desirability (to men) whereas men are defined in terms of their sexual prowess. (Contrast the meanings of the supposedly equivalent words *spinster* and *bachelor, mistress* and *master, courtesan* and *courier,* etc.) As long as we speak the language we have acquired, we are not only speaking but also thinking in sex-stereotyping ways.[21]

English and other languages structure our thinking in dichotomies that emphasize difference, suggest timeless polarities, and thus obscure the interdependence, mutability, and complexity of the social world. The ideology of scientific objectivity structures subject-object and fact-value in dichotomies and thus directs our attention away from the actual and relevant sociopolitical relations of context. Finally, the privileged status of claims to "objectivity"—like claims to "reality"—marginalizes potential critiques.

The systematic effect of thinking in nonrelational categories is to exaggerate difference, separation, and inevitability. Rather than intimate a longer story and larger picture, nonrelational categories render events and beliefs as "givens," appearing inevitable because they are ahistorical and decontextual. If we are looking through the lens of "naturally given," we cannot even ask a variety of questions and cannot take seriously other challenges. Normative questions appear irrelevant or pointless and alternative visions appear necessarily utopian. If we think only in dichotomies—of objective-subjective and realist-idealist, then our attempts to criticize objectivity and realism are rendered immediately suspect—as irrational, illogical, idealistic, unreal. And it looks as though any critique of objectivity or realism *must* entail its opposite: a complete denial rather than a partial critique.[22]

Gender is at work here because dichotomies, masculinism, and androcentrism are present. In academe as elsewhere, we rely on what men have thought, written, and concluded to establish the "givens" of our discourses. That which pertains to the lives and experience of elite males is taken as the norm and defined as good. Thus, autonomy and freedom, independence from and power over others, separation from and control over nature, military and technological mastery, exploring and taming frontiers—these are given privileged status and held to be good for everybody. However, these values not only fail to benefit everybody; they no longer (if ever) unproblematically benefit elite men. And they have never afforded accurate understandings of the world. These orientations are not all bad, but their pursuit at the expense of other values has always been costly. Without exposing and examining the trade-offs, we continue to live irresponsibly and limit ourselves intellectually.

In terms of the *organizational dimension,* gender is rendered invisible primarily by the androcentric focus on what men do. By taking male experience as the norm and privileging it as the most important to know about, we find ourselves focusing on some activities at the expense of others. This is most obvious in terms of public-private domains and the elevation of men's issues, experiences, and activities over women's. But it is also present in academe, where "hard sciences" (chemistry, biology) and fields noted for logic (physics, philosophy) and instrumentalism (engineering, business administration) are male dominated and accorded the greatest prestige and authority. Outside of the academy, we pay more attention to areas of masculine interest (heart disease, rocketry, corporations) over feminine concerns (breast cancer, contraception, child care). In world politics we focus on national and international leaders, wars and militarization, and the high stakes of global economics.

What these patterns obscure are the relationships between activities, how they are mutually structured, and how alternatives can be pursued. They also obscure the social costs of separating production from reproduction, science from social values, politics from economics, and public from private life. Losing sight of history—forgetting that we *make* our world—locks us into patterns that have never served global justice and may now threaten even the most advantaged. For example, the expansion of global capitalism is associated with the increasing power of transnational corporations and their decision-making elites as well as with a greater reliance on high technologies and the professional class they foster. These developments threaten the majority of the planet's inhabitants in at least two profound ways.

First, the concentration of resources and power in the hands of a few is always suspect; when those few are not accountable to any public constituency, the threat is even greater that they will abuse their power. Second, the consumption of resources in relation to global ecology is dramatically shaped by the operations of giant corporations. The abuse of power through its concentration and the misuse of resources through their control by a small elite in the pursuit of profit combine in today's world. This restricts the opportunities available to the vast majority in every country and throughout the world. In various ways, we *all* participate in reproducing the inequity and imbalance that maintains the status quo. And in quite different but also costly ways, we *all* are impoverished by the status quo and the structural violence it entails.

THREE

□ □ □

Gendered Divisions of Power

W hat is power? Which gender "has" it? And how does it shape "who rules the world"? In this chapter we look at how gender shapes the meaning of power and how inequalities of power have gendered effects. We focus on the gendered division of power in terms of where women are positioned (and how they get there)—in comparison to men—as state actors in world politics.

The definition of power conventionally favored in IR, as in political science generally, is one of **power-over.** Power-over is captured in Robert Dahl's classic definition: the ability of A to get B to do something that B would not otherwise do. Defining power in this way emphasizes control of material—especially military—resources and a willingness to use them in order to enforce one's preferences. It is power-over in the sense of being top-down (those on top where the most resources are concentrated are determined to have the most power) and coercive (the ability to "force" compliance is determined to be the surest sign of power). When we use only this narrow definition of power to study world politics, we neglect investigating how other dimensions of social reality—moral commitments, ethnic allegiances, sociopolitical ideologies—shape how power works and who rules the world. Finally, this definition of power is masculinist to the extent that it presupposes androcentric notions of strength, competition, aggression, and coercion and because it focuses on power understood only in terms of public-sphere activities that are dominated by men.

IR texts often draw a distinction between "high" and "low" politics. The former concerns the strategic interests of states, understood in political and military terms, and involves the activities of those who wield power in the international "public sphere." Through a high-politics lens,

45

the focal points of inquiry are national security and military might and the actors of greatest significance are heads of state and military leaders. National security and military might are preeminently masculine activities and have long been dominated by male actors. Nevertheless, throughout history, women have been crucial to the success of states and militaries and individual women have effectively exercised state power.

Because states are viewed as the primary units in traditional IR, we look in this chapter at where women are positioned as political actors within the formal power structures of states: as heads of states or governments, diplomats, foreign service and military officers, as UN and other **intergovernmental organization** (IGO) officials, and as members of national legislatures and elite administrative bodies. We address the following questions: Where are the women who wield power in public-sphere activities? What proportion of formal political power is held by women? Why do so few women aspire to or achieve public office, and how do the few manage to get there?

This chapter demonstrates how gender is systematically at work in the "high politics" of IR by engaging an apparent paradox. We begin the chapter with data on the presence of women as powerful state actors. Our listing of women who in the past held or were holding (at this writing) positions of state power challenges the gender stereotype that portrays women as uninterested in or unfit for political leadership. By contrast, in the rest of the chapter we take gender stereotypes seriously. We do so in order to analyze the gendered division of political power, that is, how a gendered concept of power and the gendered consequences of international relations interact to position men and women very differently in relation to global power. We also address how and why the gender imbalance of political power remains so invisible in conventional accounts.

WOMEN AS STATE ACTORS

Women Acting as Heads of States and Governments

Individual elite women have, throughout history, wielded considerable political power and influence. An adept international politician, Cleopatra, ruler of Egypt in the first century B.C., exemplified a tradition of politically powerful women in ancient Egypt. It was under the strong and skillful rule of Queen Elizabeth I that England first rose to power in the sixteenth century; in the nineteenth century, Queen Victoria's alliance strategies in Europe and colonizing policies abroad secured Great Britain's position as the world hegemon. Similarly, in the eighteenth century, Catherine the Great's imperialistic foreign policy achieved world power status for Russia.

Heads of government are among the world's most powerful political actors, and in the twentieth-century a number of women have held these powerful positions (see Table 3.1). On the one hand, heads of state are key executive decision-makers and policy implementors within the nations they lead. On the other, their power "within" the state has international consequences to the extent that the military, political, economic, and cultural priorities they establish reach beyond territorial borders. Additionally, heads of government "represent" their states culturally as well as politically: In varying ways they come to symbolize the values of the country they represent. Female heads of state and government are no exception.

As prime minister (1960–1965, 1970–1977), Sirimavo Bandaranaike was largely responsible for the constitution of 1972 that transformed Ceylon into the Republic of Sri Lanka; in international affairs, she also served as chair of the Nonaligned Movement. Golda Meir, having served as minister of labor, and then for ten years as minister of foreign affairs, in 1969 became prime minister of Israel and led Israel through five tumultuous years. In the Philippines, Corazón Aquino was elected president in 1986 and governed during a period of severe economic problems—exacerbated by natural disasters—and difficult foreign policy decisions. Until her assassination in 1984, Indira Gandhi ruled as a formidable prime minister of India, overseeing the defeat of Pakistan and Indian dominance of the subcontinent. In 1988 Benazir Bhutto was elected head of state in Pakistan, remaining in power until ousted in a constitutional coup two years later.

In Europe, Gro Harlem Brundtland has headed social-democratic governments as prime minister of Norway three times; Brundtland also chaired the UN World Commission on Environment and Development, which in 1987 produced a global report on the environment.[1] In France, Edith Cresson served as prime minister after important positions in the ministries of agriculture, industry, trade, and European affairs. Perhaps most familiar is the first woman prime minister of Great Britain, Margaret Thatcher. After twenty years as a member of parliament, Thatcher served as prime minister from 1979 until 1990. Her forceful response to the Malvinas/Falkland Islands dispute and resolute conservative commitments won her the attribution of "Iron Lady."

Of women at the helm of governments as of 1992, Vigdis Finnbogadottir is a member of the Women's Alliance Party; prime minister of Iceland for many years, she has promoted both pacifist and feminist causes. In a dramatic rise to power, Violeta Chamorro became president of Nicaragua in 1990. Assuming leadership in the midst of military and

TABLE 3.1   Female Heads of State in the Twentieth Century (through 1992)

Office	State	Dates
President		
Corazón Aquino	Philippines	1986–1992
Agatha Barbara	Malta	1982–1987
Violeta Chamorro	Nicaragua	1990–
Vigdis Finnbogadottir	Iceland	1980–1984; 1984–1988; 1988–
Isabela Perón	Argentina	1974–1976
Mary Robinson	Ireland	1990–
Lidia Geiler Tejada	Bolivia	1979–1980 (interim pres.)
Ertha Pascal-Trouillot	Haiti	1990–1991 (interim pres.)
Prime Minister		
Siramavo Bandaranaika	Sri Lanka	1960–1965; 1970–1977
Benazir Bhutto	Pakistan	1988–1990
Gro Harlem Brundtland	Norway	1981; 1986–1989; 1989–
Eugenia Charles	Dominica	1980–
Edith Cresson	France	1991–1992
Elisabeth Domitien	Central African Republic	1975–1976
Indira Gandhi	India	1966–1977; 1980–1984
Maria Liberia-Peters	Netherlands Antilles	1984–1985; 1988–
Golda Meir	Israel	1969–1974
Maria de Lourdes Pintasilgo	Portugal	1979 (caretaker prime min.)
Milka Planinc	Yugoslavia	1982–1986
Kazimiera Prumkini	Lithuania	1990
Hanna Suchocka	Poland	1992–
Margaret Thatcher	United Kingdom	1979–1990
Khalida Zia	Bangladesh	1991–

economic crises, Chamorro was credited by *Time* magazine with "end[ing] the *contra* war in less than a month and quell[ing] riots without bloodshed."[2] Mary Robinson assumed the presidency of Ireland in 1990; in spite of the power of the Roman Catholic Church, Robinson has advocated the liberalization of laws relating to contraception, abortion, and divorce.

UN and Other IGO Officials

It is not only national leaders who are powerful actors on the stage of world politics: Observers of IR cannot help but acknowledge the increasing significance of international organizations)—especially the United Nations—in shaping world events. To the extent that IGOs play key roles, their elite officials are powerful actors. Women have a long history of support for and participation in international organizations; some have served in leadership positions and many more are moving "up through the ranks" in order to do so. Other women wield political power by representing their states as ambassadors to the United Nations.

Nafis Sadik, from Pakistan, holds the influential position of executive director of the UN Fund for Population Activities (UNFPA). Until recently, two women served at the secretariat level, which is just below the office of secretary-general (currently held by Boutros Boutros-Ghali). Therese Sevigny was under-secretary-general for public information and Margaret Joan Anstee was director-general for the United Nation's Vienna offices. At the next level, Mercedes Pulido de Briceno served as assistant secretary-general coordinator for women from 1984 until the position was eliminated in 1986 owing to budget cuts.[3] As directors of the UN Development Fund for Women (UNIFEM), Sharon Capeling-Alakija and Margaret Snyder have served at the executive level. Letitia Shahani formerly served as Nicaraguan ambassador to the United Nations. From 1977 to 1979, Gwendoline Kwonie of Zambia chaired the UN Council for Namibia. Most familiar in the United States is Jeane Kirkpatrick, an independent thinker and outspoken public official who served as the U.S. permanent representative to the United Nations in the early 1980s.

Diplomats and Foreign Service Officers

The art of diplomacy is well recognized as a dimension of effective international relations. In providing the personal link between governments, diplomats play significant roles in promoting successful communication and negotiating mutually desirable outcomes. They are frequently key actors in preparing for and carrying out major political, economic, and military projects.

Across the world, women are state actors by virtue of serving as ambassadors. For example, in 1991 Joelle Bourgois was France's ambassador to South Africa; Sally J. Kosgei represented Kenya in Great Britain; Rita Klimova represented Czechoslovakia in the United States; the New Zealand ambassador to France was Judith Trotter; the British ambassador to Luxembourg was Juliet J. d'A. Campbell; Eugenia Wordsworth-Stevenson was the Liberian ambassador to the United States; and Margaret Nasha represented Botswana in Great Britain. For the United States, women serving as ambassadors included Shirley Temple Black in Czechoslovakia, Arlene Render in Gambia, Carol B. Hallett in Bahamas, Mary Ann Casey in Algeria, Julia Chong Bloch in Nepal, Katherine Shirley in Senegal, and Jennifer C. Ward in Niger.[4]

In addition, women have organized lobbying and policy groups that both expose and influence gender dynamics in ministries, departments, and committees dealing with foreign affairs. Such organizations include Diplomatic Service Wives Association, Great Britain (DSWA); Association of American Foreign Service Women, United States (AAFSW); and Women's Action Organization, United States (WAO).

**Bureaucratic Elites
and Members of National Legislatures**

Women elected to national legislatures shape international relations through their votes on foreign policy issues and their participation on legislative committees. At the cabinet, or ministerial, level, women holding foreign policy and/or military/defense portfolios participate directly in shaping national policy and practice; those holding other portfolios less directly, but still powerfully, influence national policies having international implications and consequences.

Around the world, the percentage of women in legislative bodies has steadily increased since 1975.[5] The political power of these women is manifested in numerous ways: committee reports, legislative objectives, policy implementation. Women who have had ministerial and cabinet posts, particularly posts with a nondomestic focus, can more directly affect international politics and even emerge as particularly significant international political actors by becoming heads of state. Cases of this include Golda Meir and Edith Cresson, who headed important ministries before assuming the position of prime minister.

In 1991 women held cabinet posts with international influence in diverse countries, among them: Australia, Ros Kelly, tourism and territories; Botswana, Gaositwe Chiepe, external affairs; Canada, Mary Collins, status of women and national defense (associate minister); Ireland, Máire Geoghegan-Quinn, European affairs; Mali, Sy Maimouna Ba, rural development and the environment; Côte d'Ivoire, Jacqueline Lohoues-Oble, justice; Seychelles, Danielle de St. Jorre, planning and external affairs; Sweden, Anita Gradin, foreign trade.[6]

The first woman to serve as a cabinet member in the United States was Frances Perkins, secretary of labor from 1933 to 1945. Also serving as secretary of labor (under Ronald Reagan) was Ann Dore McLaughlin, who previously held subcabinet appointments in the Interior and Treasury departments. Other women who have held U.S. cabinet positions include Juanita Kreps (commerce), Elizabeth Dole (transportation), Margaret Heckler (health and human services), Lynn Martin (labor) , and Carla Anderson Hills (housing and urban development under Gerald Ford; U.S. trade representative under George Bush). Most recently, President Clinton appointed Donna E. Shalala to head the Department of Health and Human Services, Hazel R. O'Leary to run the Department of Energy, and Janet Reno as attorney general. Madeleine K. Albright is now the U. S. representative to the United Nations, Carol M. Browner is administering the Environmental Protection Agency, and Laura D'Andrea Tyson is chair of the Council of Economic Advisers. Although the number of women appointed at the cabinet level remains low, women are a growing percentage of appointees to subcabinet posts and are increasingly represented in more of the cabinet departments.[7] Moreover, if Clinton's appointments are any indication, women are making inroads into departments traditionally reserved for male leadership.

The highest percentage of women in ministerial positions is found in the Nordic countries, where male-only cabinets have not been the norm since the early 1970s. Particularly striking is the approximately 45 percent of women in Prime Minister Bruntland's third Labour government. Also noteworthy is the Parliament of the European Economic Community, where women have a higher percentage of representation (approximately 20 percent) than in national assemblies and where women's increased presence appears to have made a difference in the amount of legislation benefiting women.[8]

Military Officers

Throughout history, women have played significant roles in military activities: as leaders, warriors, camp supporters (nursing and "housekeeping"), and in keeping the home fires burning. In the twentieth century, women's participation in state militaries has expanded, especially in the West. For example, in the United States women accounted for only 2 percent of the military in 1973, which marked the beginning of the All Volunteer Force. In 1991 women were approximately 11 percent, serving in all branches and most jobs: "Over 378,000 officers and enlisted women serve in the active and reserve components, many in nontraditional 'combat type' jobs, such as pilots, security police, truck drivers, and missile gunners. They have participated actively in military missions of the 1980s (Grenada, bombing of Libya, Panama invasion, etc.) as well."[9]

Thirty-five thousand U.S. women served in the Persian Gulf war, with two held as prisoners of war and thirteen losing their lives.[10] Their distinguished performance generated congressional and public support for expanding women's roles in the military, as exemplified by the Senate's overturning a forty-three-year ban on women flying combat missions. Because high command positions require cumulative experience, the number of female senior officers is slowly increasing as women achieve seniority in the military.

HOW AND WHY ARE THESE WOMEN RENDERED INVISIBLE?

The preceding identification of national leaders, governmental officials, and civil service officers suggests that there are a number of women joining the ranks of elite men as powerful national and international actors. It is hard to deny the power wielded by women who have governed First World states that hold seats on the UN Security Council (Thatcher) or Third World states that are geopolitically strategic (Aquino, Gandhi, Chamorro). Yet our lack of familiarity with the many other women named above suggests how invisible they—and the power they wield—remain. Moreover, even the presence of numerous women has not prompted gender-sensitive analyses in international relations. In other words, not only are there very few women "at the top," but even those who succeed in achieving positions of power remain largely gender invisible in conventional accounts of how power works in the world. How can we explain this failure to acknowledge gender patterns, and specifically, the absence of feminist analyses, in the face of women as global actors?

We turn first to the most obvious: Although women are approximately 50 percent of the population worldwide, the percentage of women in positions of national and international power is indeed very small: "Of the 159 United Nations member States, only six (3.8 percent) were headed by women at the end of 1990: Iceland, Ireland, Nicaragua, Norway, Dominica and the Philippines. Women also are poorly represented in the top echelons of government. Only 3.5 per cent of the world's cabinet ministers are women, and women hold no ministerial positions in 93 countries of the world."[11]

Thus gender continues to be "invisible" in part because so few women appear in the world's most powerful decision-making positions: heads of government and ministers. In addition, though most women in the world finally have the right to vote, women remain dramatically underrepresented in political institutions of "numerical representation" (on the basis of "one person, one vote").[12] In 1987, women's representation exceeded 15 percent in only 23 of 159 countries.[13] Women's participation in national legislatures has historically been highest (reaching 34 percent) in the Nordic countries, Eastern Europe, and the former Soviet Union. Elsewhere, women's parliamentary representation rarely exceeds 10 percent and is surprisingly low (5 percent) in the United Kingdom and the United States, where women's movements have been organized for several decades.

As Figure 3.1 indicates, women's participation in national legislatures was steadily increasing (between 1975 and 1987) in all regions of the world, but it was still low compared to men's. And Figure 3.2 indicates that political restructuring in Eastern Europe and the former Soviet Union has been "costly" to women's political power: Data from recent elections show women rapidly losing "representational ground." The loss of women's political representation we are witnessing in Eastern Europe is a grim reminder of the fragility of women's political power: Gains secured at great cost in one period are all too frequently abandoned, renounced, or traded away in other periods. Throughout history, women have found

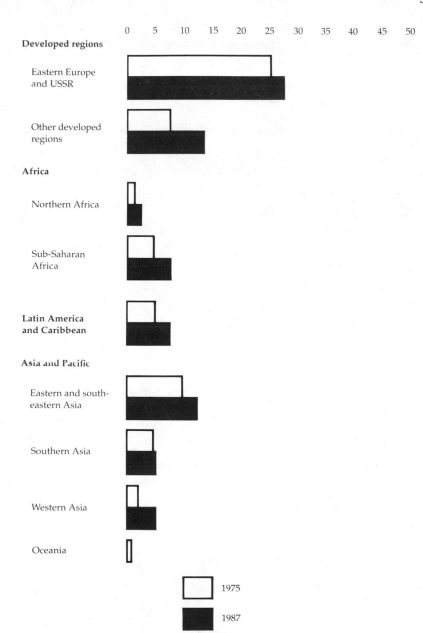

FIGURE 3.1   Gendered parliamentary representation, by region. Average percentage of women in parliamentary assemblies (unicameral assembly or lower chamber of bicameral assembly) in 1975 and 1987. *Source:* United Nations, *The World's Women: 1970–1990 Trends and Statistics* (New York: United Nations Publications, 1991), p. 32. Used by permission of United Nations Publications.

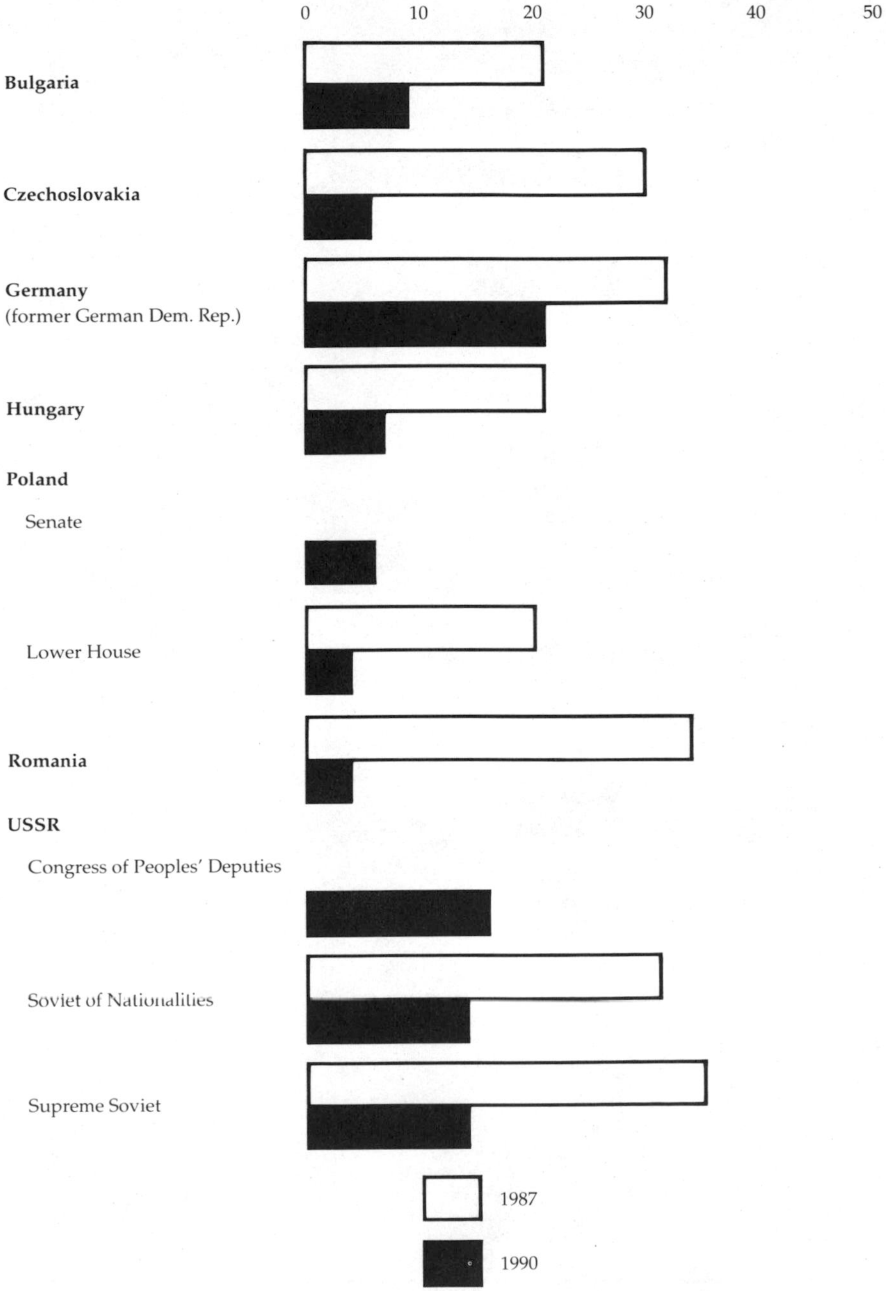

FIGURE 3.2   Recent decline in women's representation, Eastern Europe and USSR/CIS (percentages of women in parliaments in 1987 and 1990). *Source:* Data from United Nations, *The World's Women: 1970–1990 Trends and Statistics* (New York: United Nations Publications, 1991), p. 33.

themselves fighting the same battles, in different periods or contexts, for their rights and status as political actors.

The pattern of women's exclusion from traditional positions of power is replicated in IGOs, governmental bureaucracies, and institutions of economic decision-making. In the United Nations, like many large corporate institutions, women constitute only 3.6 percent of decision-making elites. Whereas women are fairly equally represented in entry-level grades, where competitive examinations determine hiring, their low representation at higher levels is due in part to recruitment practices that favor men. For example, outside recruitment depends on the submission of candidates by member states, which frequently choose from among their delegates to the United Nations; women are underrepresented in these delegations:

> In 1989, there were only 337 women [out of 1,695] in the diplomatic staffs of the permanent mission to the United Nations in New York. ... Sixty missions had no women. ... Only eight of these women held the rank of ambassador. At the UNCTAD VII Conference in 1987, there were only 173 women delegates out of 1,375 (13 percent), and 63 delegations out of 137 included no women. At [a session of the] Fourth United Nations Development Decade, 5–16 June 1989, there were 20 women delegates out of 210 (9.5 percent) and 65 delegations out of 89 included no women.[14]

Underrepresented at the top, women typically appear in greater percentages at lower levels of institutional power. They are overrepresented at the least-powerful level, clerical and support staff, where women (especially in the West) often constitute over 85 percent of workers (see Figure 3.3).

In unions, political parties, special interest organizations, and bureaucracies women may constitute a significant proportion of membership, but typically they form only a small minority (usually less than 5 percent) of officeholders or top decision-makers. In unions, women's membership varies by region and political system (see Figure 3.4), with the highest percentages in Nordic and Eastern European countries and lowest in developing countries.[15]

In developed countries, women are active in political parties but tend to remain outsiders at elite levels. Underrepresented in leadership positions, women are less likely to be put forward for office, which keeps the proportion of officeholding women low. To the extent that executive and ministerial elites are drawn from the pool of prior officeholders, women again face disadvantages, resulting in continued underrepresentation in top decision-making positions. This "route to the top" is confirmed by studies that find a strong correlation between percentages of women in legislative bodies and in ministerial positions.[16]

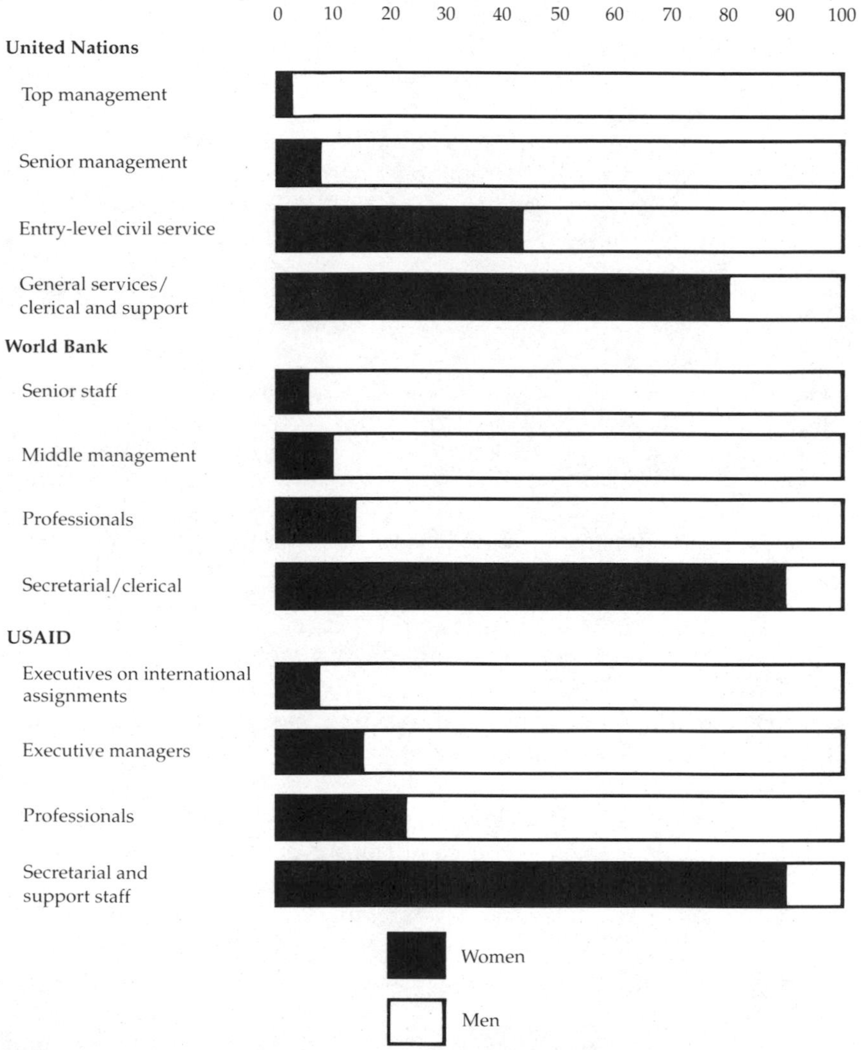

FIGURE 3.3 Gendered employment patterns: international agencies, 1980s (percentages respectively women and men). *Sources:* Data from United Nations, *The World's Women: 1970–1990 Trends and Statistics* (New York: United Nations Publications, 1991), p. 5; Joni Seager and Ann Olson, *Women in the World: An International Atlas* (New York: Simon & Schuster, 1986), map 38; Linda Schmiltroch, ed., *Statistical Record of Women Worldwide* (Detroit: Gare Research, 1991).

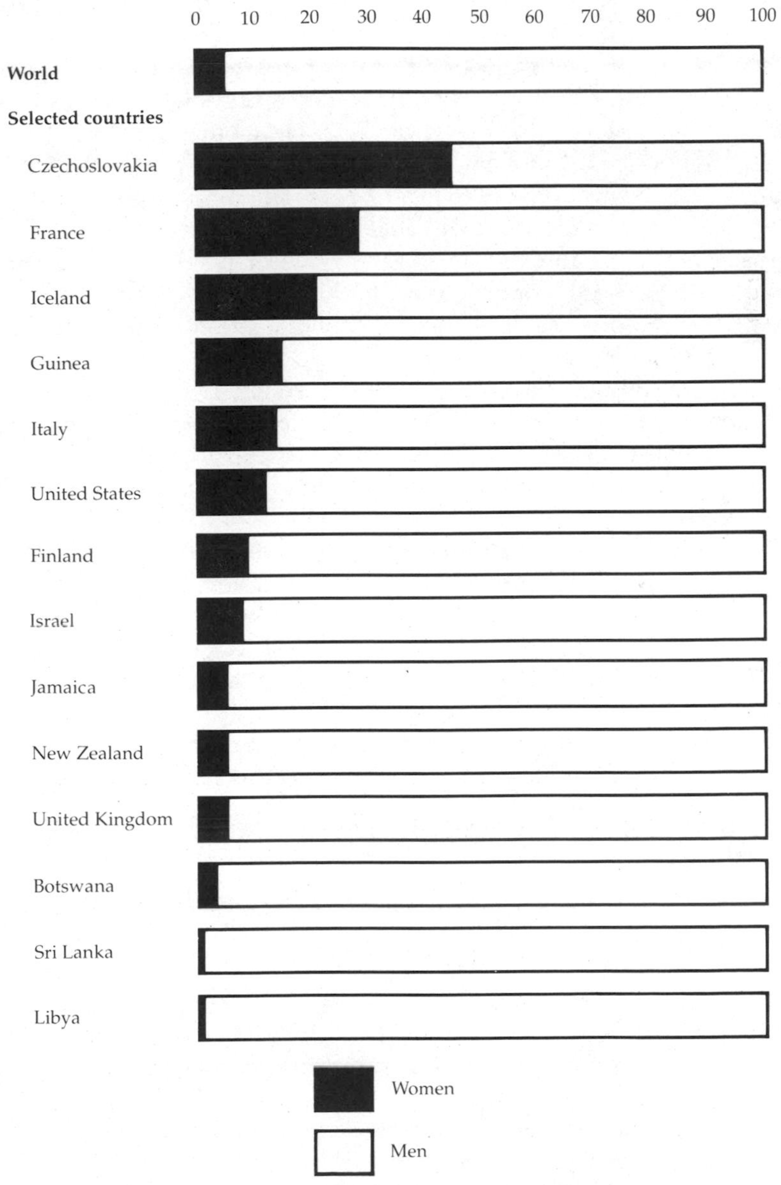

FIGURE 3.4   Gendered trade union officials: selected countries, 1980s (percentages respectively women and men). *Source:* Data from Joni Seager and Ann Olson, *Women in the World: An International Atlas* (New York: Simon & Schuster, 1986), map 20.

Women tend to be even more marginalized in business and economic-interest organizations (see Figure 3.5) than they are in "representational" channels of political power.[17] Vicki Randall reported that in 1986 only seven women were on boards of directors of the 100 leading companies in Britain, women in Western Europe are underrepresented in top offices by a factor of two or more, and even Scandinavian women hold few elite positions.[18] A 1992 report indicated that in France, only 1 percent of all corporate chief executive officers (CEOs) were women.[19] In the United States, a 1989 study of the 1,000 most valuable publicly held companies (with annual sales of $3.3 trillion) revealed only two women among the chief executive officers.[20] These proportions are far lower than women's representation among national leaders and confirm the "minuscule influence of women in the world of big business."[21]

In the contemporary world, power exercised by business both directly and indirectly shapes political power. Women's exclusion from leadership in economic decision-making bodies has considerable political significance in two ways. First, business and interest organizations produce and effectively promote candidates for political office. Second, these organizations often "come together with governments and bureaucracy to form a corporate policy-making channel."[22] As long as women are excluded from business power, their political power is diminished. This is especially the case as political power is increasingly shaped by corporate interests outside of the traditional channels of representative government.

These figures confirm that few women are situated at what is considered the apex of international political power. But they also raise the following questions: *Why* are so few women in power? *How* did women in power get there? And *what* are the gendered consequences of their being in power?

WHY SO FEW?

Explaining *why* people do or do not engage in political activities (traditionally defined "political behavior") has long been a focus of political science. Researchers have studied gender differences in political participation extensively, in particular the low percentage of women in high political office. Two conclusions emerge repeatedly from this research. First, women do not lack interest in or motivation for political action: Studies of women's participation in grass-roots organizing, community politics, election campaigns, and political organizations suggest that "women are as likely (if not more likely) to work for political causes or candidates as are men."[23] Second, a point related to the first, women's underrepresentation in political office and leadership positions is linked to gender-

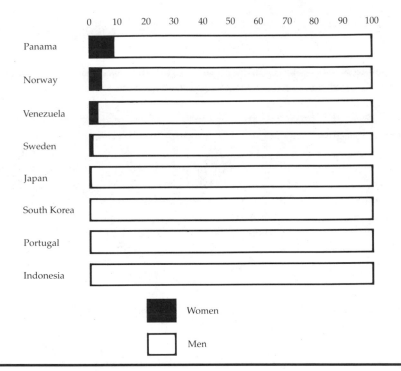

FIGURE 3.5 Gendered money management: policy-making positions in finance, insurance, and real estate, selected countries, 1980s (percentages respectively women and men). *Source:* Data from Joni Seager and Ann Olson, *Women in the World: An International Atlas* (New York: Simon & Schuster, 1986), map 21.

differentiated patterns pervasive in today's world. Gender socialization, situational constraints, and structural obstacles interact in discriminating against women as candidates for and effective holders of political office.[24]

Gender Socialization

Early studies tended to focus on the effects of sex-role stereotyping, that is, the enduring consequences of childhood socialization of girls and boys into mutually exclusive gender roles. Presumably, socialization into appropriate "feminine" behavior makes women less likely than men to pursue traditionally defined political activities. For example, feminine-identity formation is inextricable from cultural expectations that motherhood is the primary role of women, that women's domestic role is antithetical to public-sphere activities, and that traits associated with political efficacy (ambition, aggression, competitiveness, authority) are distinctly *unfeminine*. To the extent that women internalize these stereotypical norms, they are unlikely to perceive themselves as political actors or aspire to public office.

As a corollary, socialization into appropriate "masculine" behavior makes men more likely than women to identify with political activities. Just as important, gender stereotypes, because they are held by men *and* women, create a "climate" that encourages male participation while discouraging female participation in politics. Thus, individual women who seek leadership positions must struggle not only with their own internalized stereotypes but also with the fact that gender stereotyping in general fuels *resistance* to women as political actors. Finally, for women who do achieve positions of power, expectations of appropriately "feminine" behavior are often in conflict with qualities required for successful leadership. In short, gender stereotypes suggest that appropriately feminine women (passive, dependent, domestic; engaged in meeting private, familial needs) are by definition inappropriate political agents (active, autonomous, public oriented; engaged in meeting collective, not personal, needs).

Situational Constraints

Gender socialization produces different male and female orientations toward political participation. Gender stereotyping produces behavioral patterns that result in different concrete living situations for women and men that also constrain women's participation. Hence, we are better able to explain gendered political participation if we look at the *interaction* of stereotypes, for example, how women are assigned domestic and mothering responsibilities, and gender-differentiated living situations, for example, how the gendered division of labor limits women's involvement in traditional or "formal" politics. More than any other obstacle, the time and energy demands of having primary responsibility for children are identified as the main constraints on women's political participation, especially their pursuit of political office. This makes sense in light of recent data showing that the average employed, married woman in the United States works eighty-four more hours per month than her husband.[25]

All over the world, women who earn income are burdened by a **double workday.** Not only are they responsible for work that produces income; they are also held responsible for work that ensures the reproduction of the family unit and the physical maintenance of the household. Moreover, it is not simply the longer workday that inhibits women's participation in politics; it is also women's lack of control over *when* they will be available and whether (or how) family obligations will interfere with political pursuits.[26] In general, the more demanding the form of political participation (e.g., officeholding versus voting) the more it conflicts with women's mothering responsibilities—though some women, in spite of these constraints, are officeholders. It does appear that women who seek high-level administrative and political careers are more likely than men to remain unmarried, to be divorced, or to enter politics at a later age, when mothering responsibilities have diminished.

These patterns reveal the difficulties *for women only* of combining family responsibilities and political office.[27] Men are not forced to make these choices because their political activities are considered separate from their domestic relations. Women, in contrast, are so closely identified with the domestic sphere that when they take on political activities it is considered in combination with, not separable from, their role in the family. As a telling example, a West German high court in 1986 ruled that "politics and childrearing were incompatible" and, on that basis, Green party executive member Margarete Wolf-Mayer was denied custody of her child.[28]

Structural Obstacles

Clearly, stereotypes and situational constraints shape the gender of political activism, but the recurring differences in women's and men's participation must also be examined in relation to large-scale, interacting, and enduring social structures. Here we refer broadly to sets of power relations and/or social-cultural institutions that determine the boundaries of individual behavior. Understanding why so few women hold political power requires understanding how social structures and their interaction make it much more difficult for women (than men) to seek and secure political office. Although primary gender socialization occurs in childhood, the hierarchical dichotomy of masculine-feminine is enforced throughout our lives. The gender dimensions of multiple social structures interact and, in effect, "discipline" individual behavior to conform to stereotypes.

For example, traditional religious belief systems and institutions play an important role in perpetuating images of women that deny them leadership positions. All too frequently, women are portrayed as either the source of evil (the uncontrollably sexual whore) or the model of saintliness (the self-sacrificing virgin). Neither is an appropriate identity for political *leadership*. In addition, the vast majority of religious institutions themselves exclude women from top leadership roles. No matter how this exclusionary practice is legitimized, it in fact sends a clear and unequivocal message that reinforces gender stereotypes: that women are not equal to men and that they cannot be trusted with or lack the qualifications for positions of authority and power.

Religious beliefs interact with and may reinforce other cultural sources of gender stereotyping. This is generally the case in regard to identifying the home/family as woman's sphere and the public/politics as man's sphere. It can also be quite explicit, as in the seclusion of women (purdah) practiced in many Islamic countries.[29] The point is that the structural separation of public and private has gendered consequences. Religious, educational, and judicial institutions tend to reproduce the ideological division of public and private and its gendered dynamics. Both informal and formal public-private separations affect women's political participation negatively by identifying women exclusively with the private sphere.

Thus, our expectations of different behaviors for men (appropriate for politics) and for women (inappropriate for politics) make it difficult, first, for women to see themselves comfortably in conventionally defined political roles and, second, for men and women generally to see and accept women as political agents. In the latter case, negative attitudes toward women's political participation are expressed as lack of confidence in and support for female candidates and politicians.[30] In sum, to the extent that we perpetuate the stereotype of "a woman's place is in the home" (or in the bedroom), we ensure that women will be seen as "out of place" in political office.

As Figures 3.6, 3.7, and 3.8 indicate, gender divisions of labor reflect the effects of gender stereotyping. Although the specific jobs assigned to women and men vary cross-culturally, "women's work" worldwide is associated with lower status and pay and less power than "men's work." As Hilary Lips pointed out: "Traditional stereotypes work against gender equality in the workplace because they help to promote the idea that women and men are suited for different kinds of work—and that the jobs for which women are best suited are the least powerful, lowest-paying ones."[31]

The horizontal and vertical segregation of both men and women in the work force affects women's access to political power. Horizontally, women are concentrated in fewer occupations than men and in jobs where women are the majority of workers—clerical work, elementary teaching, nursing, waitressing. Moreover, these are not occupations from which political candidates are traditionally recruited. In general, the work women do for pay is an extension of the feminine role assigned to women and replicates work women are expected to do as mothers and wives: care for dependents, serve the needs of others, provide social and physical necessities, and be docile, flexible, emotionally supportive, and sexually attractive.[32] Not only are women clustered in certain jobs but they are also expected to be "feminine" in whatever job they hold.

The workplace is also segregated vertically, with women concentrated in pink-collar jobs (men in blue-collar), in domestic services (men in protective services), and in light industry (men in heavy industry).[33] Vertical gender segregation ("the higher, the fewer") occurs both within and across industries: Women generally are concentrated in part-time, temporary, nonorganized, lower-status, lower-paying, and less-powerful positions. As a result, women earn less money, have less-secure jobs, and

63

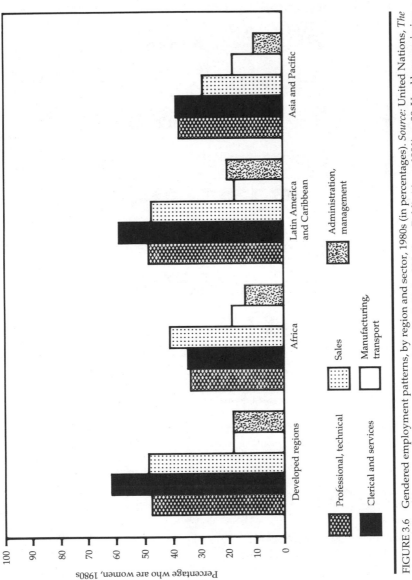

FIGURE 3.6 Gendered employment patterns, by region and sector, 1980s (in percentages). *Source:* United Nations, *The World's Women: 1970–1990 Trends and Statistics* (New York: United Nations Publications, 1991), p. 88. Used by permission of United Nations Publications.

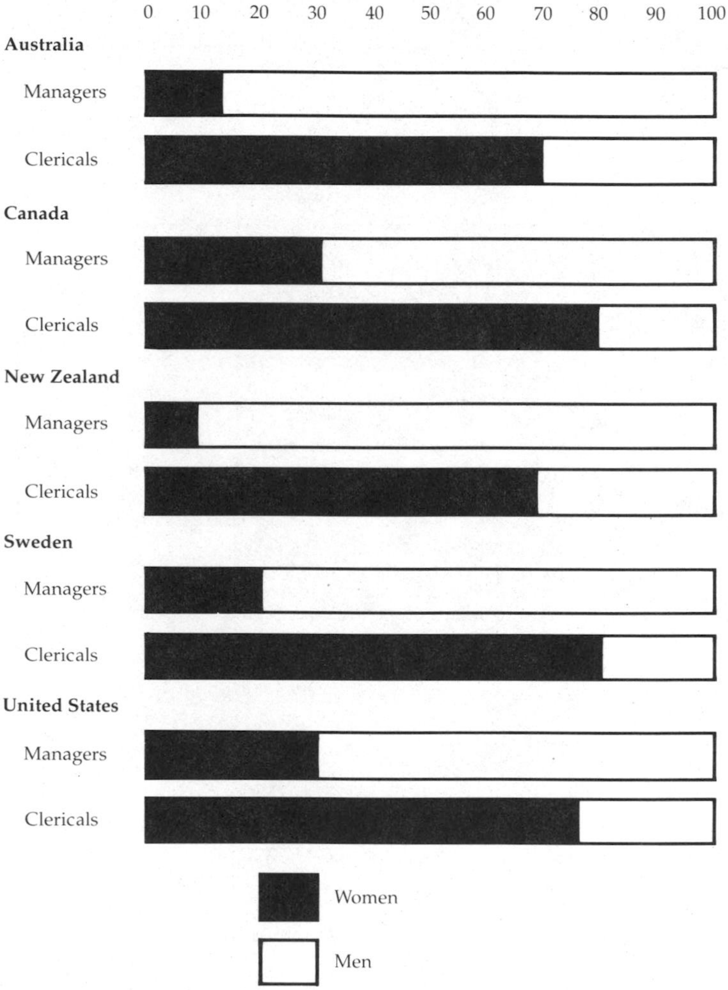

FIGURE 3.7   Gendered employment: five developed countries, 1980s (percentages respectively women and men). *Source:* Data from Linda Schmiltroch, ed., *Statistical Record of Women Worldwide* (Detroit: Gare Research, 1991), p. 468.

rarely climb into powerful executive ranks. Race, ethnicity, and class discrimination interact with gender discrimination to exacerbate the self-perpetuating cycle of elite males holding on to power at the expense of all other groups.

Gendered divisions of labor affect women's political participation in multiple ways. Most obviously, women's structural disadvantage in the labor market translates into their having fewer resources, less status, and

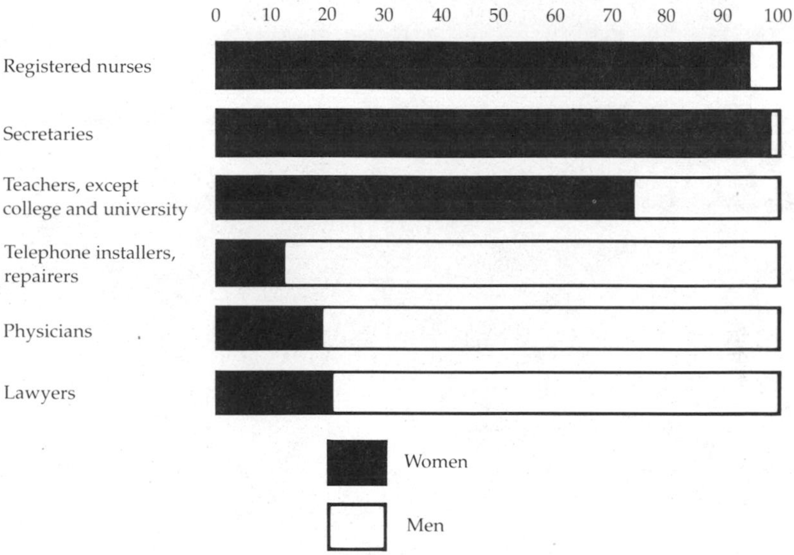

FIGURE 3.8 Gendered labor force: selected U.S. occupations, 1990 (percentages respectively women and men). *Source:* Data from U.S. Department of Labor, Bureau of Labor Statistics, *Working women: A Chartbook* (August 1991), p. 43.

less experience "wielding" power when competing with men for political office. And when it comes to recruiting and promoting people for political office, educational and occupational structures interact to exacerbate women's disadvantage. Women receive not only a *different* education than men do but, in most of the world, a good deal *less* education than men. Because education is so closely related to occupational opportunities, lack of educational training fuels the gender segregation of the work force and its negative consequences for women. Moreover, certain professions have historically been associated with or appear particularly compatible with achieving and maintaining political power: law, military, career civil service, big business. It remains the case that women are underrepresented in these occupational areas and are especially "absent" at the top levels from which political leaders are often recruited.

Other obstacles to women's political participation include direct and indirect legal barriers. Gaining the right to vote is a first step. France did not legalize women's suffrage until 1944; Switzerland held out until 1971. Women are still not permitted to vote in Kuwait and Saudi Arabia. The right to be elected is a second step. Women did not gain that right until 1952 in Greece, 1961 in El Salvador, and 1974 in Jordan. Women were not permitted to run for Parliament in the United Kingdom until 1918,[34] and married women were barred from the civil service until 1946; in the

"Secretaries." Cartoon showing the factors contributing to the feminization of poverty. CATHY copyright 1992 Cathy Guisewite. Reprinted with permission of UNIVERSAL PRESS SYNDICATE. All rights reserved.

United States, until 1971 women foreign-service career diplomats were required to resign if they married. And although women had held offices in Arizona for some time, it was only in 1988 that Arizona voters *legally* removed a requirement that state officeholders be male. It should be noted that 19 percent of voters in 1988 voted *against* repeal.[35]

The gender patterns of military service also shape who reaches political office. A strong correlation between military (especially combat) experience and access to political leadership is typical in developing countries under military domination (approximately 64 countries were so identified in 1990)[36] but is not restricted to militarized states of the Third World. Since the time of Washington, combat experience—which still excludes nearly all women—has seemed almost a mandatory qualification for those seeking the U.S. presidency. As of 1992, twenty-seven (of the forty-two) U.S. presidents had served in the military; eleven had held the rank of general; until Clinton's election in 1992, every president since 1944 (Truman), had had military experience.[37]

In the 1992 campaign, Bill Clinton's failure to have served in Vietnam was used to challenge his trustworthiness as well as his ability to play the role of commander in chief. In the 1984 campaign, vice presidential candidate Geraldine Ferraro was asked repeatedly whether she "had what it takes" to push the nuclear button; Dan Quayle was rendered suspect by his avoidance of active duty; and George Bush drew on his bailing out of a B-29 to counter the "wimp factor" in his public image.[38] Similarly, it is no accident that as soon as "victories" were reported in the Gulf war, U.S. military leaders were proposed as presidential candidates.[39] For women, who remain a small percentage of the military and are largely excluded from combat, the military path to political power excludes them. In fact, as long as military experience is perceived as the requisite criterion of manliness for high political office, the only way women can "demonstrate" the required militancy is by adopting an *excessively* "tough lady" image. Ironically, the few women in power may feel pressured to "outmacho" their male counterparts and render invisible whatever "feminine" qualities they may have brought to the job.[40] In sum, gender stereotypes and the *interaction* of situational constraints, domestic responsibilities, and religious, educational, economic, legal, and military structures discriminate against women's political participation and, especially, their access to high political office.

From another angle of vision, political institutions themselves can be seen to impede women's participation. Vicki Randall identified three institutional barriers in her discussion of political recruitment and promotion.[41] First, at each level, political advancement requires "appropriate" political, leadership, educational, and/or occupational experience: As noted above, these criteria discriminate against women who are structurally likely to have different and fewer resources and/or start later in their pursuit of office.

Second, the institutions associated with politics and power and the norms and practices of these institutions are those of "a man's world." Exclusively male until recently and still dominated by men, they are masculinist in the following senses: Behavior traits deemed suitable, sometimes essential, for political success are stereotypically masculine (ambition, leadership, rationality, competitiveness, authority, toughness); meeting times and locations, as well as socializing (networking) activities, are in practice convenient for men's (not women's) schedules and geographical mobility; and issues of central importance are not those most immediately relevant to most women's lives ("women's issues" are treated as peripheral to conventional politics).[42]

Randall identifies a third institutional barrier in the direct expression of male prejudice: outright discrimination against women.[43] Forms of discrimination in the workplace vary, but the presence of gender hierarchy and sexism creates a less favorable environment for women, who must then struggle harder than male counterparts to be successful.[44] As long as the workplace and political office are identified as "male terrain," women constantly confront and must deal with resentment of their unwanted presence. Women are most frequently reminded of their outsider status when they are viewed not as colleagues but in terms of their gender and sexuality. Subtle and not-so-subtle references to women and sexuality produce an atmosphere of male dominance in which women must either become "like men" or become invisible.[45]

HOW DO WOMEN GET TO THE TOP?

Having identified multiple, interacting factors that impede women's access to office, we will now consider how women, especially those at the apex of political power, managed in fact to get there. Candidates for elite office are traditionally recruited from prior leadership roles in political parties, local or regional government, unions, interest groups, business, civil service careers, and/or the military. We have seen that women are at a disadvantage in regard to these traditional routes to power: In general, women have less access to and leadership experience within the institutions that "feed" candidate pools. Yet women do reach the top. By examining the routes they take, we learn more about the gender division of power.

Most important, both men and women at the apex of national and international power tend to be well educated (the women, often in nontraditional areas), affiliated with "political families," and come from backgrounds of relative wealth and privilege. Some women follow the political party stepping stones to power: advancing through local, regional, and national party activities and building on previous electoral successes (Thatcher, Meir, Cresson, Eugenia Charles). Other women rise to power during transitional periods: when a compromise (and conciliatory) candidate is sought (Chamorro, Aquino) or when grass-roots issues have gained prominence and prompted a search for fresh leadership (Brundtland, Finnbogadottir). Finally, some women (Gandhi,[46] Bhutto, Khalida Zia, Aquino, Chamorro, Bandaranaike, Isabela Perón) acquire political office initially through their relationships to politically prominent men[47] (see Figure 3.9).

WHAT ARE THE GENDER
CONSEQUENCES OF WOMEN IN POWER?

What do these patterns reveal about gender relations? On the one hand, we observe that a frequent route to high office for women is through family connections and specifically, the death of a father or husband. In these cases, women *enter* office less on the basis of political experience, especially political leadership, than on the basis of their relationship to men of political stature. Coming from prominent families, acting as "male surrogates," and often symbolizing national unity in conflict-ridden situations, these women may find it difficult to establish themselves as leaders in their own right. There are several dimensions of gender at work here. Being female is not *always* a disadvantage: When symbols of unity, compromise, or conciliation are sought, women may have an advantage over men. That is, stereotypes of women can work to the benefit of female leaders in situations where crises or transitions require a caring, ameliorative figure. Especially in Latin America, women have used the image of "supermadre" to gain political power and promote alternative political agendas.

At the same time, however, the very effectiveness of the stereotypes serves to reproduce, rather than challenge, gender dichotomies. When women act "like women," even though they are at the helm of national governments, the traditional picture of gender is not disturbed. Similarly, when women assume national leadership as a result of their success in grass-roots activism, their association with "soft issues" (the environment, peace, feminism) can reinforce the traditional *dis*association of women with "hard issues" (national security, economic competition) and the masculine traits assumed necessary for dealing with them (fearlessness, cold reason).

It is not surprising then that often women who "get there on their own" (Thatcher, Meir) are identified as especially masculine. Some research suggests that women aspiring to or holding political office play

FIGURE 3.9 A female "statesman." Indira Gandhi worked as an aide to her father, Jawaharlal Nehru, then rose through the ranks of the Congress Party and became a formidable prime minister. She was often referred to as the "mother" of her nation. Courtesy of Information Service of India, Embassy of India, Washington, D.C.

down feminine qualities in order to appear more appropriate for "states-manship."[48] Certainly Margaret Thatcher conveyed in her attitude and enacted in practice a disdain for feminism. She denied its relevance in her life, and as prime minister she undermined social services for women. During her eleven years of power she did not appoint even one women to a ministerial post. Moreover, we must acknowledge the rationality of this behavior: "Those who argue that it should not be necessary for successful women to adopt so-called masculine attributes ignore the fact that, given social definitions of 'male' and 'female' identity traits, this may be the only possible strategy to gain acceptance as a woman in an authority role."[49]

The overall picture remains one of continued gender dichotomies: Women succeed through their identification as "traditional" (feminine) women facilitating male-defined projects, as trivialized "soft leaders," or as manlike by their playing down any association with feminine "weak-ness." It appears that being seen as politically *powerful* in the traditional sense requires that women become "like men. " Two points emerge from this brief discussion of women in the highest state offices.

First, as long as female political actors are perceived either as tradi-tional women or "invisible women" (because they are acting like men), gender expectations are not really disrupted. Paradoxically, even when women wield the highest state power, by continuing to behave in gender-stereotypical ways, they reinforce rather than challenge the politics of gender. Even though gender is at work here (shaping pathways to and the exercise of power), it remains "invisible" to observers of world politics. In other words, by appearing as traditional women or honorary men, female politicians do not challenge the categorical distinction between feminin-ity and masculinity and do not politicize this gender dichotomy.

Second, and related to the first, there is no simple, one-to-one relation-ship between the presence of women in power and the extent of feminist politics. If traditional gender relations remain in place, more women in power need not translate into a politics that is "better" for women in a feminist sense. This is easiest to see when we consider the case of adding women who behave like men. As noted earlier, it is not simply the paucity of women at the top but also that the power of gender remains invisible even when (and where) women are in power.

We cannot understand the continued invisibility of gender simply by reference to how women politicians "choose" to present themselves (as suggested above). We must situate those choices within the larger context of "international politics." We can do this by examining how interna-tional leadership, politics, and power are defined and by locating women as political actors within this context.

"Now, dear! Don't let the weaker sex undermine your resolve ..."

"Gender and power." Cartoon published during the Falklands War showing women leaders as warrior-states"men" who disdain feminine weakness in times of war. Copyright © Express Newspapers PLC. Reprinted by permission.

WHAT MAKES ACTORS/AGENTS
POWERFUL? WHO GETS ATTENTION?
FOR WHAT?

Feminists have documented the pervasive bias of androcentrism in political science and international relations. One effect of this bias is the assumption that political actors are men. Another is the narrow definition of politics as exclusively public-sphere or governmental activities. Yet a third effect is the narrow definition of power as the capacity to enforce one's will (power-over in contrast to empowerment or "power to").

These effects are not simply an academic concern because the definitions they take for granted are promoted outside of academic disciplines as well. Consider the focus of television news on "spectacular" (rather than everyday) events: wars, weapons, violence, crises, men as leaders/protectors and women as dependents/victims. The leaders we see tend to be heads of government of countries that are geopolitically powerful or of foreign policy significance. Otherwise, international news is almost exclusively viewed through the lens of various crises: seemingly hopeless extremities of governmental, military, economic, refugee, population, health, food, water, fuel, and/or ecological breakdown. (The exception is international sports, which foster instead nationalist "ownership" of outstanding performances of individuals and teams—virtually all men except during the Olympics.)

In these accounts gender issues remain invisible in various ways. Attention to wars and spectacles is at the expense of everyday, maintenance activities that in fact are a precondition of the world's continuing to "work." The latter are largely ignored, yet they are the activities occupying women's—most people's—lives. To the extent that women appear in depictions of politics, they tend to be acting "like men" (Thatcher) or in supporting roles to the main/male actors (for instance, as wives, secretaries). In depictions of crises, women (or what Cynthia Enloe termed "womenandchildren")[50] are the ever-present victims in need of protection by men or through male-defined programs. Not inconsistent with the crisis picture, women occasionally appear as saviors and saints, whose model of sacrifice and commitment spurs men on to greater feats of protection (or competitive performance). Here, the "value given to female roles emphasizes gender polarity, thus strengthening male roles as the dominant structure."[51]

Again, not only are women and their activities depicted as secondary to (or merely in support of) men's public-sphere pursuits, but also the *way* in which women make an appearance tends to reinforce rather than challenge conventional gender stereotypes. Left in place are androcentric accounts that obscure women as powerful actors/leaders, that deny the politics of private-sphere activities, and that mystify the role of masculinism (ideologically and structurally) in women's continued subordination. The gender dynamics of politics—especially international politics—remains invisible as long as women "appear" only when they adopt masculine principles *or* epitomize feminine ones.

LOCATING POWER: NATIONALLY AND INTERNATIONALLY

Gender Divisions in Defining and Holding Power

We can begin to see how politics is gendered and how women's choices are structured, if we examine where women are located as political actors. At the national level, as suggested above, women located at the head of governments are typically perceived as "like men" (exceptional women!) or "mothers of their countries." Located as parliamentary/legislative leaders and ministers, women hold significant national power but rarely do so in the most "masculine" areas: defense, foreign policy, finance, justice (see Figure 3.10). Although there are individual exceptions, a clear pattern emerges of women's location in areas associated with "social

74

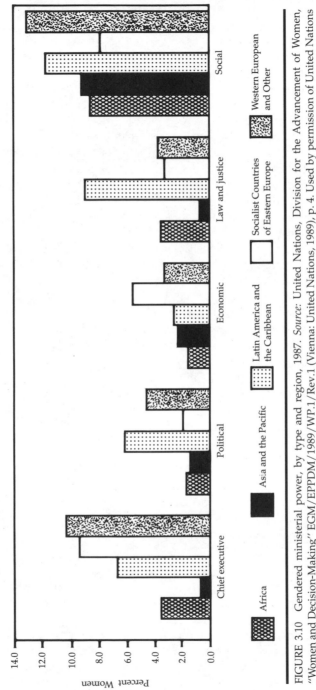

FIGURE 3.10 Gendered ministerial power, by type and region, 1987. *Source:* United Nations, Division for the Advancement of Women, "Women and Decision-Making" EGM/EPPDM/1989/WP.1/Rev.1 (Vienna: United Nations, 1989), p. 4. Used by permission of United Nations Publications.

functions" (education, health, welfare).[52] It is difficult to assess to what extent women are forced into these particular areas by gender stereotypes that preclude women's leadership in more-"masculine" fields. However brought about, women's location outside of conventionally defined "power" domains contributes to their invisibility as powerful political actors.

Although consideration of the location of women as political actors within national contexts is illuminating for our discussion, we should not forget that nations themselves are variously located in terms of political tradition, geopolitics, economic development, regional dynamics, religion, colonial history. We will briefly consider how some of these dimensions, which in fact interact with each other, affect the proportion and visibility of women's political participation.

Gender Dimensions
of Varying Political Systems

Women's representation in national legislatures is most favored in countries with liberal-democratic or socialist-communist traditions, and there is some evidence that electoral systems based on **proportional representation** (PR—allotting seats according to the proportion of votes received for a slate of candidates) additionally favor women.[53] However, only in the Nordic countries do women fare reasonably well both in national legislatures and elite governmental office (heads of government, ministries). In the former socialist-communist countries of Eastern Europe, women's representation in national legislatures was quite respectable (as in their unions), but this was not matched by strong representation in elite decision-making. It is worth noting again that what the media refer to as the "democratization" of these countries has had devastating effects on women's political representation and reproductive rights.

In the United States and United Kingdom (UK), where liberal democracy and women's rights have considerable history, women's representation in national assemblies remains surprisingly low (rarely exceeding 5 percent) and women "at the top" of government (Thatcher notwithstanding) are extremely rare. In sum, women's representational power (both legislative and governmental leadership) is consistently visible only in Nordic countries; elsewhere (including the United States and the UK), women appear as governmental leaders only exceptionally.

Gender Divisions as a Function
of Regional Distinctions

Many data sources simply provide aggregate figures by region. For present purposes, regional comparisons suggest that women's overall political participation is stronger in developed countries (the First World), weaker in Latin American and Asian regions, and least evident in Africa and the Middle East (in short, weaker in those areas referred to as developing, or Third World countries). It would be misleading, however, to assume that **development** (conventionally measured by a country's degree of industrialization) alone promotes female participation in politics. Reporting to the United Nations, the Division for the Advancement of Women concluded that "level of development as measured by gross domestic product (GDP) is unrelated to percentage of women in decision-making positions."[54] (The **gross domestic product** is a measure of the total output of goods and services produced within the nation's borders.) It is the level of gender equality rather than level of development that matters. In brief, there appears to be an interactive effect: "An increase in the general level of equality in a society leads to more women in decision-making which increases policies to promote general levels of equality."[55]

Thus, conventional distinctions between developed and developing countries fail to explain gender patterns. We can see this by considering that women have similar proportions of parliamentary representation in Japan (1.4), Iran (1.5), and Paraguay (1.7); in the United States (5.3), Brazil (5.3), and Peru (5.6); in Canada (9.6), Bangladesh (9.1), and Zimbabwe (9.0); in Italy (12.9), Iraq (13.2), and Rwanda (12.9); and in Iceland (20.6), North Korea (21.1) , and China (21.2).[56]

Similarly, it is often assumed that levels of literacy, education, and paid employment are positively correlated with acceptance and promotion of women as equals and with equal rights to political participation. This easy (liberal) generalization obscures the different ways that religion, colonial history, electoral system, alliances, militarism, and so forth, interact to generate historically particular gender relations that may or may not enhance women's identification with politics.

Particularly significant are ways in which cultural belief systems (sometimes based on religion) shape gender stereotypes and determine appropriate gender activities. This is most obvious when cultural beliefs prevent women from assuming roles outside of the family/household sphere: Where women are defined primarily as mothers and wives, and social structures confine their activities to the private sphere, opportunities for women's "political" action are severely limited. Predominantly Islamic countries tend to restrict women to family-oriented activities, so they have little presence—or power—in public-sphere activities. Women in countries strongly influenced by the Roman Catholic church are similarly restricted, in this case by expectations that they conform to stereotypes of women as maternal and/or saintly. These are *not* the components of "conventional" political power, though individual women may sometimes take on "moral" leadership by embodying the qualities of saintliness.

It is also worth noting the negative effects that **colonization** (the imposition of European rule throughout the Americas, Africa, and Asia) and externally imposed **modernization** (industrialization, urbanization, and export-oriented economic strategies) have had on women's status, including, in some cases, the elimination of political rights and power previously held in "traditional" societies.[57] In Norway, which has the most-balanced gender representation, a long tradition of legal equality—dating from the Viking period—has facilitated the relatively strong legal position of women and their right to political participation.[58] Nigeria also has a long tradition of women as politically and economically powerful agents, but its colonial experience had negative effects on the power women previously held through political leadership and/or women's centrality in the marketplace. Eurocentric constructions of masculinity and femininity transformed indigenous political practices and gender divisions of labor in ways that denied the legitimacy of women's public roles and diminished their economic power.

In general, processes of industrialization in the First World and **dependent development** (or **underdevelopment**, by which economies and societies of the First World benefit at the expense of those in the Third World) have two negative gender consequences. First, these processes involve the expansion of monetary exchanges as the basis for social systems, often referred to as the development of cash economies. In contrast to men, women's association with the private sphere restricts their participation in wage labor, especially in high-wage labor. Industrial capitalism's focus on paid labor diminishes the significance of "women's work" and contributes to a deterioration in women's status. The second negative consequence is closely related to the first. Not only paid labor but also public-sphere activities gain in prestige during processes of industrial capitalism. But the gendered division of public and private spheres tends to exclude women both formally and informally from the sphere of activities that is gaining status. As noted earlier, the public-private dichotomy works in many ways to exclude women from political activities and to minimize the significance of power relations—and therefore politics—in the private sphere. Women lose out as the public sphere of waged labor and political power becomes increasingly distinguished from and considered superior to the merely "private" sphere.

CONCLUSION

In this chapter we have explored gendered divisions of power by examining "the presence of women, " specifically, how women and men are differently located as political actors in state structures. By comparing where men and women are situated, we show both how world politics affects gender and how gendered concepts, practices, and institutions shape who exercises power. By asking gender-sensitive questions—Why are there so few women? How do the few succeed? What effect do they have? What makes actors powerful?—we reveal how gender is rarely acknowledged but always at work in the study and practice of world politics.

The gender dimensions of socialization, situational constraints, and institutional structures pose formidable obstacles to women's participation in formal politics. In large part, for women to acquire state power and be visible as state actors they must conform to gender stereotypes and thus leave gender dichotomies unchallenged. Most women at the helm of governments adopt the gender of state power and state agency: They "become like men," fulfilling androcentric definitions of power and politics. Some women derive legitimacy for their leadership by reference to maternal stereotypes associating women with national conciliation or advocates of "soft issues." Both strategies tend to render gender hierarchy invisible because they reproduce rather than challenge gender dichotomies and their gendered effects.

Adding women as agents of state power certainly changes the presence of women in world politics. But how much it changes the power of gender is a more complicated question. It is not simply increases in women's representation but also decreases in masculinism that positively affect global gender issues. In Chapter 4, we continue to explore the presence of women by examining the gender-differentiated effects of divisions of violence, labor, and resources. And we continue to reveal how the power of gender interacts with and reproduces these gendered divisions.

FOUR

□ □ □

Gendered Divisions of
Violence, Labor, and Resources

The gendered division of power makes possible not only the relative denial of formal power to women in the international system but also the exclusion of women's struggles and "women's issues" from the world politics agenda. To see how the gendered division of power both oppresses women and minimizes their struggles against oppression, we need to explore two interrelated aspects of power—the gendered nature of the concept of power and the gendered effects of this concept of power.

The gendered nature of the concept of power refers to the assumption in world politics of power-over. We argue that this form of power is masculinist because it presupposes the stereotype of masculine "nature" and behavior—competition, aggression, and coercion—often backed by physical or military force. This concept of power keeps most women from being taken seriously as national and international leaders unless they adopt masculine leadership styles while remaining feminine enough to uphold traditional symbols of motherhood and family that undergird the nation. Moreover, because the gendered or masculinist concept of power visualizes it as operating from the top down, women's political struggles—usually carried out at the grass-roots level or from the bottom up—are rendered practically invisible.

The gendered effects of power refers to the ways that men and women are treated unequally in the international system, in which formal top-down power is held largely in the hands of men. These effects have translated into limited access to state power for women and little attention to women's issues by states and international organizations, which perceive "women's issues" as separate from and inferior to "political issues."

Therefore states and international organizations reduce issues like reproductive rights, rape, and wife battering to domestic or even personal
problems, which then appear irrelevant to the so-called real politics of
war and economic competition.

The gendered conception of power produces gendered effects. In a
male-dominated world where power-over is valued, those who are neither able nor inclined to engage in aggressive and coercive practices are
seen as weak, less important, and even expendable. Because women are
associated with feminine characteristics of passivity and compliance,
their needs, interests, and even lives have been rendered invisible or unimportant. Broadly speaking, these are the gendered effects of power.
They result from the masculinist construction of power as power-over,
which gives greater access to power to men, who, then, "overpower"
women. To explain this generalized power imbalance between men and
women further, in this chapter we examine other gendered divisions—of
violence, labor, and resources—that work to consolidate and reproduce
gender inequalities.

Conventional definitions of power stress that to have power, to exercise control over others, one must have certain resources at one's disposal.
For an individual, this often means possessing a lot of physical strength,
money, and property. For a state, this usually means possessing a strong
military, a highly industrialized economy, and significant natural resources. Persons or states lacking any or all of these attributes are seen as
less powerful or even powerless. According to this conventional definition of power, women seem largely powerless.

For example, if we look through the lens of the gendered division of violence, we see that women are stereotyped as smaller and weaker than
men and represent a very small proportion of the world's militaries. Thus,
women typically do not possess or have access to most means of destruction and, as a result, are more often victims than perpetrators of direct violence. Through the lens of the gendered division of labor, we see that
women's unemployment and underemployment outpace men's in every
country, and that women and children constitute the poorest of the poor
in every country. In almost every occupational category, women are paid
less than men for doing the same job; yet women work more hours than
men the world over, both in their paid employment and in the home. In
short, women lack significant control over the means of production and
have too much responsibility for and often too little control over the
means of reproduction. Finally, if we look through the lens of the gendered division of resources, we discover that women own only 1 percent
of the world's land and, thus, have very little private property and minimal access to or control over natural resources. In fact, women are often
treated as natural resources whose bodies are free or as cheap labor that

can be exploited to amass wealth for states, corporations, and individual men.

These manifestations of the gendered divisions of violence, labor, and resources subject women disproportionately to various forms of direct and structural violence and also hinder women from aspiring to or attaining conventional or formal power in homes, communities, workplaces, national governments, and international organizations. Dealing with the gross inequities created by the gendered divisions of violence, labor, and resources is not high on the agendas of domestic and international policy-makers. In this chapter we will argue, however, that these gendered divisions are not only harmful to women because they produce and reproduce the power imbalance of gender inequality but are also harmful to all of us because they contribute to global crises.

Whereas Chapter 3 examined how the gendered division of power marginalizes women's status in conventionally defined politics, this chapter examines how gendered divisions of violence (security issues), labor (economic issues), and resources (equity and ecology issues) construct and reproduce a gender-differentiated world. To organize the discussion, we identify three interacting components of each gendered division and the issue area it constitutes. The components are (1) the gender dichotomies at work (the underlying assumptions and expectations), (2) the differential effects of these dichotomies on men and women (the roles they are assigned in relation to militaries, economies, and environments), and (3) the systemic consequences of these gender dichotomies (exacerbating global problems). The patterns we identify through the examples we offer (which are, by no means, exhaustive) paint an overwhelmingly negative picture of the gendered effects of world politics; however, it is necessary to understand the full impact of the gendered divisions of violence, labor, and resources and the interactions among them to appreciate the varied struggles against these processes that we document in Chapter 5.

VIOLENCE:
WAR AND SECURITY ISSUES

Throughout history there have been numerous examples of women warriors, and women fighters exist today. In spite of this, there is a pervasive gender dichotomy that divides women and men into "life-givers" and "life-takers."[1] Most male-dominated societies have constructed elaborate sanctions and even taboos against women's fighting and dying in war. As a result, men have gained almost exclusive control over the means of destruction worldwide, often in the name of protecting women and children, who are either discouraged from or not allowed to take up arms to protect themselves.

As life-givers women are not only prevented from engaging in combat, but are also expected to restore "life" after a death-dealing war is over. Women are expected to mourn dutifully the loved ones who fell in war and then produce new lives for the nation to replace its lost members. Thus, after the devastation they must "pick up the pieces" and create the conditions for repopulating society. These conditions include creating more men—who too often serve as soldiers—and more women—who too often bear sons only to lose them through war. The work of men as life-takers thus creates perpetual work for women as life-givers.

In this sense, women are not separate from either the production or consequences of war even though they are often prevented from engaging in direct combat. Yet in spite of their participation, women remain associated with war's opposite—peace. The characterization of "woman" as passive and submissive is often translated into the idea that women are pacifist by nature. This reinforces the stereotype of women as life-givers and portrays them as insufficiently fit or motivated to be life-takers. The assumption that women have a natural revulsion against war makes them undesirable partners in combat: How can women be trusted on the battleground if they are unwilling to fight and kill? Men, in contrast, are stereotyped as naturally aggressive and competitive, which presumably prepares them to kill or be killed. In addition, it is assumed that the presence of women on the battlefield will distract men from fighting successfully, perhaps by turning their aggressions away from fighting and toward sexual conquest or by tying them down to protect "weaker" female comrades, thereby endangering the pursuit of body counts. On this view, men might lose the war by pursuing or protecting women on the battlefield rather than fighting successfully to protect their women at home.

After the battle, women are expected to take care of returning soldiers, salving their wounds and psyches as well as meeting needs—for food, clothing, and shelter—previously met by the military. When the "boys come home," women are expected to serve them—and to do so with gratitude for those who fought and took life on behalf of their women and their nation. If women fail in these duties, then male protectors are often given tacit approval for "disciplining" their women, through physical violence if necessary. Such physical violence is learned on the playground when boys play "war" in preparation for their adult roles as potential soldiers. And it is honed when men are actually trained by militaries and participate in "real" wars. Life-takers have no responsibility for "unlearning" these skills during peacetime; global statistics on domestic violence suggest that men may use these skills against the women and children they protected in wartime if the latter do not please them in the home. Thus, those who are denied access to the means of destruction to protect themselves during wartime also have little protection against the wartime protectors who may turn violent in the home.

We now begin to see how gender dichotomies such as the following are at work in reproducing the gendered division of violence: soldiers-mothers, protectors-protected, aggressive-passive, battlefront–home front, batterers-victims. How are these dichotomies related to the different roles and positions of men and women worldwide? How do they shape our perceptions of war and security issues? How are men and women situated differently in relation to processes of militarization, even when war is absent? And how does a gender-sensitive lens enrich our understanding of systemic militarization as a global problem?

In societies where masculinity is equated with violence, men are under constant pressure to prove their manhood through acts of aggression. There are, of course, a variety of forms of male aggression that have been deemed unacceptable or illegitimate within civil societies (such as murder, assault, gang warfare, and, at least in terms of the laws of some countries, wife battering and child abuse). However, in one highly legitimated and organized institution within most societies men can attempt ultimately to prove their masculinity—the military.

State militaries serve many functions. According to conventional world politics wisdom, militaries serve to protect the borders of states and the citizens within them from outside aggression inevitable given the anarchic **interstate system,** which is based on **power politics,** not the rule of law. On this view, militaries are deemed necessary for the maintenance of national security, either as deterrents to would-be aggressors or as effective fighting machines capable of vanquishing actual aggressors.

Some world politics perspectives see militaries serving other less laudable functions, such as protecting repressive state elites from rebellion by their own people. This is often described as maintaining the **internal security** of states at the expense of nonelite citizens. Also, militaries are implicated in maintaining permanent war economies arising from the infamous **military-industrial complex,** which organizes a state's economy around producing weapons rather than civilian goods. Under such conditions, the military can become one of the few sites for "employment," not only for the poor and least educated, but also for large numbers of middle-class voters.

Less appreciated or analyzed, even by more critical world politics observers, is the role the military plays in reproducing masculinity and femininity as a result of its dependence on these gender divisions. As Cynthia Enloe argued, militaries not only need men to act as "men," that is, to be willing to kill and die on the behalf of the state to prove their "manhood," but militaries also "need women to behave *as the gender 'women.'*"[2] This means that women must be properly subservient to meet the needs of militaries and of the men who largely constitute them.

These needs are enormous. According to Ruth Leger Sivard, "World military expenditures from 1960 to 1990 add up to $21 trillion ($21,000,000,000,000) in 1987 dollars, equivalent in size to the value of all goods and services produced by and for the 5.3 billion people on the earth" in 1990.[3] Despite a small—5 percent—reduction in military expenditures since 1987 (the peak of worldwide military spending) and the end of the cold war, there remained in 1990 "26,000,000 people in the regular armed forces, another 40,000,000 in military reserves, a stockpile of 51,000 nuclear weapons, 66 countries in the business of peddling arms, 64 national governments under some form of military control—and 16 wars under way."[4] These numbers may steadily decrease over the next decade as a result of a variety of "build-down" agreements, most notably between the United States and the Commonwealth of Independent States. However, Sivard, based on the build-down trends as of the beginning of 1991, predicted that it would take "125 years before annual education expenditures per school-age child match the current level of military expenditures per soldier."[5]

What effects will military expenses—assuming that militaries will continue to consume large amounts of resources to the detriment of the civilian population for some time to come—have on the positions of men and women in the international system? In 1988 a little over half the world's state militaries excluded women.[6] States that exclude women from their militaries are found primarily in Africa, the Middle East, and to some degree in Latin America and Asia.[7] Women also tend to be excluded from militaries in states that are ruled by military regimes. However, even in democratic and socialist states under civilian authority, women typically make up less than 10 percent of the state military. As can be seen in Table 4.1, the United States has one of the highest rates of female participation in the armed forces (11 percent), followed by Canada (9.15 percent) and Israel (9 percent).

Given the relatively low rates of female participation in state militaries worldwide, it is obvious that most women are not direct recipients of military spending.[8] Also based on these statistics, few women can claim combat experience (indeed, most women serving in the armed forces are excluded from combat), which (as we noted in Chapter 3) has often served as a prerequisite or a test of leadership skills for those seeking high political office. Some feminists, particularly in the United States, have responded to these problems by insisting that the armed forces work to recruit more women by further breaking down discriminatory practices, such as the combat exclusion and the prohibition against homosexual men and women serving in the armed forces. They argue that these steps

TABLE 4.1   Women in State Militaries, Selected Countries, 1988 (in percentages)

Belgium	3.840	South Africa	3.300
Canada	9.150	Zimbabwe	3.800
France	2.690	Australia	7.000
Greece	0.860	Fiji	1.100
Netherlands	1.480	Japan	1.200
Portugal	0.012	New Zealand	8.550
United Kingdom	5.100	Philippines	0.400
United States	11.000	Argentina	0.050
Switzerland	0.003	Nicaragua	8.000
Israel	9.000	Uruguay	4.400

SOURCE: Selected data from Francine D'Amico, "Women as Warriors: Feminist Perspectives," paper presented at 32nd Annual Convention of the International Studies Association, Vancouver, British Columbia, March 20–23, 1992, pp. 11–14. Used by permission of Francine D'Amico. D'Amico's data were compiled from government-reported figures, mostly found in International Institute for Strategic Studies (IISS), *The Military Balance, 1987–1988* (London: IISS, 1988), and ILO, *Yearbook of Labour Statistics* (Geneva: ILO, 1977–1987).

will balance the gendered division of violence, which currently accords military men more access to formal positions of power and to the resources garnered by military spending.

Other feminists, however, question this strategy. For example, Francine D'Amico found that state militaries "want women to meet personnel needs under conditions of high militarization and to fill the *man-power* shortage, not to promote sex equality."[9] In fact, at a time when women in the United States have been joining the armed services in unprecedented numbers, they have been experiencing continuous resistance and repeated setbacks to their demands for equality in all other spheres of life. Susan Faludi's bestseller, *Backlash: The Undeclared War Against American Women*, documents the real war most American women are facing.[10] She asks, for example, "Why do American women, in fact, face one of the worst gender-based pay gaps in the developed world?" "Why do they represent two-thirds of all poor adults?" "Why are nearly 80% of working women still stuck in traditional 'female' jobs—as secretaries, administrative 'support' workers and salesclerks?" "Why are their reproductive freedoms in greater jeopardy today than a decade earlier?" And given that "battering was the leading cause of injury to women in the late 1980s," why is it that "federal funding for battered women's shelters has been withheld and one third of the one million battered women who seek emergency shelter each year can find none"?[11] It should be noted that five hours of military spending in the United States, which constituted about $200 million in 1985, could have funded 1,600 rape crisis centers and battered women's shelters.[12]

Not surprisingly, D'Amico found that women's experiences in most state militaries mirror these civilian realities rather than depart from them. Most women perform "support" functions, occupying the lower echelons of the military largely as clerical workers. Moreover, sexual harassment of female soldiers by male military recruits and officers is very common, as evidenced most recently at the 1991 Navy Tailhook Convention.[13] Wife beating, too, is believed to be particularly high among military men, according to a report on domestic violence in the United States.[14] In addition, between 1977 (the Hyde Amendment) and 1993 (President Clinton's order removing the restriction), women in the U.S. armed services had no access to safe and legal abortions through military health clinics. Finally, there is little evidence so far that women's military experience, either as members of state militaries or fighters in national liberation struggles, is catapulting them into positions of power. Thus, D'Amico argued that women's presence in the military may reflect the militarization of society, not the achievement of women's equality:

> Women's increasing presence in the military does not change the fundamental gendered construction of the institution, which at its core is coercive, hierarchical, and patriarchal. In fact, the increasing presence of women serves to legitimize the institution by giving it a facade of egalitarianism. When women accept the "warrior mystique," they soften the image of the military as an agent of coercion/destruction and help promote the image of the military as a democratic institution, an "equal opportunity employer" like any other, without reference to its essential purpose.[15]

This essential purpose is organized, direct violence, which we and others have argued, depends, in part, upon the structural violence of organized gender inequality. The only times that women have direct access to the largess that the world's militaries command is during periods of increased militarization, a process that costs most women, children, and men far more than what a few women and a much larger number of men gain from their military participation. For example, unprecedented military expenditures over the past three decades have led to reductions in health, education, and social service sectors, in which women predominate as workers and social welfare recipients. Since 1975, when the UN Decade for Women began, there have been small and uneven improvements in overall rates of literacy (although the number of female illiterates has actually grown in the Third World), infant mortality (which is still very high in parts of the Third World and among minorities in the United States), life expectancy (which for women is only forty-three years in Afghanistan, East Timor, Ethiopia, and Sierra Leone), and women's employment in the formal labor force in most regions (although they remain more unemployed worldwide than men).[16] However, during the same period, military spending far outpaced education and health spending in both the developed and developing worlds. In effect, the current gendered division of violence operates to ensure that life-taking activities are better funded than life-giving ones (see Table 4.2).

The negative impacts of militarization go far beyond the extraction of public funding from the meeting of basic human needs. Human rights, too, are sorely compromised. A recent report by Amnesty International vividly documents examples of military and police forces around the world terrorizing, imprisoning, and even torturing women who seek information about family members who have "disappeared" at the hands of government-sponsored death squads or who are active members and/ or leaders of peasant land-reform movements, women's rights organizations, ecological groups, community associations, national liberation struggles, and political parties (see Figure 4.1).[17] In fact, such women are often tortured both in spite of and because of the gendered construction of women as vulnerable.[18]

On the one hand, women who challenge government authority are perceived by their torturers as unworthy of protection because they have stepped out of their supposedly passive and apolitical role. On the other hand, government torturers reserve special forms of torture for activist women, such as rape and other forms of sexual abuse (especially when they are pregnant) in order to intimidate women into returning to their assigned passive role. (Indeed, according to rape crisis and battered women's shelter activists and researchers, the goal of most violence against women, whether it be by government forces or individual men, is to return them to subservient positions in the home, workplace, and polity.) Sexual torture of women, sometimes in front of the men who love them, is also used to deter male activists from revolutionary activity. The assumption is that these men will not further risk the lives of their "more vulnerable" female family members, whom they will fail to protect if they continue to challenge government authority. In this respect, the gendered division of violence acts to keep repressive regimes in power.

Militarization is also implicated in high rates of prostitution, which raise issues of public health, economic disruption, and racial tension. In the mid-1980s, there were approximately 3,000 military bases "controlled by one country but situated in another country."[19] Many military men have come to expect sexual servicing not just as a perk but as a right and even a necessity during their stints overseas. Perhaps the most notorious case is that of the Subic Bay Naval Base in the Philippines. In the late 1980s, Filipino feminist organizations reported that, as a result of high unemployment and extreme poverty, more than 20,000 Filipino women and about 10,000 Filipino children regularly acted as prostitutes for U.S. servicemen at Subic Bay.[20] This situation contributed not only to the spread of AIDS but also to racial tensions and nationalist fervor: Filipinos

TABLE 4.2 The Economy of Death

Amount	Paid For	Could Have Paid For
$20 million	20 Patriot missiles	Vaccines to protect all the women in Africa from tetanus
$65 million	1 E-2C Hawkeye aircraft	The estimated total amount of external funds spent on AIDS in Africa in 1990
$450	1 M-16 rifle	The training of a primary health care worker to respond to such community needs as immunization, oral rehydration, antibiotics, safe births, and postnatal care
$350 million	Two days of air combat	UNICEF's 1990–1991 budgeted expenditures (plus $48 million)
$12.3 billion	Noncombat costs, January–March	The total current annual amount of investment in water supply in the developing world
$500 million	One day of air and ground combat	Oxfam's operating budget—forty-six times over—for 1989–1990
$6.9 million	1 CH-47D army transport helicopter	All of Save the Children's refugee programs in Indonesia and Thailand, 1989–1990 (providing services for 25,000 people)
$20,000	1 Stinger missile	Basic medical equipment and building materials for a maternity center in Mali

If you were to spend $1.2 million a day for ten years you would spend $44 billion, the estimated amount spent on the Gulf War alone (not including long-term costs of operating a base in Saudi Arabia or reconstructing Kuwait).

SOURCE: Ms., May/June 1991, p. 15. Data from Center for Defense Information, PATH (Programs for Appropriate Technology in Health), Oxfam, UNICEF, and Save the Children. Compiled by Julie Feiner. Reprinted by permission of Ms.

denounced militarized prostitution as a symbol of their compromised sovereignty. Subic Bay base is now closed (the Philippine government revoked its lease in 1991), but the nexus between military bases and prostitution continues elsewhere, furthering the gendered division of violence that capitalizes on poverty and leaves despair, disease, and international tensions in its wake.

The logical conclusion of militarization—war—claimed the lives of more than 13 million men, women, and children, most of whom were noncombatants, in more than eighty-one conflicts between 1960 and 1987.[21] Robin Morgan argued that killing noncombatants, which "had become a 'legitimate' military tactic in conventional warfare," has invoked what we call **terrorism,** the "random murder of average citizens, including those in no way connected to power."[22] She also noted that whether it is state terrorism or terrorism perpetrated by insurgent groups against states, terrorists are predominantly male. In contrast, the majority of the millions of refugees in the world, fleeing from war or terrorism are

FIGURE 4.1   Abuse of women's human rights. The poster demands "liberty for prisoners of conscience, impartial trials for political prisoners, abolition of torture and the death penalty all over the world"—demands that only begin to address the human rights abuses visited upon women. Copyright © Amnesty International. Reprinted by permission.

women and children.[23] Moreover, Susan Forbes Martin reported that frequently women, once in refugee camps outside or inside their own countries, are raped by military personnel guarding the camps, insurgent forces who infiltrate the camps, and male refugees.[24]

If all of these consequences are the "essential purpose" of militarization, it is hard to see how participating in it can be liberating for women or men. Even so, we still confront the problem of analyzing the recurring linkages between masculinity and violence and femininity and passivity. Judith Hicks Stiehm argued that achieving gender parity in the U.S. armed forces might ultimately force an acknowledgment that war is not "manly" and that women can protect themselves. On this view, women's equal participation might destabilize the ways in which the gendered division of violence and the gender inequality upon which it rests contribute to militarization. However, Stiehm's own study suggested that this seems unlikely because when economic conditions deteriorate, there are more un- or underemployed men available for recruitment, thereby reducing the need for women to fill "manpower" shortages.[25] Moreover, if militaries are reduced in size, particularly in those countries that allow women to serve, recruitment needs will be reduced as well, so there will not be any "manpower" shortages. D'Amico found that feminist agitation in the West for including more women has not been a major factor in military personnel decision-making.[26] Thus, gender parity seems an unlikely development in any state military.

Other feminists have argued that although comparatively few women are soldiers on the battlefront, many more serve the military on the home front, for example, as workers for defense contractors. Enloe found that in California's Silicon Valley, which received $2.3 billion in contracts for military electronic systems from the U.S. Defense Department in 1979–1980, "80 per cent of assembly plant workers are women, a majority of whom are black, Hispanic, or Asian."[27] If we consider that approximately "40% of a new navy cruiser is composed of electronics,"[28] one could argue that the cheap labor of these women contributes more to life-taking than individual male and female soldiers on the battlefront.

War has never been an exclusively male enterprise. It depends significantly on female labor, often of working-class women of color, who represent between one-quarter to one-half of all enlisted women in the U.S. armed forces.[29] Add to this the "support" work of millions of military wives, nurses, and prostitutes, and we begin to see how militaries are dependent on women. The gendered division of violence, however, continues to obscure this fact through the mechanism of sexism (as well as racism and classism). In fact, it is the gendered division of violence that separates men and women into "Just Warriors" who protect and "Beautiful Souls" who are protected,[30] thus pressing both men and women into serving the world's militaries in respectively gendered ways. This keeps women and men from questioning the essential purpose and the negative effects of war, militarization, and violence on their own and others' lives.

LABOR: ECONOMIC ISSUES

Women's economic security is seriously compromised by military security. In fact, divisions of labor, based on notions of what constitutes "women's work" and "men's work" in nearly every society, typically stem from the gendered division of violence in which the reproductive work of child-bearing and child care—life-giving—is reserved for women, while the work of war making and hunting—life-taking—is reserved for men. However, beyond this tendency for women to do work related to their biological ability to bear children and for men to perform functions related to their upper-body strength, gendered divisions of labor have varied greatly over time and across cultures.

Prior to Western colonization, divisions of labor in many cultures were fairly elastic, as evidenced by anthropological studies of such diverse, pre-Western-contact cultures as the Igbo of Nigeria, the Hawaiians, and some Native American civilizations.[31] Women participated in productive labor, such as agriculture, creation of artifacts, and trade and were often allowed to own land and amass wealth in their own right. In addition, women's reproductive functions translated into religious and political authority in many pre-Christian cultures that perceived women's fertility as powerful and sacred. Some women in precolonial cultures became warriors when they had no children or had passed childbearing age. In such cultures, men also transgressed what we, in the "modern" West, have come to define as traditional gender roles. Under conditions of relative equality and elasticity of gender roles, gendered divisions of labor were perceived as complementary—in the sense that those tasks that were gender segregated were viewed as equally valuable to the life of the society.

Western colonization introduced a more rigid, less equal, and, thus, less complementary conception of how labor should be divided between the sexes. This has not totally undermined alternative, more flexible notions of the work men and women perform, but a more unitary, global, gendered division of labor based on the Western model has emerged in what is now a world capitalist system. In the latter framework, the division of women's and men's work is rooted firmly in patriarchal conceptions of women's and men's "nature." Many Western political theorists, from the Greeks to the Enlightenment philosophers, assumed that women's child-bearing capacities not only made them more fit for the reproductive work of child care and work in the home, but also made them unfit for the productive labor of business, commerce, and governance occurring outside the home. Moreover, although a few of these theorists saw reproductive work as important to sustaining the good society and the good polity, most viewed productive work as far more important and higher in status. Similarly, they argued that men, who were not identified with the supposedly emotional and irrational realm of biological reproduction, were more fit for high-status work in the economy and the polity. Often displacing more "complementary" arrangements, the Western gendered division of labor set up a rigid separation between women's and men's work and simultaneously devalued women's work.

This rigid separation was justified on the basis of supposedly self-evident "facts" about women's and men's bodies. But this obscures the gender ideology at work, which projects onto the bodies of men and women a series of fixed and oppositional attributes, traits, and societal positions that have little to do with biology. Indeed, biology itself is never static because bodily functions, abilities, and even meanings change significantly over time in response to different social arrangements and technological interventions. In spite of these fluctuations, the Western gendered division of labor was constructed ideologically and practically on the following supposedly "natural" and unchangeable oppositions: production-reproduction, public-private, skilled-unskilled, formal labor–informal labor, paid work–unpaid work, breadwinner-housewife, and family wage earner–"pin money" wage earner.

Through colonization, this Western division of labor was imposed on many cultures in the Americas, Asia, and Africa from the fifteenth to the twentieth centuries. As a consequence, the economic status and well-being of many women in diverse cultures around the world were diminished. For example, in her classic study, *Woman's Role in Economic Development*, Ester Boserup found that prior to colonization, farming in many African countries was almost exclusively women's work, and men were largely responsible for clearing fields, hunting, and warfare.[32] Western colonizers first usurped African men's traditional roles by controlling land and then attempted to make these now "lazy African men" engage in farming, which under Western patriarchal ideology, was viewed as men's work.[33] This process involved a systematic transferral of land rights from women to men in many African countries (see Figure 4.2). It also ensured that only men, who were deemed heads of households, were schooled in Western agricultural techniques and provided with Western agricultural technologies.[34]

This is not to suggest that colonizing practices were generally beneficial to most African and other colonized men. In the wake of Western colonization, many indigenous peoples—both women and men—lost access to ancestral lands for farming and hunting. Giving some men titles to small plots of land not usurped by Western plantation owners and turn-

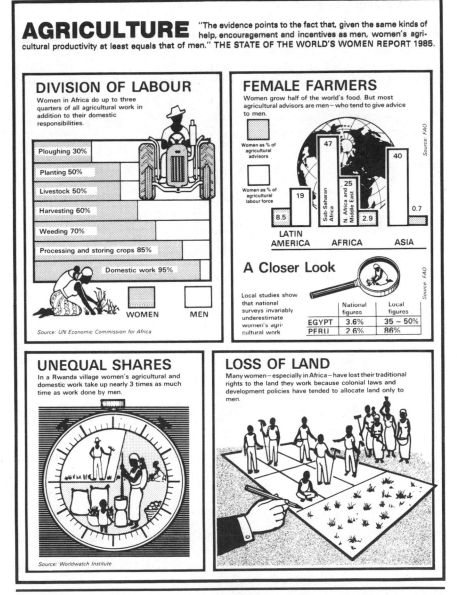

FIGURE 4.2 Gendered development policies. This series of charts shows how much agricultural work women perform in the Third World, often with the least amount of time and resources. From Jeanne Vickers, *Women and the World Economic Crisis* (London: Zed Books, 1990), p. 21. Courtesy of the United Nations "The State of the World's Women 1985."

ing men as well as women into farm laborers (either as slaves or minimally paid workers) did not mean **empowerment** (enhanced capacity) for colonized men. However, colonized women became even more marginalized, relative to colonized men, under patriarchal colonial rule. As Gita Sen and Caren Grown observed, "The colonial period created and accentuated inequalities both 'among' nations, and between classes and genders (also castes, ethnic communities, races, etc.) 'within' nations."[35]

In spite of this massive intervention to make Africans and other Third World peoples conform to the Western gendered division of labor, women still perform between 40 and 80 percent of all agricultural labor throughout the Third World.[36] Yet Western efforts to develop or modernize the postcolonial Third World through aid, loans, and technical assistance have continued to favor landowning men as recipients of assistance, while disregarding Third World women's vital role in food production. In fact, development efforts have actually worsened the conditions of female farmers and contributed significantly to the problem of world hunger.

For example, studies of women and development indicate that Western approaches stressing large-scale, highly mechanized farming to produce crops for export have undermined female farming systems that had been central to the maintenance of food self-sufficiency in many Third World countries. Deprived of good, arable land through their loss of land rights and the introduction of cash crops, female farmers have been reduced to growing a few subsistence crops on small, marginal plots of land. Meanwhile, the emphasis on cash crops for export has meant that the majority of food grown in Third World countries is not for local or even national consumption. Unfortunately, the prices of agricultural commodities on the world market have steadily declined in the postwar period, generating insufficient cash resources for importing food and other goods necessary to serve the basic needs of vast numbers of poor Third World peoples. Moreover, even when imported food is available, impoverished rural and urban people cannot afford to buy it. Women's subsistence farming for their families in rural areas provides practically the only relief from starvation, yet this activity is increasingly limited by the use of more land for cash crop production.

Even experiments to accelerate food production for national consumption have failed to meet the basic needs of poor people. An example is the **green revolution,** which relied on highly mechanized, large-scale farming techniques that further displaced subsistence farming women.[37] Architects of this revolution assumed that moving women off the land would enable them to fulfill the Western ideal of housewifery, with more time to care for their husbands and children. In fact, the reverse happened. With the loss of subsistence crops cultivated by women to feed their families, women were forced into working on "green revolution" farms to supplement their husband's income so their families could purchase sufficient food. Thus, women's extrahousehold labor increased. Not only were they responsible for reproductive work and whatever subsistence farming they could carry out, but they also became wage laborers, in effect working a triple day, in contrast to men's single responsibility to earn a wage.

The imbalance between women's and men's work was also exacerbated by the urbanization and industrialization resulting from Western approaches to Third World development. Western development agencies assumed that Third World countries could modernize only by following the general pattern of growth in the West, that is, of moving from an agrarian to an industrial economy. Thus, Western-funded development projects in the Third World focused on building large-scale industrial and urban infrastructures often at the expense of developing the agricultural sector. As a result, food was short in the cities, whose populations were swelling because of the influx mainly of men from rural areas who had left the land in search of more jobs and higher wages.

Unfortunately, most men who migrated to the cities did not make enough money to be the breadwinners for wives and children left behind in rural areas, who had to try to survive through marginalized subsistence farming. Often this situation led to men's abandonment of their families, producing a significant rise in the number of poor, female-headed households. By the latter part of the 1980s, up to 40 percent of the households in much of the Third World had fallen into that category.[38] This systematic impoverishment of rural women and their children produced a marked deterioration in nutrition and health, undermining even further the ability of women to meet basic needs for themselves and their children (see Figure 4.3).

By the 1970s, Western development agencies began to recognize the heavy costs of neglecting and even undermining women's roles in the development process. These agencies began to shift their focus from industrial projects to "basic needs" assistance programs, dealing with nutrition, health, housing, education, and home-based income generation. These focused not just on "productive" labor but also on "reproductive" labor and led to the creation of Women in Development (WID) policies and programs within, for example, the U.S. Agency for International Development (USAID), the UN Development Programme (UNDP), the World Bank, and such private agencies as the Ford Foundation.

However, a study of these agencies' performance, in terms of providing direct assistance to women or integrating women into development projects, found very uneven and disappointing results. During the period between 1972 and 1988, the Ford Foundation (women made up 53.2 percent of its professional staff in 1986) had the best record. It granted $27.5

96

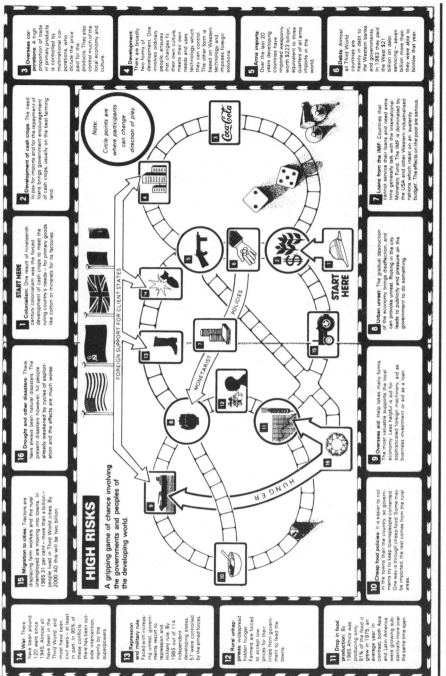

FIGURE 4.3   High risks of development. This high stakes "game," played by world political, financial, and military elites at the expense of vast numbers of people in the Third World, is most costly to poor women and children. From Jeanne Vickers, *Women and the World Economic Crisis* (London: Zed Books, 1991), p. 109. Copyright © *New Internationalist*; reprinted by permission.

million to women-related projects, which ranged from research on women's roles to direct assistance in the areas of "women's economic activities, legal rights and advocacy, and women's reproductive health."[39] One should note that this constituted only a fraction of the foundation's $6.6 billion annual budget (as of 1987). The World Bank, which funds about 250 projects per year (its annual budget is $16–$18 billion), claims to have involved women in about 300 projects during the five years between 1979 and 1984; however, only 54 percent of those made women the "major beneficiaries."[40] UNDP had the worst record. Although UNDP funds about 5,000 projects per year, only 65 examples of women-related projects funded between 1978 and 1989 could be identified—and of these, only 68 percent required women's participation or made women the direct beneficiaries.[41]

Examples of UNDP-funded projects that directly assisted women include a Liberian self-help village development project and an Agricultural Extension Services Project in Yemen, both of which involved providing women with income-generating skills, credit, nutritional information, and household technologies as part of a larger effort.[42] UNDP-funded projects that directly involved women include "projects such as Organizing Mothers' Clubs and Cooperatives in Bolivia and the Women's Handicraft Centre in the United Arab Emirates."[43] World Bank–funded projects with WID components tended to be concentrated in the areas of agricultural and rural development and education and were most often located in Africa.[44]

Nuket Kardam concluded that development agencies are, for the most part, not interested in empowering women, only with providing them, minimally and unevenly, with "welfare and access."[45] In effect, they generally resist doing anything that might disrupt the gendered division of labor that privileges productive work over reproductive work, that assumes women perform only reproductive work, which itself is viewed as unimportant to the growth and sustainability of a nation's economy, and, thus, that keeps many women impoverished and relatively powerless. Of major funding sources, only the Ford Foundation has backed projects that might enhance not only the conditions under which women labor but also the choices women have about what labor they do.

In sum, Eurocentric trade and development policies have gender-differentiated consequences. Third World men have been negatively affected by these policies, but Third World women have been systematically and more dramatically impoverished.[46] Currently, the choices available to these women are few and grim. For women who can no longer scratch out an existence in the countryside, there are essentially four options: prostitution, domestic service, street vending, and factory work. As we shall see, each of these gendered occupations, although on the bottom rungs of the international division of labor, nevertheless serves to "make the world go round" (in Cynthia Enloe's words)[47]—but not for the benefit of women.

Sexual Work

Prostitution, which has always been present officially or unofficially around military bases, has now taken the form of big business by being tied to the most lucrative industry in the global economy—international tourism. In Bangkok alone, more than 250 hotels routinely offered prostitutes to their guests in 1978, and conservative estimates in 1980 indicated that approximately 3 percent of all Thai women were engaged in some kind of prostitution.[48] Tragically, the percentage of children and teenage girls was double this amount. The labor of these women and children is used to provide sexual services to European, North American, and Japanese businessmen and to male tourists, who constituted 73 percent of international visitors to Thailand in 1986.[49] Although some prostitutes working for escort services and massage parlors can make far more than the average semiskilled women, the larger number of women and children who work the streets and go-go bars make considerably less than highly-paid prostitutes. For the most vulnerable, prostitution may take the form of indentured service.[50] Those who really control and reap the most profits from prostitution are men in the Thai military and police forces, male owners of local and transnational hotel chains, male pimps, and men who run international sexual-slave-trade operations. In 1984, as many as 16,000 Thai prostitutes were "exported" to Japan, Europe, and the Middle East because of the demand for their "special" services.[51]

What makes Thai and other Southeast Asian prostitutes valuable commodities on the world market is a facet of the gendered division of labor. Western gender ideology is infused with racist categorizations that assign different types of "natures" to different types of men and women. In the area of sexuality, white women are construed as prudish and almost asexual, and black women (and men) are seen as wild and even oversexed. Asian women, however, have been marketed as "perfect" sexual playthings for Western or Westernized men. They are described as childlike and virginal and thus appropriately submissive and nonthreatening; yet they are also presented as extremely responsive and sexually experienced. The combination suggests that Asian women want only to please men and, moreover, know how to do it. This ideology "naturalizes" Asian prostitution, effectively hiding the coercive processes of poverty, the state, international capital, and militarization that sentence so many women to the occupation.

Domestic Work

Domestic work has also become an "international business." For poor Third World women who opt to become maids, the largest markets for their services usually lie outside their countries, in places like North America, Europe, and the Middle East where there are substantial numbers of middle- and upper-class families. In 1984, about 18,000 Sri Lankan women were working overseas, mostly as domestic servants.[52] In 1988, 81,000 Filipino women were serving as domestic workers abroad, providing "between $60 and $100 million in foreign exchange" for the Philippine government; the women were supporting as many as five dependents back home.[53] This trade in cheap domestic labor can of course be economically beneficial for the sending country and the host families, but domestic workers themselves have been subjected to various kinds of indentured servitude and sexual abuse by their employers, against whom they usually have no recourse as noncitizens in foreign countries.[54] Thus, the gendered division of labor operates to produce domestic servants who will remain subservient wherever they go.

Informal Work

Compared with the perils of prostitution and domestic service, other types of informal work—street vending and home-based piecework—may appear attractive options for poor, displaced women. But the reality is stark. Market women typically sell small, inexpensive commodities ranging from vegetables to cigarettes. In effect, they make supplementary incomes as street retailers for male merchants who control the market. The women are often subjected to sexual and police harassment as well as to merchant exploitation—and typically have to hand over their incomes to their husbands. Home-based piecework does offer income-generating opportunities for women who are confined to the home in highly sex segregated societies. However, this kind of work is arduous, isolating, and also poorly paid.

Consider the 100,000 to 200,000 lace makers of Narsapur, India, who "work 6–8 hour days for an average payment equal to 19 percent of the minimum wage for women." Male traders and exporters have become rich selling this handicraft on the world market.[55] The gendered division of labor has ensured that these lace makers are viewed and view themselves as "housewives," not "workers," and their labor is not even counted in their country's official statistics. As Marilyn Waring pointed out, "The service of housewives and other family members, household maintenance and production, and illegal transactions are all outside the UNSNA's [United Nations System of National Accounts] production boundary," which supposedly is an accounting of everything of value in or to the market in every country.[56]

Whereas women predominate in the informal work force in both the developing and developed world, they also constitute between 35 and 40 percent of the formal, paid labor force around the world (with the exception of the largely Muslim regions of the Middle East, North Africa, and western Asia, where women's formal labor force participation reaches only 17 percent). However, according to the United Nation's recent report, women's pay worldwide averages 30 to 40 percent less than that of men, even though women typically work longer hours than men.[57] Thus, at the same time that women are entering the paid labor force in record numbers, the global phenomenon of the "feminization of poverty" is increasing.

Factory Work

The paradox of women's increased labor force participation and increasing poverty is attributable to several world economic factors that are related to the global gendered division of labor. Through gender stereotypes, women are perceived as particularly compliant workers who need only make "pin money" to supplement their families' income. Although many women are the sole support of their families and have been active in agitating for better working conditions, the ideology of the gendered division of labor is used to rationalize the use of women as cheap labor. This ideology also typically construes women as either unskilled or particularly good at detail work that requires manual dexterity, thereby "ghettoizing" them into pink-collar service occupations or light-industry assembly work. As a result of the decline in heavy manufacturing (at least in the West) and the increase in high-technology information-based industries, service and light industry jobs are the fastest-growing occupations in the world economy. Women are in high demand to fill these positions, which are typically low paying, nonunionized, and relatively unregulated in terms of health and safety requirements. Among poor and working-class Third World and First World women, such jobs are typically the most sought-after option for making a living. Unfortunately, the rise of these occupations has translated into increasing rates of female labor-force participation, but the latter has not necessarily led to livable wages for women and their families.

For example, 85 percent of the workers in the world's seventy-nine light-assembly and manufacturing **export-processing zones** (EPZs—enclaves favoring MNC activities) operating in thirty-five countries in the mid-1980s were women. Pressed to work at a much faster pace and 50 percent more hours than Western workers, these women earned 20 to 50 percent less than men doing comparable work and received as little as 40 cents an hour.[58] As one Mexican worker observed, one can work in the *maquiladoras,* or Mexico's EPZs, for ten years and still live in abject poverty, complete with cardboard roofs, no electricity or safe drinking water, and little to eat.[59] It is rare, however, that women last ten years working in EPZs. The typical female worker is between sixteen and twenty-five years of age. By the time she reaches her mid-twenties, she is "burnt out" by the pace of the work, the long hours, and the toxic chemicals that are heavily present in such unregulated industries.

She also may be losing her eyesight from the unabated close work required to sew intricate garments or from looking through a microscope for as long as twelve hours a day to assemble microchips (see Figure 4.4). Moreover, during her "productive" years, she will be subjected to sexual harassment by supervisors—"the 'lay down or be laid off' policy"[60]—and will be responsible for supporting and doing the reproductive labor for her family, as a single parent or as a daughter. If she rebels against her lot through labor organizing, she is pressured into submissiveness by her employers, her government, and even her male family members who rely on her for this meager—but often only—wage.

Meanwhile, U.S. transnational corporations (TNCs), which in the mid-1980s owned 90 percent of the *maquiladora* plants in Mexico, have been reaping huge profits as a result of the use of this cheap nondomestic labor.[61] Moreover, this exploitation of Third World women factory workers has cost the jobs of many working-class women in the United States, who are concentrated in labor-intensive occupations. Between 1979 and 1983, 35 percent of the workers who lost their jobs because of plant closings in the United States were women, and this is considered a conservative estimate: It did not cover companies of 100 workers or fewer, which are heavy employers of women.[62] The dramatic erosion in manufacturing jobs for U.S. women has significantly contributed to the impoverishment of the growing numbers of female-headed households in the United States. In 1991, 88 percent of white, 93 percent of black, 93 percent of Hispanic, single-parent households were female headed.[63]

The plight of both Third World and Western women has been exacerbated by the **debt crisis,** which arose in the 1980s and continues to wreak havoc in the world economy. The origins and nature of the debt crisis will not be described here, but its net effects—negative economic growth in the developing world and a decline in the economies of many developed countries—are important to our discussion. Already suffering significant reductions in real income and employment as a result of the worldwide recession that reduced the price of commodity exports, workers in the Third World faced even harsher treatment when their governments were forced to accept International Monetary Fund (IMF) **structural adjustment** or austerity programs in order to qualify for more development

Gary Massoni/AFSC

Gary Massoni/AFSC

FIGURE 4.4   Women on the global assembly line. The working conditions of these young Mexican women in *maquiladoras* in Tijuana, Mexico, reveal that these workplaces are the new "sweatshops" of transnational corporations that rely primarily on women's cheap labor. Photos courtesy of the American Friends Service Committee. Photographer Gary Massoni.

loans. Essentially, such programs require countries to increase productivity and exports while decreasing government spending on social welfare. Studies show that Third World working-class women and children bear the brunt of structural adjustment policies, which mire them in deep poverty while enabling their governments to make payments on foreign debts.[64] Similar patterns are observable in developed countries where conservative governments are imposing structural adjustment policies (undermining unions and slashing social welfare programs) to increase economic competitiveness.

Under such conditions, more and more women are forced to seek and accept low-wage jobs in the formal labor market, and even greater numbers enter into or step up their participation in the informal labor force as street vendors, domestic servants, or prostitutes. At the same time, they remain almost exclusively responsible for the reproductive labor of child and elderly care as well as housewifery. Moreover, this reproductive labor is made more demanding and more difficult by government cuts in social services in both the developing and developed worlds. In the face of high debts and deficits, governments are forcing working women to perform the caretaking for which the public sector is abandoning responsibility. This stepped-up reproductive labor is getting harder to perform under the conditions of scarcity created by over a decade of structural adjustment policies.

June Nash reported that wives of industrial workers being laid off in massive numbers in the United States are having to turn to the peasant practices of their European ancestors—growing food on meager subsistence plots and canning it for storage. She also reported that those who have always lived in gathering-and-hunting subsistence economies, such as the indigenous peoples of the Brazilian rain forest, are struggling to survive as their sources of food and shelter are being destroyed by intensified logging, slash-and-burn agriculture, and even the creation of industrial EPZs in the middle of the rain forest. Under these conditions, men deprived of their jobs or usual sources of livelihood are engaging in more domestic violence against their wives and children. Such men also are flooding into the informal economy, usurping some of the income-generating activities women, particularly as heads of households, have traditionally turned to in an effort to feed themselves and their children.[65]

In short, the gendered division of labor ensures that crises in the world economy are, in great measure, absorbed by mostly poor and working-class women and that male-dominated TNCs and Western banks reap large profits at the expense of these women, their families, their societies, and ultimately, world society. However, it is only after ten years of structural adjustment policies that we are seeing in sharp relief how deadly the intertwining of the gendered divisions of violence, labor, and resources can be for women, children, men, and the planet.

RESOURCES:
EQUITY AND ECOLOGY ISSUES

At first glance, the issue of the use and abuse of the global environment and its natural resources seems to have nothing to do with gender. At one level, it can be argued that all human beings have an impact on the natural environment and all human beings are affected by the degradation of the environment by "man-made" pollution. At another level, we have come to think of natural resources as the property of states (and corporations), whose relative power in the international system depends upon the extent of the resources under their control and their ability to both exploit and preserve them for economic purposes. Through these lenses, there is no room for seeing or thinking about what we call the gendered division of resources. However, if we look more closely at the way in which resources are divided within states, which resources are valued, how resources are used and by whom, and where pollution is most concentrated, we begin to see gendered patterns. Looking still deeper, we also begin to see that the very relationship that "man" has with nature in the late twentieth century the world over has been formed, in part, by a Western gender ideology that is becoming increasingly global and quite harmful to the earth and its inhabitants.

The Indian physicist and ecofeminist Vandana Shiva argued that before the rise of Western colonization and Western science, indigenous peoples throughout the world had close and relatively harmonious relationships with the natural world, viewing it as sacred and alive with spirituality.[66] Typically, natural forces were seen as feminine because they represented to these cultures the generative power of fertility and birth. Many of these pre- or non-Christian cultures worshipped goddesses who were embodied in all manner of natural objects, ranging from volcanoes and bodies of water to birds and animals. What Shiva called the **feminine principle** ensured that people used—but did not abuse—the natural environment. In fact, the "feminine principle" was itself a reflection of women's particular relationship with nature through the productive and reproductive work they performed in these cultures. Not only did women bring new life into the world through childbirth, but they were also responsible for gathering and cultivating the staple foods consumed for the perpetuation of life.

As we noted earlier, in many places the rise of Western colonization undermined communal land use and women's land rights. This disrupted carefully balanced and ecologically sound relationships between peoples and their lands. In addition, the rise of Western science transformed peoples' notions of nature, and a worldview that saw nature strictly as a resource for "man-made" projects replaced belief systems in which nature was revered as the manifestation of divinity. Early Western science, coupled with Christian ideology, turned the feminine principle upside down. Nature was still thought of as feminine, but rather than powerful and goddesslike, nature was seen as a passive resource from which men could take anything they needed or wanted without care for the effects of their interventions. This reversal in gender ideology and environmental thinking paved the way for rapacious land-use patterns and technologies, which have led to numerous ecological crises since the advent of the industrial revolution.[67] Western gender ideology construes nature as a passive resource to be controlled, used, and even abused. As this ideology has become increasingly widespread, environmental crises have followed, ranging from the problems of acid rain and global dumping to ozone depletion and global warming.

Gender ideology is by no means the sole cause of these problems, but if we look through the lens of the gendered division of resources, we see that gender ideology contributes to the growth and perpetuation of these problems. Although there are still cultures that retain some reverence for the feminine principle of nature, the increasingly global aspects of the gendered division of resources rest upon the following dualisms: culture-nature, active-passive, subject-object, users-resources, advanced-primitive, and exploitation-stewardship. These dualisms are manifested in the contemporary situation, where women have a great deal of responsibility for caring for the environment but little say in how it will be used and for what purposes.

Denying women any appreciable role in decision-making about use of the environment has led directly to what Gita Sen and Caren Grown called the **food-fuel-water crises** in the rural areas of the Third World.[68] These crises result from resource depletion that threatens the survival of people in subsistence economies. Women's displacement from the land by large-scale agricultural development for export has contributed to high levels of famine, particularly in Africa. But there are additional consequences of this displacement, contributing not only to continued hunger but also to deforestation and desertification. Women are the main food producers and processors in most of the rural areas of the Third World, and they must have access to clean water and firewood for fuel. As their land is lost to corporate farms and water sources are polluted by agricultural runoff from fertilizers and pesticides, rural women are forced to travel farther and farther in search of clean water—sometimes as far as twenty kilometers from their home. Because the amount they can carry is limited, they may have to fetch water several times a day, adding more hours to their hard labor to sustain the meager diets of their families (see Figure 4.5).

Diane Shandor/AFSC

FIGURE 4.5   Gendered ecology. (*Top*) This photo of a Chadian refugee woman in Sudan shows how deforestation results from pushing people off their land. UNHCR/S. Errington. (*Bottom*) A view of a workers' shantytown outside a *maquiladora* in Tijuana, Mexico, shows the degraded environment in which women workers and their families must live as a result of the industrial pollution surrounding these "homes." Photo courtesy of the American Friends Service Committee. Photographer: Diane Shandor.

Similarly, as forests are cut down for large-scale agricultural enterprises, women must go further afield to look for the firewood needed to cook and to boil water, making it safe to drink. When water and fuel sources are being depleted, not only does food become scarce, but also the basis for ecologically sound agricultural practices is eroded. First, female subsistence farmers are forced to cultivate small plots of land over and over again rather than engage in crop rotation. This depletes vital soil nutrients and can eventually even lead to small-scale desertification. Large-scale desertification is the result of the overuse of crop lands by corporate farmers who do not rotate crops, and who overwater and salinate the soil and/or grow crops using methods that destroy fragile topsoil.

Second, when the soil is too depleted to produce crops, rural populations are reduced to consuming the seeds for future crops, destroying their capability to produce their own food. Another alternative is to seek food, as well as fuel and water, further away from their homes. This pushes rural peoples into marginal and therefore sensitive ecosystems, even conservation areas and parks. Different interests motivate the poor rural peoples, who have few alternatives for survival in the short term, and the ecologists, who take the longer view toward saving the environment but who do not work on remedies for the unequal distribution of land and resources that forces poor people to seek food, fuel, and water in protected areas.

This unequal distribution of land and resources arises not just from class status but also from gender divisions in a world in which women own only 1 percent of the land. The Western assumption that women are not farmers has led both to the loss of women's land rights and to the failure to provide technological assistance to women who work the land. As we have learned from the unforeseen consequences of high-technology experiments like the green revolution, not all technology is good or appropriate for every socioeconomic and environmental context. Development mistakes (mistakes for the large number of people impoverished by them) might have been avoided if women, who are the most reliable "natural resource managers," had been consulted about how best to use the land and what technologies are most appropriate.[69]

Most women agricultural workers are not formally educated in modern, Western agricultural techniques. However, they work closely with and on the land and have developed significant informal knowledge about ecosystems and appropriate land-use patterns. As farmers, women often know which plants have the most nutritional value and what forms of cultivation lead to the least soil erosion and water consumption. As traditional healers, women often know which plants have medicinal value and what practices sustain the biodiversity of an ecosystem to ensure that such healing vegetation is preserved. As fuel gatherers, women know they are dependent on forests to provide renewable sources of firewood.[70] International and national development planners and agencies that ignore women's knowledge and introduce inappropriate technologies can do much more harm than good.

Of course, women are not always kind to the environment, especially when they become members of consumer-oriented cultures. Western gender ideology encourages women to adopt a consumer life-style through which they can beautify their bodies (according to Western standards), dress fashionably (as defined by male fashion designers), and stock their homes with modern "conveniences" (some of which actually create work). Beauty products are implicated in all manner of ecological harm, ranging from inhumane animal testing of makeup and shampoos to ozone depletion from aerosol spray use. Fur coats are products of the brutal destruction of animals for their pelts. Sanitary napkins and disposable baby diapers decompose slowly and release toxic chemicals in garbage dumps. Finally, "keeping up with the Joneses" keeps women (and men) enamored of the idea that they must have more cars, dishwashers, laundry machines, microwaves, refrigerators, and other devices that take much energy to produce and run, result in a great deal of air and water pollution, and create a significant amount of garbage when they are thrown away to make way for new, improved models.

Whereas middle- and upper-class consumers in "throw-away" societies are heavily implicated in resource waste and environmental pollution, poor and working-class women worldwide suffer the effects of environmental degradation and pollution. The poor and working class are concentrated in crowded and often highly polluted residential areas and largely unregulated, toxic workplaces. For example, women working in Mexico's *maquiladoras* report high levels of illness-causing dust in unventilated garment-industry sweatshops and open trays of cancer-causing chemicals next to them in electronic-industry workrooms.[71] In the rural villages of the Third World, women have the greatest exposure to the harmful gases released from their cookstoves.[72] And given the rise in poor, female-headed households, a large number of women and children live in remote rural areas and urban slums, where toxic-waste dumps are common. This is frequent in Third World countries that accept toxic refuse from the First World in order to earn foreign exchange.

Women's reproductive organs are harmed by exposure to industrial toxins in workplaces and residential communities, resulting in ovarian cancer, infertility, miscarriages, and birth defects.[73] Recognition of women's susceptibility to industrial toxins has led to some restrictions on where women are allowed to work. However, data on sterility, cancers, and genetic damage indicate that men's reproductive health is also put at risk by working in toxic environments. This suggests that the gendered solution of barring women from certain workplaces is simply an "industrial protection racket" that draws attention away from polluting industries as the real problem.[74] Similarly, women's reproductive failures have called attention to the hidden effects of nuclear testing and nuclear power plant emissions and accidents. States and industries should be held accountable for the extensive reproductive harm and genetic damage their nuclear programs have produced.[75]

In a world where the global population will reach 10 billion by 2025 if present demographic rates continue, more than 100 million couples who want to limit their family size do not have access to family-planning services.[76] States, the many men (and a few women) who run them, and various fundamentalist religious groups who enjoy state support must be held accountable for the denial of reproductive rights to women around the world. Over 60 percent of the people of the world live in places where there is no access to safe and legal abortions on request.[77] Even in many developed countries with liberalized abortion laws, there are significant restrictions ensuring that only middle- and upper-class women can afford abortions. The denial of reproductive rights is directly related to environmental and equity issues, most visibly in regard to population pressures and health crises for women.

The World Health Organization estimates that more than 500,000 women die from pregnancy-related causes every year, including 200,000 who die from complications arising from illegal abortions. For every woman who dies, 30 to 40 more suffer lifelong health problems as a result of abortions attempted outside the law.[78] As Table 4.3 illustrates, for Third World women the risk of dying from pregnancy-related causes is over 100 times greater than that for women in northern Europe. Clearly, there are significant costs for women, their families, and their societies resulting from the gendered division of resources that denies women reproductive rights and services. In economic terms alone, this denial entails staggering medical, nutritional, and welfare service costs (see Figure 4.6).

For example, by spending $412 million on family-planning services in 1987, the United States saved $1.8 billion in costs associated with dangerous pregnancies, unsafe abortions, and unwanted children.[79] Such savings are even more critical in the Third World, which has few and overburdened health-care facilities. Freeing up these services from mostly preventable maternity-related illnesses and deaths would translate into more resources for treating other catastrophic illnesses such as AIDS.

AIDS is now "the leading cause of death for women ages 20 to 40 in major cities in the Americas, Western Europe, and sub-Saharan Africa."[80] The gendered divisions of violence, labor, and resources have conspired to make this so, putting young urban women at tremendous risk through

TABLE 4.3   Lifetime Risks of Dying from Pregnancy-Related Causes, by Region, 1987

Region	Risk
Africa	1 in 21
Asia	1 in 54
South America	1 in 73
North America	1 in 6,366
Northern Europe	1 in 9,850

Some examples of the costs of denying women full reproductive rights ranging from accessible and affordable prenatal care to safe, legal, and accessible birth-control and abortion services.

SOURCE: *Ms.*, November/December, 1991, p. 16. Data from Ann Starrs, *Preventing the Tragedy of Maternal Deaths: A Report on the International Safe Motherhood Conference* (Nairobi, Kenya: 1987). Reprinted by permission of *Ms.*

prostitution, rape, poverty, poor health care, and lack of contraceptive services and "safe sex" education. These factors have minimized women's power to control their own bodies, making them highly susceptible to contaminants and disease, which they end up passing on to their children, who, in turn, become damaged global "resources."

Under the gendered division of resources, women not only have little access to resources that might make their lives longer and easier but also are treated as resources themselves, to be used and abused when it suits the purposes of powerful men, states, and industries. What women need and want is rarely considered in the calculus of how resources are defined, divided, and used. As a result, not only women but also the planet and its other inhabitants suffer from this far-from-benign neglect.

CONCLUSION

The gendered divisions of violence, labor, and resources are interrelated and reinforce each other. The global forces of militarization, capitalist accumulation, and resource extraction and exploitation both produce and depend on these gendered divisions, which, in the final analysis, benefit only a small percentage of privileged men. The vast majority of men are susceptible to violence perpetrated by other men who are proving their "masculinity," receive wages commensurate with those of underpaid women in the global economy, and are subject to deteriorating health, the result of environmental degradation and the destruction of the "feminine principle." Thus, women and men, ultimately, share similar interests in confronting and struggling against these global forces and the gendered divisions on which they depend.

Unfortunately, gender ideology sustains inequalities between women and men and obscures the common causes that should unite them. In effect, gender ideology divides women from men and weakens the strug-

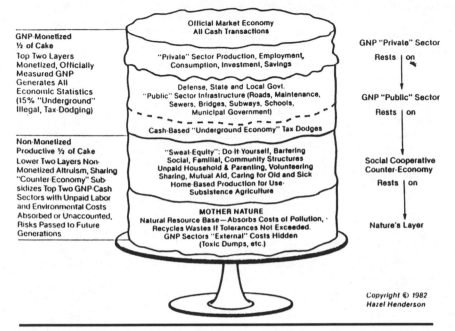

Total "Industrial Cake" diagram labels:

GNP-Monetized ½ of Cake
Top Two Layers Monetized, Officially Measured GNP Generates All Economic Statistics (15% "Underground" Illegal, Tax-Dodging)

Non-Monetized Productive ½ of Cake
Lower Two Layers Non-Monetized Altruism, Sharing "Counter-Economy" Subsidizes Top Two GNP-Cash Sectors with Unpaid Labor and Environmental Costs Absorbed or Unaccounted, Risks Passed to Future Generations

Official Market Economy
All Cash Transactions

"Private" Sector Production, Employment, Consumption, Investment, Savings

Defense, State and Local Govt.
"Public" Sector Infrastructure (Roads, Maintenance, Sewers, Bridges, Subways, Schools, Municipal Government)

Cash-Based "Underground Economy" Tax Dodges

"Sweat-Equity": Do-It-Yourself, Bartering Social, Familial, Community Structures Unpaid Household & Parenting, Volunteering Sharing, Mutual Aid, Caring for Old and Sick Home-Based Production for Use-Subsistence Agriculture

MOTHER NATURE
Natural Resource Base—Absorbs Costs of Pollution, Recycles Wastes If Tolerances Not Exceeded. GNP Sectors "External" Costs Hidden (Toxic Dumps, etc.)

GNP "Private" Sector
Rests on

GNP "Public" Sector
Rests on

Social Cooperative Counter-Economy
Rests on

Nature's Layer

Copyright © 1982
Hazel Henderson

FIGURE 4.6 The industrial cake. This image depicts how dependent the male-dominated formal economy is on exploitation of women's productive and reproductive labor and degradation of the planet. From Hilkka Pietilä and Jeanne Vickers, *Making Women Matter: The Role of the United Nations* (London: Zed Books, 1990). Copyright © Hazel Henderson and *Paradigms in Progress* (Indianapolis, Ind.: Knowledge Systems, 1991). Reprinted by permission.

gles of us all against global violence, world poverty, and planetary destruction. Fortunately, gender ideology is being challenged all over the world by women's movements that have made the link between gender inequality and the many local and global problems to which it contributes. In the next chapter, we turn to these struggles, whose success depends upon both women and men making the connection between gender hierarchy and global crises.

FIVE

□ □ □

The Politics of Resistance:
Women as Nonstate, Antistate,
and Transstate Actors

The gendered division of power and its subsets, the gendered divisions of violence, labor, and resources, severely restrict the effects that women can have on world politics. As Chapter 3 indicated, the few women who have made it into the corridors of power as state actors have done little to dispel prevailing gender ideologies and divisions. Typically, they have adopted masculine leadership styles for themselves without disrupting feminine stereotypes more generally. These "steel magnolias" simply combine and, thus, reinforce the gender divisions of masculine and feminine. They do not challenge them.

At the same time, there are other female political actors who *do* challenge gender dichotomies. Because they typically organize outside of state structures, these actors tend to be invisible through the conventional state-centric lens on world politics. Such women are found in women's, peace, socialist-revolutionary, economic welfare, and ecology movements. Their activities are concentrated below the level of the state and are often geared toward agitating against oppressive state structures and policies. Women also tend to be involved in issues and movements that cut across state boundaries, for example, global-environmental groups and feminist networks. This chapter focuses on women in their roles as nonstate, antistate, and transstate actors who, to varying degrees, do challenge the gendered divisions of power, violence, labor, and resources. We focus on the multiple political roles that women play as well as on the systemic effects of their political activities to shift attention away from "fit-

FIGURE 5.1 Feminisms in action. (*Top left*) The April 5, 1993, March for Women's Lives in Washington, D.C., which supported reproductive freedom in the United States. Photographer: Anne Sisson Runyan. (*Bottom left*) Dutch women protest the deployment of cruise and Pershing II missiles in the Netherlands in 1985. They are marching outside the palace of Queen Biatrix in Amsterdam to show her that senior citizens are opposed to nuclear arms. Photographer: Jan Phillips. (*Top right*) A woman demonstrates against political repression in Chile in 1986. The protest sign reads "For life and for peace, stop the murders." Photo courtesy of Amnesty International. (*Bottom right*) A woman worker silently resists sexist exploitation by her employers by proclaiming on her T-shirt that her body is her own. Photo courtesy of American Friends Service Committee. Photographer: Gary Massoni.

ting women into" traditional IR frameworks and toward an understanding that accommodates and empowers women's struggles against the hierarchical consequences of practicing "world politics as usual." Yet as we document the liberating dimensions of these struggles, we are reminded that they can perpetuate at the same time that they challenge gender dichotomies.

WOMEN'S MOVEMENTS

No woman is born, and not all women become, feminist, but some women *and* men do. How one becomes a feminist varies with each individual, but the impetus for developing a feminist consciousness often arises when a person experiences a contradiction between who that person thinks she or he is and what society wants her or him to be. It may arise out of a contradiction in the opportunities a society says it offers to an individual and what that individual actually experiences. In advanced (post)industrial societies, women are typically told that, under the law, they have equal opportunities (in the liberal democratic sense) to compete for political and economic power. However, in fact, indirect or structural barriers to full political and economic participation reduce most women's rights and choices. In more-traditional societies, particularly those that experienced some kind of colonial or neocolonial rule, colonially imposed laws and certain cultural and religious traditions combine to deny equal opportunities to women, even under the law. The gendered division of power in both cases circumscribes women's choices to be and do things deemed outside of their assigned gender roles.

Throughout history women—individually, collectively, and sometimes with men—have struggled against direct and indirect barriers to their self-development and their full social, political, and economic participation. In the modern era, they have often done so through organizing women's movements that have addressed many issues and, thus, taken many forms (see Figure 5.1). People associate women's movements with campaigns to gain equal rights for women under the law. But women have often sought more-transformative changes in social, political, and economic systems because prevailing masculinist systems undermine women's struggles for gender equality despite formal equal rights. As a result, it is sometimes difficult to separate women's movements from other political movements agitating for social, political, and economic transformation. In this text, we regard as feminist those political movements in which participants self-consciously and deliberately link gender inequality with other forms of social, political, economic, and/or ecological injustice.

Liberal Feminists

Feminists engage in many kinds of strategies to erode or explode gender dichotomies.[1] Liberal feminists, who are most active in equal rights movements, seek to eliminate these dichotomies by eliminating the emphasis on gender *difference* and replacing it with an emphasis on sameness. They argue that women are equal to men because they are essentially the same as men in regard to capacities for aggression, ambition, strength, and rationality. This argument is at odds with the idea that women are naturally the opposite of and inferior to men. But the problem is that this perspective accepts masculine traits as the norm to which women can and should aspire. As a result, it challenges the gendered *division,* but not the gendered *notion* of power. It leaves intact and even reinforces the idea that power equals aggression, ambition, strength, and rationality. A system of power-over is thus perpetuated, ensuring that women and men who appear lacking in these traits will not be admitted to the corridors of power. Instead, they will remain the objects of power to be manipulated and coerced.

In short, the question that liberal feminists must grapple with is "equal to whom and for what?" As our earlier discussion indicated, this question is particularly pertinent with respect to the issue of women in the military. Even if women were to be admitted into state militaries in numbers equal to men's and as equals of men (neither of which is likely in a power over system), the problem that state militaries are organized hierarchically and for the purpose of engaging in direct violence and/or "backing up" systems of indirect violence still remains.

Radical Feminists

Radical feminists approach gender inequality quite differently from liberal feminists. Rather than insisting that women are the same as men because they share masculine capabilities, radical feminists celebrate feminine traits and argue that men should adopt them. In fact, radical feminists see masculinity, with its emphasis on aggression and violence directed by men against women and men, as the problem, not the solution for liberating women and other subordinated groups. Thus, a strategy of some radical feminists, often referred to as cultural feminists, is to revalue previously denigrated aspects of femininity, making them the norm to which all people should aspire in pursuit of a better world.

For example, cultural feminists seek to remove the negative connotations from such feminine traits as passivity, nurturance, emotionalism, and dependence and to redefine them more positively. Women's purported passivity—destructive if it keeps them from acting politically against their oppression—is positive to the degree that it promotes a desire for accommodation and thus a nonviolent resolution of conflicts. Similarly, women's supposed proclivity to nurture—problematic when it comes to tying women exclusively to reproductive labor—is positive as an ethic of care that extends to children, the poor and victimized, and the planet as a whole. Indeed, radical feminists generally argue that the near worship of masculine rationality has promoted an instrumentalism that threatens the very life of the planet and its inhabitants. Cultural feminists within radical feminism go on to theorize that women's greater tendency toward emotion and intuition offsets this rationalistic calculus that has no feeling for life and, thus, no concern for the destructiveness of instrumentalism.

Whereas radical feminists criticize women who depend on men in ways that too often leave the women victimized, they point out that (inter)dependence, not autonomy, is essential for human and planetary survival. People and nature are bound up in webs of interdependency that entail responsibility and care for others. Thus, radical feminists insist that interdependence be revalued and redefined in a way that promotes the establishment of mutually respectful relationships among women and men, among peoples, and with nature—a mutual respect that recognizes the inescapable interdependence of all life.

For many radical feminists, the politics of sexuality is paramount. According to this view, a fundamental source of women's oppression is male domination of women's bodies, both ideologically (through pornography, demeaning stereotypes, sexist jokes) and practically (through androcentric marriage and property laws, denial of women's reproductive rights, sexual violence). Here the personal is political in the sense that even women's most "private" and intimate experiences are shaped by institutions and structures that privilege male-defined pleasures and masculinist principles. As a corollary, these radical feminists are critical of **heterosexism,** which assumes heterosexuality is the only "normal" and therefore legitimate pattern of sexual and social relations.

As a result, much of the activist work of radical feminists is geared toward intervening in destructive relationships through the establishment of rape crisis centers and battered women's shelters in many parts of the world. They are also active in peace, ecology, reproductive rights, antipornography, and gay and lesbian rights movements. Their aim in all these movements is to undermine systems of power-over and replace them with systems of empowerment.

In short, radical feminists have no interest in being equal to men, if being equal means becoming like or the same as male oppressors. Thus, for example, they criticize the liberal feminist strategy of supporting the entry of women into state militaries. They argue instead that neither women nor men should enter the military, which, in their view, is a patriarchal institution designed to exaggerate masculinity, oppress women, and destroy human and planetary life.

Socialist Feminists

Socialist feminists, while supporting many of the goals of liberal and radical feminists, question the latter's continued use of problematic gender categories. Like radical feminists, they argue that the divisions between private and public, reproduction and production are patriarchal constructions, but they believe that the answer is not to revalue the private sphere and reproductive work but rather to show how the private, reproductive sphere and the public, productive sphere are not only interrelated but also less distinctive than they seem. For the majority of people in the world—that is, non-Western, poor and working-class women and men of color—a rigid distinction between who can and cannot work in the public, productive sphere is impossible. Poor and working-class women have never had the dubious luxury of being confined to the private sphere of home and family.

In addition, socialist feminists argue that it makes no sense to separate productive and reproductive labor and give no value to the latter, as has been the case under capitalism (and in states' calculations of the gross domestic product [GDP]). Reproductive labor, including the labor that women perform in the informal, home-based economy, is productive work and should be counted as such. If it were, then attention would be drawn to the impoverished circumstances under which most women labor, which affect the overall productive capacities of societies. It would also expose the costs to society extracted by capitalist reliance upon women's cheap or free labor to make a profit. In other words, if capitalist industries had to pay the actual costs of women's reproductive labor (based on the prices charged for providing equivalent services, such as day care and housecleaning), we would see that the ways in which these industries currently are organized are not, in fact, efficient or competitive, but wasteful and expensive.

Under the current system, workers' wages can be kept artificially low because they do not have to be used to pay for women's reproductive labor in the home. Thus, resources and wealth can be concentrated at the top of corporate hierarchies, where the least productive (and reproductive) work is done. Thus, to take women's reproductive labor seriously means that the very nature of corporate organization and production would have to change. First, the wage structure would have to be adjusted to ensure that more money and resources are distributed to productive and reproductive workers. Second, there would be greater demand for the production of things that meet the basic needs of households rather than luxury items that can be consumed only by the few. States, too, would have to have a very different orientation, focusing their programs on assisting reproductive labor rather than subsidizing exploitative, luxury-oriented industries.

In sum, socialist feminists encourage us to rethink, rather than embrace, gender dichotomies. In the process, work and welfare are redefined by expanding the idea of work and exonerating the notion of welfare. The latter would no longer be a system of meager handouts but a societal priority to increase all people's productivity in equitable, healthful, mutually respectful, and life-affirming ways. Thus, socialist feminists are interested in undermining the power-over system of capitalist patriarchy through empowerment. However, they believe this can be accomplished best by a societal and global redistribution of power, as opposed to placing their hopes in the empowering capacity of feminine traits. As a result, socialist feminists are most active in socialist revolutions and women's economic movements, organizing around such issues as women on welfare, women in development, and women in the "global factory." Through this work, socialist feminists, like radical feminists, have also criticized state militaries. However, socialist feminists tend to emphasize that the military-industrial complex impoverishes women by extracting resources from state and global economies that should go to meet basic needs. Women entering the military in greater numbers will not change this imbalance of resources between the military and the civilian economy.

Postmodernist Feminists

Postmodernist feminists, found most often in academic circles, but also in feminist political movements, also want to see an end to women's oppression in all spheres. These feminists are critical not just of gender dichotomies and categories but also of the concept of gender itself, at least as it has been used within other feminisms. They are concerned that the concept of gender, like sex, still contains within it traces of biological determinism and "essentialism." They argue that other feminisms, even when they criticize how gender is used by capitalism, militarism, and other power-over systems, tend to speak of gender as if it stems from women's and men's essential natures and seemingly unalterable roles. They worry, for instance, that the cultural feminist tendency (within radical feminism) to glorify feminine traits does not alter masculinist assumptions that women must nurture and must be protected. By the same token, they argue that socialist feminist proposals to improve the conditions of women's reproductive labor leave intact the idea that only women do reproductive labor by virtue of their roles as wives and mothers.

Postmodernist feminists extend their critique of gender categories by challenging us also to rethink our use of the terms *woman* and *man*. Their point is that we are all more complicated beings than these unitary labels suggest and our experiences of being gendered—as woman or man—vary along dimensions of race, class, nationality, ethnicity, sexuality, and so on. All these identities with which we are labeled, either individually or in hyphenated form (such as white-poor-French-woman), are social constructs that are created, given meaning, and reproduced by the differing, yet interlocking, systems of power in which we are embedded. That is, these identities do not arise from our genitals or skin color (although, historically, physical attributes have been made politically salient). Rather the identities arise from and are perpetuated by social and psychological interpretations of physical differences among people—interpretations that are used to organize people hierarchically all over the world. Postmodernist feminists do not question the existence of pervasive sexism and racism. But they urge feminists and other political movement activists to avoid speaking of women and men, blacks and whites, and so on, *as if* they were unitary, essential categories that do not change in meaning over time and across cultures.[2]

Because postmodernist feminists are concerned with complicating, not reproducing, gender (and even sex) categories, they are wary of feminisms that posit a natural sisterhood of women, presupposing a universally shared experience of oppression. They argue, instead, that women have different experiences of oppression (according to their socioeconomic, cultural, and political locations) and that any solidarity women may develop should arise from women's consciously choosing to work together on an issue. They do not expect that such coalition building will be free of conflict among different women (and/or men) working together—or that it should be. Whatever consensus is built will arise from a struggle to see and value each other's perspectives, and whatever actions are taken may only apply to the specific context of the struggle.

In short, this does not mean that there can be no large-scale, transstate or transcultural movements to address global problems. It suggests instead that local and localized solutions, geared for subverting power-over in the multiple sites where it is developed and deployed, might produce the most just outcomes in the struggles against multiple global problems. For example, postmodernist feminists, although generally critical of state militaries for the violence and economic impoverishment they have visited upon most women, recognize that women are no more inherently peaceful than men are inherently aggressive. They also recognize that peace does not always bring justice. Thus, postmodernist feminists believe that women should have the maneuvering room to "fight" in their struggles for a peace predicated on equality and justice.

Practical and Strategic Gender Interests

Women, feminist or not, who become involved in political activities often do so as a result of what Maxine Molyneux called "practical" or "strategic" gender interests.[3] In Molyneux's words, **practical gender interests** "are usually in response to an immediate perceived need, and they do not generally entail a strategic goal such as women's emancipation or gender equality."[4] By contrast, **strategic gender interests** are derived from a more general analysis of women's subordination and involve the formulation of system-transforming, or strategic, objectives to overcome that subordination.[5] According to this distinction, women who organize spontaneously to protest food shortages, sex discrimination in the workplace, or lack of adequate health care for their families are generally acting upon their practical gender interests. That is, they are seeking a change in conditions without insisting on a change in the larger system of gender dichotomies. Stated differently, even though practical gender interests do in fact arise out of gendered divisions and hierarchy, they are distinguished from strategic gender interests by not fundamentally challenging those divisions and hierarchy.

When women participate in political movements as a result of their practical gender interests, they may develop an awareness of their strategic gender interests by self-consciously confronting their subordination as women. In the process, they come to the understanding that their practical gender interests are not being satisfied because their strategic gender interests are being thwarted. This insight enables them to link gender inequality and the problems—often of sheer survival—that they face in their daily lives.

It can be argued that movements arising out of women's practical gender issues constitute reformist politics, whereas movements arising out of strategic gender interests constitute transformative politics. But we must remember that both forms of politics are necessary—not only to ameliorate the oppressive conditions under which most women live but also (eventually) to eliminate these conditions altogether. Moreover, movements arising out of practical gender interests can have revolutionary, or transformative, consequences; and movements arising out of strategic gender interests may result only in reform, and only for a few women. Finally, women can and have been known to engage in rather reactionary politics, usually in response to their practical gender interests, but sometimes in pursuit of their strategic gender interests.

Women who become fundamentalist, antifeminist, and/or militarist may do so because they think that their traditional roles of wife and mother, from which they gain a certain amount of protection and esteem, are threatened (whether by atheists, feminists, or Communists). Some feminists alienate others by actions that have tended to exclude rather than include. For example, women of color and poor women have accused white, Western, middle-class women of failing to work with them to place the critique of *all* social hierarchies at the center of feminist theorizing and activism.

By referring to practical and strategic gender interests, we hope to show the relationships among local, state, and global feminist movements. Most political resistance is a response to local and immediate conditions that are perceived as obstacles to the realization of practical interests. But oppressive conditions at the local or state level are often a manifestation of more-encompassing systems of hierarchy (racism, capitalism, sexism). As activists become aware of the relationship between local struggles and larger systems of hierarchical relations, some pursue system-transforming strategies. In this way, participation in local resistance actions can lead to participation in (or at least support for) larger and sometimes global social movements. To the extent that local actions are linked to system-transforming movements, they have implications for world politics.

There is no perfect formula for eradicating women's global subordination arising out of gendered divisions of power, violence, labor, and resources. Moreover, there is no guarantee that women's gender interests, whether they be practical, strategic, or both, will lead to the effective and progressive mobilization of women and men to combat gender and other hierarchies. Nevertheless, in the sections that follow, we look at a variety of women's nonstate, antistate, and transstate struggles that attest to the fact that women all over the world are political, are active, do challenge gender dichotomies, and do change world politics by their political agency—even though very few women are state actors.

ANTIWAR AND PEACE MOVEMENTS

The discipline of international relations, which essentially began after World War I—the war that was supposed to end all wars—has been preoccupied with the question of how to prevent or stop war. With the rise of peace studies during the Vietnam era, IR has also began to ask what peace is because surely it must be more than simply the time between wars. Women have long been involved in analyzing how to stop war and how to create peace, though they have received no attention for these activities in past and most contemporary international relations literature. Instead, their peace efforts have been ignored or trivialized—largely by men who stereotype women as soft-headed, irrational pacifists. This characterization is political because it excludes women's perspectives from the study of war and peace. Instead, that subject is reserved for and addressed by "realists": ostensibly hard-headed, rational men, especially those with military experience.

In addition, the gendered division of violence positions women as life-givers, expected to mourn the toll of war quietly, pick up the pieces when it is over, and not undermine the war effort by asking, for whom? and for what? Women who do ask questions are seen as ungrateful for the protection courageously delivered by men and states through their military might and actions. In spite of this gendered state of affairs, women have protested loudly and often against war and for a more just and peaceful world (see Figure 5.2).

Examples extend from the fifth century B.C. Athenian play *Lysistrata*, in which women refused to sleep with men who went to war, to the International Women's Gulf Peace Initiative in 1991 against hostilities in the Persian Gulf. However, it was not until the rise of the first wave of feminism, during the latter part of the nineteenth century, that the political linkage between peace and women's emancipation was made. This pre–World War I period is considered the golden age of peace movements in the West. Predominantly white, middle-class women formed a variety of peace societies (such as the Union Internationale des Femmes, the Ligue des Femmes pour Desarmament, the Alliance des Femmes pour la Paix, and the Société d'Education Pacifique in France), which were used as models for women's peace societies elsewhere in Western Europe, the United States, and even Japan.[6] Liberal feminist peace activists made their presence known at major international peace conferences, including the first and second Hague conferences in 1899 and 1907.[7] Socialist feminists organized their own international conferences, such as the First and the Second International Conference of Socialist Women, held in 1907 and 1910 respectively, at which they endorsed resolutions against the militarism of imperialist powers.[8]

In 1915, predominantly white, middle-class feminists in the United States under the leadership of Jane Addams formed the U.S. Woman's Peace party (WPP). The WPP tapped both practical and strategic gender interests by calling for women's suffrage (the right to vote) and arguing that women's role as mothers gave them a special moral responsibility to oppose war. Not all suffragists supported a platform of peace, especially after World War I had broken out. But in 1915, 1,136 delegates from twelve countries made a dangerous wartime journey to The Hague to attend the International Congress of Women to protest against the war. The congress passed twenty resolutions on the destruction of humanity, the use of sons for cannon fodder, and the victimization of mothers/women that war inflicted.[9] The congress also founded the Women's International League for Peace and Freedom, which continues to exist, with headquarters in Geneva and thousands of chapters all over the world.

During the interwar years, white, middle-class women in large numbers joined organizations such as the British Peace Pledge Union and within these organizations formed their own women's committees and peace campaigns.[10] As World War II loomed, such organizations collapsed when both women and men were drawn into the war effort by

FIGURE 5.2   Women for peace. This graphic, which appeared outside the Peace Tent at the NGO Forum during the final conference of the UN Decade for Women in 1985 in Nairobi, Kenya, quotes British novelist and essayist Virginia Woolf. Writing between World Wars I and II, she believed that women had common cause, enabling them to transcend borders and end wars. Courtesy of the International Women's Tribune Centre, Inc. Illustrator: Anne S. Walker.

their governments. Governments appealed to women's practical and strategic gender interests. They encouraged women to support their "boys" by mothering the nation through rationing, buying war bonds, and doing volunteer work for the duration. They also offered women jobs in wartime industries that had previously been closed to them.[11] Yet this combination was not in fact liberating. Even though women went out to work in large numbers, they were still expected to fulfill the maternal role for servicemen and the nation.[12]

As a result, when men came home from war, most women were laid off from higher-paying jobs in wartime industries and were expected to go back to being full-time homemakers. However, this was a "luxury" affordable only to white, upper-middle-class women: Actually, 84 percent of all U.S. women working during 1944–1945 were doing so out of economic necessity,[13] and only 600,000 women had left the paid work force by 1946.[14] Nevertheless, 58 percent of U.S. women in 1943 felt that they could "best help the war effort by staying at home."[15] The onerous task of combining work with family led many married women to leave their jobs readily, albeit under pressure from husbands, unions, and bosses who were hostile to their presence in the work force when the war ended. In this sense, the disruptions of World War II did not really challenge or undermine gender roles and dichotomies, which were ultimately deepened and reinforced.

At the same time, the fact that women—especially white, middle-class women—were encouraged to take their role as wives and mothers seriously during the 1950s led some of them into antimilitary movements from the 1960s through the 1980s. For example, the 1960s saw the rise of Women Strike for Peace in the United States and the Voice of Women in Canada, which organized to "End the Arms Race, Not the Human Race."[16] Women Strike for Peace organized a one-day strike on November 1, 1961, in which 50,000 women left their homes and workplaces to protest the arms race. So threatening was this action to cold war orthodoxy that in 1962 the House Committee on Un-American Activities accused leaders of this grass-roots women's movement of being Communists.[17]

During the 1980s, a host of women's antinuclear groups emerged in response to the post-detente resurgence of the arms race and the U.S. testing and deployment of cruise missiles. These groups ranged from the Oxford Mothers for Nuclear Disarmament (UK), Women Opposed to Nuclear Technology (UK), and the Women's Pentagon Action (U.S.), to women's peace camps set up outside nuclear installations throughout Europe and North America. These women's peace encampments, including Greenham Common and "Molesworth in England, Comiso in Italy, Hunsruck in West Germany, Seneca and Puget Sound in the United States, Nanoose in Canada, Soesterburg in Holland, Pine Gap in Australia, and others"[18] attracted many thousands of women who insisted that life on the nuclear precipice was intolerable to them, their children, and their grandchildren. This perspective encouraged many women to demand an end to East-West hostilities by staging "peace walks" from Stockholm to Moscow and organizing international women's peace conferences like the one called "The Urgency for True Security: Women's Alternatives for Negotiating Peace" held in Halifax, Nova Scotia (Canada), in 1985 and the subsequent Women's "Peace Tent" experiment at the Non-Governmental Forum for the end of the UN Decade for Women Conference in Nairobi, also in 1985.[19]

At the same time, groups like the Mothers of the Plaza de Mayo in Argentina and Mothers of El Salvador organized to bear witness to brutal regimes that had made their children "disappear" (see Figure 5.3). Women in Northern Ireland, like Mairead Corrigan and Betty Williams,

FIGURE 5.3 Women against political violence. The Mothers of the Plaza de Mayo in Argentina demand an end to the political violence. Photo courtesy of Amnesty International.

who won the Nobel Peace Prize in 1977, rallied to stop the bloodshed between Protestants and Catholics. The Mothers of the Heroes and Martyrs in Nicaragua cried out against the U.S.-sponsored contra war against the Sandinista government and its people; the Shibokusa women of Mount Fuji in Japan protested the expropriation of land by the U.S. and Japanese militaries; the Sri Lankan Voice of Women for Peace was calling for the end of the civil war between Sinhalese and Tamils; women of Fiji appealed to the French government to stop nuclear testing in the South Pacific; and black South African women continued their struggles against the violence of apartheid.[20]

The motivation of much of this past and contemporary peace organizing by women has been their identification with and assigned responsibility for mothering. Many of these women have been interested in protecting their children and future generations from the ravages of war and war preparation, whether nuclear or conventional. But they also have been calling attention to the fact that their reproductive work in terms of providing food and shelter for their families is being made much more difficult and even impossible by war machines that eat up people and resources. Thus, women's political action on behalf of peace often arises from "practical" gender interests that enhance women's assigned roles in the so-called private sphere.

On the face of it, these women's struggles for peace do little to disrupt gender dichotomies because they leave in place the image of men as aggressive and bellicose life-takers/killers in contrast to women as pacifist life-givers/reproducers/mothers. However, these struggles do call into question certain other aspects of gender hierarchy produced by the gendered division of violence. For example, by the very act of "leaving home" and taking on so-called public-sphere institutions and issues—often at the risk of death and imprisonment or, at the very least, censure by governments and mainstream societies—these women challenge the idea that women are weak, passive victims who can only mourn their fate on the home front. At the same time, such actions belie the idea that it is only men who die from the ravages of war and war preparation and that these deaths only occur on the battlefield. In fact, women's protests against war and all other kinds of state violence reveal generally hidden and unfamiliar costs of modern total warfare.

Moreover, the horrors that women identify completely undermine the notion that men are protectors and that women are protected. Because the male-dominated state security apparatus is the cause of their suffering and that of their children, many of these female peace activists ask, Who is going to protect us, or how are we going to protect ourselves, from the protectors? It is in the struggle to answer this question that many women have become "soldiers for peace," a contradiction itself that forces us to rethink gender categories, identities, and practices.

Within these movements as well are women struggling on behalf their strategic gender interests. Peace activists who identify themselves as feminists are less likely than those who do not so identify themselves to promote or celebrate motherhood as the basis for women's peace activism.[21] Feminists are aware that women's responsibility for mothering has often brought them into the struggle for peace, yet they warn us that until reproductive labor is no longer the sole or major responsibility of women, there will be no real change in the priorities of states, international organizations, and the mostly elite men who run them. Moreover, as long as women remain tied to the currently devalued "private sphere," their protests will be marginalized by those in power, who will continue to expect the women to "pick up the pieces" in the wake of continual destruction. Indeed, feminists ask whether there can be any peace worth having in the absence of gender, race, and class justice.

Finally, feminist peace activists argue that neither women nor mothers are innately peaceful (here they agree with postmodern feminists) or necessarily life-givers. On the contrary, women, like men, have always served militaries and supported wars—as spouses, workers, soldiers, government officials, and parents. When we dispel the notion that the struggle for peace is not some innate feminine attribute that is "soft" and available only to women, the way will be opened up for many more to join the struggle for peace *and* justice that will make world politics enhance, rather than undermine, the survival and equality of all.

REVOLUTIONARY MOVEMENTS

The fact that women take up arms in national liberation struggles contradicts the stereotype that women are naturally peaceful. Throughout recorded history we find stories of women fomenting and engaging in populist violence as leaders and followers. For every female revolutionary leader such as Joan of Arc, Olympes de Gouge, Rosa Luxemburg, Alexandra Kollantai, Dora Maria Tellez, and Winnie Mandela, there have been millions of women who have participated in countless uprisings, guerrilla movements, and revolutions—ranging from the French, American, Russian, and Chinese revolutions to more recent revolutionary struggles throughout Latin America, the Caribbean, Africa, and the Middle East.[22] Not all these women have taken up arms. More typically they have worked in underground movements to hide and heal guerrilla fighters, pass information and weapons, and organize communities in support of the revolution. Still, most revolutionary women have supported armed struggle as a necessary, although not the only, facet of revolutionary action.

Although often motivated by the same concerns as men—a desire to overthrow corrupt regimes, to fight colonialism and imperialism, and to build nationalism and a national economy not controlled and impoverished by foreign elites—women also join or are encouraged to join revolutionary struggles on behalf of their practical and strategic gender interests. In the testimonial literature that chronicles women's experiences in revolutionary struggles, we find examples of women revolutionaries who were drawn into the struggle both as mothers responsible for providing for their families and as women seeking greater equality with men, first on the battlefield and then in the government of the new state-to-be. Like the pattern with peace movements, women tend to become involved in revolutions initially because of their practical gender interests and then work for their strategic gender interests when they run up against sexism in revolutionary movements.

An example is the role of women and women's associations in the revolutionary struggle against the Somoza regime in Nicaragua. Gloria Carrion was active in the Association of Nicaraguan Women Confronting the Nation's Problems (AMPRONAC) and became the general coordinator of the Luisa Amanda Espinosa Nicaraguan Women's Association (AMNLAE) after the victory of the Sandinista National Liberation Front (FSLN). Lea Guido was also an organizer with AMPRONAC and later, the minister of public health in the National Reconstruction government. In interviews, both Carrion and Guido reported that women were drawn into the struggle on the basis of their family and maternal roles.

Carrion described women as "the centres of their families—emotionally, ideologically and economically" who do not see themselves "'simply' as housewives" subordinated to husbands.[23] Guido told of a women's campaign around the slogan "Our Children Are Hungry, Bring Down the Cost of Living." She argued that the parties of the traditional Left had failed to mobilize women because they did not address women's practical gender interests. The women's campaign was successful "because we learned how to involve women in the national struggle while at the same time organizing around problems specific to women."[24]

AMPRONAC and, later, AMNLAE brought many women into nonviolent aspects of revolutionary struggle on the basis of their practical gender interests. Engaging in revolutionary violence generated particular problems for women. By becoming guerrilla fighters, women transgressed their traditional gender roles and were often seen as threatening to revolutionary men. Confronting the sexism of their comrades, many women were awakened to strategic gender interests. Monica Baltonado, a guerrilla commander of the Nicaraguan Revolution, pointed out that the extent of sexism among men of the FMLN varied:

> Some comrades were open to dealing with sexism while others remained closed. Some said women were no good in the mountains, that they were only good "for screwing," that they created conflicts—sexual conflicts. But there were also men with very good positions. Carlos Fonseca, for example, was a solid comrade on this issue. It's been a long struggle! We won those battles through discussions and by women comrades demonstrating their ability and their resistance.[25]

Women, who constituted over 30 percent of guerrilla combatants, did prove their mettle in the insurrections against Somoza's regime.[26] However, after the triumph, they made up only 6 percent of military officers in the Sandinista People's Army (EPS), which discouraged women's participation on the basis that women's first obligation is to motherhood.[27] After protests from AMNLAE, three women's *reserve* battalions were set up. The majority of women who wanted to defend the revolution were active in two organizations: the Sandinista Popular Militias (MPS), designed to defend farms and factories against sabotage by U.S.-supported contra forces, and the Sandinista Defense Committees (CDS), which organized neighborhoods to create better living conditions. The

MPS and the CDS were viewed—by male leaders and often by women themselves—as more consistent with women's mothering roles and family responsibilities. Indeed, although AMNLAE's symbol was a picture of a young woman with a rifle on her back and a baby in her arms, in actuality most Nicaraguan women were encouraged to put down the gun and pick up their baby after the triumph.

That mothering was incompatible with violent revolutionary action was recognized by women fighting for the independence of Zimbabwe in the 1970s. One young female guerrilla reported that women were able to convince their male comrades to accept the use of contraceptives by arguing that "to be sent back to Mozambique for five months to have a baby was a setback to the war."[28] The women who made this "practical" argument, however, had undergone deeper transformations that tapped their strategic gender interests, especially in regard to reproductive rights: "Our attitudes to contraception and abortion changed during the years of struggle. The girls really adopted a new way of living after what they've seen in the bush, the contacts they've had with other people from European countries, from the books they've read."[29]

Revolutionary struggles, indeed, create "new women" who transgress proscribed gender roles, but these women remain disadvantaged in terms of the gendered division of power and resources when the revolution is over. A spokesperson for the Omani Women's Organization, which was active in the People's Front for the Liberation of Oman in the mid-1970s, put it this way: "Many men had received education and political experience ... before they joined the Front, while women had their first education and political experience when as young girls they joined the Revolution."[30] Because women had less formal training than men before the revolution, they were again left out of the picture when military demobilization proceeded. In sum, women are more easily demobilized and sent back home, whereas men assume positions of power in new regimes when revolutions are successful.[31]

A "successful" revolution is, conventionally, one in which a dictator or ruling regime is toppled and a new regime is put in its place. Rarely is a positive change in the condition and status of women viewed as a key measure of a revolution's "success." Nevertheless, there have been instances where conditions that intersect with women's practical gender interests have improved. Not infrequently, successful revolutions bring improvements in meeting basic human needs. For example, delivery of improved health care reduces rates of infant mortality, the provision of education expands work opportunities, and better nutrition supports a generally healthier population. Such gains particularly benefit the large numbers of poor women who are finally provided some assistance in meeting their assigned responsibility for sustaining the family.

In the area of women's strategic gender interests, some revolutionary movements and later governments have instituted reforms intended to break down sexual stereotypes and inequalities. For instance, Cuba's revolutionary government wrote a new Family Code that afforded women equal rights in marriage and divorce and called for equal responsibilities in the household, including shared housework.[32] Nicaragua's Sandinista government passed similar legislation in 1981. Even prior to this measure, the Sandinistas responded to demands made by AMPRONAC by legislating a ban on the sexist use of women in advertising and by outlawing prostitution—in the hopes of integrating women into alternative employment.[33]

Unfortunately, these and other such measures, although progressive in comparison to measures in many other countries, were not motivated solely or primarily by feminist concerns. More typically, the governments wanted to get more women into the productive labor force to increase the country's gross domestic product (GDP), combat Western cultural imperialism in the form of pornography and sensationalist press, and inculcate revolutionary "morals," particularly in Catholic countries. Indeed, abortion remained illegal in Nicaragua throughout the revolutionary period despite the fact that thousands of women died or were maimed there by back-alley abortions every year and despite AMNLAE's demands, beginning in the mid-1980s, for legalized abortions.[34] Moreover, the shared-domestic-responsibility clauses in both the Cuban and Nicaraguan family codes were rarely enforced, and men in these societies for the most part fail to participate equally in household decision-making and continue to do little reproductive labor. These responsibilities still fall heavily on women's shoulders. Finally, the gains women made as a result of socialist revolutions—either of the practical or strategic variety—have been seriously eroded. This is a consequence of both internal and external dynamics: the economic, political, and social turmoil created by foreign military intervention and economic embargoes, civil wars, and the overthrow of socialist regimes in Eastern Europe, the Soviet Union, and Latin America.

The failure of socialist regimes and their "democratizing" successors to place women's strategic gender interests at the center of their concerns is related to what feminist analysts call **gendered nationalism.** On this view, nationalist struggles have been gendered because they involve the manipulation of gender identities and symbols and gendered divisions of power, labor, and resources.

Nationalist fervor has served as the driving and unifying force behind liberal, socialist, and, most recently, anti-Communist revolutions. Struggles for economic and political justice have typically been framed within the context of national self-determination and autonomy—concepts that have a decidedly masculinist cast and, up to the present period, have for the most part translated into self-determination and autonomy for men and, especially, male leaders. As we have seen, this lauded self-determination and autonomy has been made possible largely through women's undervalued and unheralded reproductive labor, which "frees" men for the seemingly greater heroics that shape *the* national identity. As Enloe observed, "The notion of what 'the nation' was at its finest hour—when it was most unified, most altruistic—will be a community in which women sacrificed their desires for the sake of the male-led collective."[35]

Under this construction of the nation, women's feminist aspirations are forced into conflict with their national allegiance, and revolutionary male-run governments are able to ignore and even vilify feminist demands. An extreme example of gendered nationalism infused the 1978 Iranian Revolution, in which large numbers of women contributed to the downfall of the shah only to become the primary targets of sexual "purification" campaigns to limit their autonomy under the right-wing Islamist regime of the Ayatollah Khomeini.[36] But the pattern of gendered nationalism is in fact widespread. Virtually without exception, women have been used—as symbols of national morality, as behind-the-scenes support workers, as guerrilla fighters—to win nationalist struggles. But with victory, the practical and strategic interests of women are subordinated to masculinist priorities.

Thus, women's struggles on behalf of revolutionary movements, whether as combatants or as less-violent resistance workers and populist protesters, have not brought them "liberation" from gender oppression. To the degree that revolutions improve general conditions for meeting basic human needs, women's practical gender interests have been served. However, despite the personal transformations experienced by female revolutionaries who stepped outside their traditional roles, structural or systemic transformations in line with women's strategic gender interests have not been a consequence of male-led revolutions.

One reason for this lies in the failure of revolutionary women's struggles to undermine fundamental gender dichotomies. No matter what women do in combat, they are still expected, after and even during revolutions, to give life. Their primary roles as reproducers and mothers remain unquestioned. Men are not expected to perform this dual role during revolutions or to cease being the protectors when it is over. Nowhere is there a poster with a revolutionary man shouldering a gun while holding a baby. And nowhere has he picked up the baby when the gun is no longer necessary.

Jean Bethke Elshtain pointed out a second reason that women revolutionaries fail to undermine gender dichotomies. Under the gendered division of violence, "female violence is what happens when politics breaks

down into riots, revolutions, or anarchy: when things are out of control,"
whereas the violent revolutionary male "can restore order, including the
order he violated."[37] In other words, women's violence is exceptional, but
men's violence is an accepted component of men's role as consolidators
and sustainers of the political order. Robin Morgan conveyed this point in
her discussion of terrorism. She argued that the stateless male terrorists of
today are simply the statesmen of tomorrow, who will—as statesmen—
purvey state terrorism, as history has amply shown us. In contrast, female
terrorists—especially the bomb-planting and bomb-throwing variety
who are not portrayed safely with babies in their arms—continue to be
unnerving figures that represent the worst kind of disorder. They symbolize what lies outside and even threatens the conventional image of the
transfer of power from terrorist men of the state-that-is to their heirs apparent, terrorist men of the state-that-would-be.[38]

We cannot, however, undermine the gendered division of violence
simply by becoming more comfortable with the image and reality of the
female "terrorist." That image in fact perpetuates the gendered division
of violence because women's revolutionary action undertaken in the context of the struggle between men of the state-that-is and men of the state-
that-would-be reinforces that which produced this contest.

Contemporary revolutionary movements tend to take the state system
for granted, their leaders typically seeking to form a new state or seize
power in an existing state. As a consequence, women's activities in these
struggles also remain state focused.[39] Women are crucial both to mobiliz-
ing mass support for revolutionary struggle and to achieving victory
through home-front and battlefront activities. Yet to women the benefits
of successful revolutions are always tempered by the retention of
masculinist principles.

After revolutionary movements achieve the status of "new states," no
one denies their international significance because states are central actors. To understand how the gender dynamics of revolutionary movements affects world politics, we need to appreciate the linkages between
the personal (gender-differentiated experiences in revolutionary struggle), the political (gender-differentiated costs and benefits), and the global
(gendered interstate and transstate institutions and movements).

What begins to emerge when we look at these events through a gender-
sensitive lens? One point is that women are essential to the success of revolutionary struggles. To the extent that these struggles shape international relations, the presence of women and the power of gender should
be analyzed as significant determinants of world politics. Another, and
broader, point is that women (and men) who engage in revolutionary activities are, by definition, challenging the status quo. Put into question are
gender stereotypes as well as oppressive conditions, corrupt regimes, and

economic exploitation. In the process of struggle, participants presumably develop a clearer understanding of how societies function and how structural change can be promoted and/or resisted. As our examples illustrate, women consistently find their interests subordinated to or denied by masculinist nation-states. This raises—often explicitly—the following questions: What should the priorities of a society be? How do societies sustain themselves? Are state orders capable of instituting justice and equity? How are the costs and benefits of struggle divided? Who wins as long as the gendered division of violence remains intact? These questions increasingly appear on the agenda of nonstate, antistate, and transstate movements, and the debates and actions they fuel are increasingly a dimension of world politics.

ECONOMIC MOVEMENTS

Women's protests in regard to economic conditions are perhaps the most durable and pervasive example of their being political actors. As we have seen, women are at a disadvantage owing to the gendered division of labor within the home and family (the unpaid labor force), the gendered division of labor in the workplace (the paid labor force), and the gendered international division of labor (the global economy). These processes have relegated large numbers of women, especially those with children, to poverty and have given most women few options for earning a living wage or for moving up the economic ladder. The struggle to provide for themselves and their families on a day-to-day basis limits women's time and energy for political activism. But it has also served as a motivating force for even the poorest of women to leave their homes to protest the unfair economic straits in which they find themselves. These economic protests take many forms and sometimes bring women into related struggles, such as women's, peace, revolutionary, and ecological movements. Like their participation in other movements, women's participation in economic movements often emerges from practical gender interests.

The gendered division of labor within the home holds women primarily responsible for the well-being of the family. As a result, women are usually quick to challenge authorities when the mainstays of life are threatened. It is the gender stereotype of women as life giving and life sustaining that positions women as primary caretakers and makes them the first to protest when economic conditions keep them from providing that care.

There are many examples of women taking to the streets collectively—in "bread riots," seizures of grain or foods, protests against the sale of overpriced goods, and/or demands for a just price for market products.[40] For instance, in the Flour War of 1775 that precipitated the French

Revolution, women "took positive and often violent action to rectify intolerable conditions—conditions threatening to family and community stability."[41] In 1929, women in Nigeria responded in force against colonial taxation and marketplace policies: "Tens of thousands of Igbo women marched, dressed in symbolic war attire, danced, chanted, sang, 'sat on' offending men, destroyed courts and prisons, freed prisoners, cut telegraph wires, set up their own courts and offices, closed down markets, collected money to sustain their actions, and set up or revived organizations for mutual support."[42]

Such actions are especially common in nonindustrialized contexts where the marketplace is dominated by women as producers, exchangers, and consumers of basic goods. There, traditional gender assignments make the provision of basic goods women's domain and serve to legitimize women's acting on behalf of family and community to protest against basic goods shortages. Also in these contexts traditional gender assumptions that women are vulnerable and in need of protection serve, to some degree, to inhibit violent reprisals directed by authorities against their unauthorized demonstrations. However, women's participation is no guarantee that officials will not act swiftly and violently against economic protests, as the killing of fifty women in the Igbo "women's war" makes clear.[43]

In industrialized contexts, where most poor, urban women cannot produce basic goods and are made dependent on state welfare systems, women's protests against the impoverishment of their families often take the form of welfare rights movements. For example, from 1966 to 1970, the Brooklyn Welfare Action Council (B-WAC) organized thousands of welfare recipients to fight for minimum welfare standards that would guarantee the right of every family to have the essentials for survival and modern life. B-WAC members staged a number of visible and theatrical protests outside welfare offices and inside shopping complexes. They demanded supplemental payments and department store credit for welfare recipients who could not live from check to check. For a brief period of time, B-WAC succeeded in getting more funds to welfare recipients to pay for such modern essentials as "costs of laundry; graduation; layettes; confirmation, camp, gym, and spring clothes; and washing machines."[44]

These cases and many more like them suggest that women's struggles against the consequences of the gendered division of labor in the home—women's practical gender interests—are primarily local and short-term engagements. Because women are acting in their traditional roles as family caretakers, they are focused upon their most immediate economic needs and usually seek only relief, not social transformation. As a result, their gains are typically temporary. The basis of their struggles does not challenge—but rather reinforces—their gender roles, leaving them still responsible for reproductive labor, even under the worst economic conditions. The point is that as long as reproductive labor is viewed as a private matter to which women are assigned, neither men as individuals nor the agencies of the state are under any obligation to do more than provide temporary—and usually insufficient—relief in response to women's economic protests.

In the face of meager and grudging assistance to women responsible for "unpaid" reproductive tasks, some women are challenging the notion that women's reproductive labor is just a private matter that does not even constitute "work." Some women's economic movements emphasize the fact that reproductive labor is the precondition of all other human activities: We cannot exist without the work women do in food production and preparation, emotional and physical caretaking, and maintaining the material and psychological dimensions of what we think of as home. Domestic work is essential, yet we deny its value to ourselves as individuals whose emotional and material "basic needs" must be met and to our societies, which would perish without this unpaid labor. Just how extensive and valuable is this labor? The United Nations estimated that "if unpaid housework were valued at the cost of purchasing comparable goods and services ... the measured value of GDP in countries would increase by 25–30 percent.[45]

Denying the centrality and value of domestic labor has various consequences for women's and men's lives. The most basic reality is that women, who spend more time working than men, are accorded less status for what they do, and men increasingly accumulate control over cash resources. "Tilting first under rules that say women must do all domestic work, the scales are tipped further by men's greater opportunities to earn wages. Advantage builds on advantage until today they are tilted so steeply that almost all of the world's wealth is on man's side, while most of the world's work is on woman."[46]

Women have protested the devaluation of domestic work and men's increasing economic control in diverse ways. The risk of divorce, loss of economic support, and the threat of violence (against themselves and/or their children), makes going on strike in the home a risky option for women. But women do resist by following strategies of "refusing to cooperate." For example, men grow maize (corn) and women grow groundnut (peanuts) in Zambia. When maize profits soared, women did not shift production in their fields to the more lucrative maize "because they—and not their husbands—kept the money from sales of groundnut."[47] Women also challenge the devaluation of their domestic work by insisting that they be paid for it. In the past several decades, "wages for housework" campaigns have been a feature of feminist debate and political action, especially in Europe and North America.

In a parallel vein, feminists have recently challenged national and international (UN, World Bank, IMF) accounting methods that keep women's domestic work invisible by according it no value in estimating national productivity. Women's groups in Canada, Trinidad, Australia, New Zealand, Norway, and India are promoting national studies to assess women's economic contributions to national income.[48] As Carol Lees pointed out, the effects of national accounting are not gender neutral: "As a result of the exclusion of women's labor from information gathering we are denied proper access to programs and policy at every level of government in every country"[49] (see Figure 5.4).

These actions, because their goals are not only better conditions for women to perform reproductive labor but also equity in the cash resources available to women and men, extend beyond women's practical gender interests. By redefining women's reproductive labor as work on which the public sphere depends and by demanding payment for this work, women are attacking the ideological and structural barriers that impoverish them relative to men. However, revaluing domestic work does not necessarily challenge the stereotype that only women should do it, nor does it disrupt the idea that men are better suited for more highly paid jobs in the public sphere.

The gendered division of labor in the work force has stirred many women to join trade union movements in the hope of improving general working conditions and wages as well as receiving pay equity relative to men in the same or comparable jobs. Berenice Carroll reminded us that it was women who initiated the earliest industrial labor strikes during the first half of the nineteenth century and a strike by women was the first of the rebellious actions that culminated in the Russian Revolution.[50] From the 1912 Lawrence, Massachusetts, textile workers strike that inspired the formation of the International Ladies Garment Workers Union to the Women Workers Movement founded in 1984 in the Philippines to protest labor conditions for women in export-processing zones, women have been active organizers and their efforts have had international implications. However, as these examples suggest, women often have created their own trade unions because they were marginalized or silenced by male-dominated unions concentrated in heavy industries, where women workers are in the minority.

Because of most women's locations within the wage labor market—in low-wage, light-industry and service jobs as well as in the so-called informal labor force of street vendors and subsistence agricultural producers—their labor organizing is more difficult, but also more varied, than the typical workplace-centered organizing that goes on in male-dominated industries. For example, in India, women street vendors formed the Self-Employed Women's Association (SEWA) to demand better wages from

FIGURE 5.4   Women for appropriate development. As illustrated by this poster for the Tech and Tools exhibit at the NGO Forum for the End of the UN Decade for Women conference in Nairobi, Kenya, in 1985, Third World women want development technologies that are appropriate for empowering themselves and sustaining their societies. Courtesy of International Women's Tribune Centre, Inc. Illustrator: Anne S. Walker.

commodity suppliers. Traditional trade unions do not organize such workers, but SEWA developed an imaginative strategy. Women street vendors organized other women street vendors by visiting them on the street and in their homes and providing literacy training so that they could participate more fully and equally in decision-making. The Honduran Federation of Peasant Women, another group that was over-looked by industry-based union movements, did not seek better wages from their employers (multinational, or transnational, corporations pay-ing them the equivalent of U.S. $2.00 a day) but rather alternative income-generating opportunities that would release them from having to work for MNCs.[51]

These examples show women's labor organizing to be oriented toward increasing women's autonomy as workers. Women's preference for more-flexible, self-directed, and home-based work reflects their practical gen-der interests in having more time and energy to perform their reproduc-tive labor. However, the strategies employed to achieve these ends often lead women to challenge a host of institutions and policies that traditional labor organizing fails to confront. For example, in order to promote safer worker conditions for women in the Philippines, the feminist organiza-tion Gabriela has supported women's demands for health care and immi-gration policies offering some protection from the effects of the presence of U.S. military bases and foreign servicemen.[52] Gabriela also promotes income-generating activities, community development, vocational-training and educational programs, and opportunities for feminist re-search. In this way, women's strategic gender interests are awakened and mobilized in the process of fighting for working conditions that better meet their practical gender interests.

These national and local women's struggles in the waged labor force are linked through transnational women's economic movements that challenge the international gendered division of labor that shores up the current capitalist global economy. Formed in 1974, the Women's International Information and Communication Service (ISIS/WICCE), at different times based in Switzerland, Uganda, Italy, Philippines, and Chile, has connected more than 10,000 women's groups in 130 countries. Among the many issues and strategies ISIS/WICCE deals with are the or-ganizing of women's groups against economic development policies that marginalize and exploit women workers.[53] Since 1978, the American Friends Service Committee, through its Women and Global Corporations Project, has linked workers, activists, and researchers worldwide who are promoting legislation to stop TNC practices that are reducing jobs and wages for women workers in the North and exploiting women's cheap la-bor in the South.[54]

"Default Isn't Ours." In this cartoon, poor Third World women and their families defy the structural and adjustment policies of their governments and the International Monetary Fund. From Jeanne Vickers, *Women and the World Economic Crisis* (London: Zed Books, 1991), p. 7. Originally produced for *A Journey Through the Global Debt Crisis* by the Debt Crisis Network, Washington, D.C. Reprinted by permission of the Debt Crisis Network. Cartoonist: Harold Saunders.

The debt crises and structural adjustment programs imposed by international lending institutions have had particularly negative consequences for women. Therefore, a variety of global and regional women's and development organizations have focused on combatting these gender-differentiated effects. These groups include DAWN (Development Alternatives with Women for a New Era), founded by Third World and First World women researchers and activists, which produced its first analysis of development strategies and their gendered consequences for the Nairobi meeting that concluded the UN Decade for Women.[55] More recently, DAWN's Latin American Region Research Group has connected Latin American women's groups developing alternative economic strategies with poor women and their local organizations. This networking includes "the Centro de Estudios de la Mujer in Chile and in Argentina; La Morada, also in Chile; Flora Tristan in Peru; CIPAF in the Dominican Republic; IDAC in Rio de Janeiro; the Rede Mulher in São Paulo, CEAAL throughout Latin America; the SOS Corpo in Recife and innumerable other groups."[56] DAWN is also working with WAND (Women and Development Unit) in the Caribbean, and AAWORD (African Association of Women for Research and Development) in West Africa "to evaluate standard macro- and micro-economic analyses, document their negative impact on women, and develop alternative frameworks."[57]

Women in many countries are engaging in an unprecedented global and regional organizing effort to confront a host of economic exploiters— from development agencies to multinational corporations to sex tourism operators. Women's nongovernmental organizations are committed to grass-roots organizing by poor and working-class women, whose struggles are backed up by research by, but not led by, more privileged academic women. Although the immediate goal of these struggles is to meet the practical gender interests articulated by poor and working-class women, the analysis that informs these struggles goes to the heart of every woman's strategic gender interests. That analysis exposes the gendered division of labor in all its forms and shows that this division keeps most women from having an equitable share of local, national, and global wealth, despite the fact that they are now the primary breadwinners the world over.

ECOLOGY MOVEMENTS

Perhaps the newest form of women's political action is in the area of saving the environment. From the tree-hugging Chipko Movement in India to the tree-planting Greenbelt Movement in Kenya and the nature-worshiping ecofeminist movement in North America, women are on the move to stop the rape of Mother Earth. For Third World rural women, saving the environment is crucial to their economic survival. As the primary food, fuel, and water gatherers, these women have particularly strong interests in reversing deforestation, desertification, and water pollution. When these processes threaten women's abilities to draw upon natural resources for themselves and their families, the women act in the only way available to them—putting their bodies on the line:

> In 1974, village women of the Reni forests of the Chamoli district in Uttar Pradesh decided to act against a commercial enterprise about to fell some 2,500 trees. The women were alone; the menfolk had left home in search of work. When the contractors arrived, the women went into the forest, joined hands and encircled the trees ("Chipko" means to hug). The women told the cutters that to cut the trees, they would first have to cut off their heads. The contractors withdrew and the forest was saved.[58]

Like women's struggles against immediate economic threats posed by the gendered division of labor, creative responses to the gendered division of resources may be effective in the short term, but they fail to address long-term systemic issues. In the Chipko case, the responses did not undermine forces of global capitalism that are among the major causes of deforestation, nor did they challenge the idea that only women need be the stewards of the environment because they are closer to nature than men. These spontaneous strategies also fail to redistribute in favor of women the resources necessary for more effective long-term organizing (see Figure 5.5).

The Greenbelt Movement in Kenya, formed by Wangari Maathai, of the National Council of Women, has begun a resource-generating process through which women can become more effective stewards of the environment. After instituting an effective national tree-planting campaign, the movement established a tree nursery. "Women are involved in rearing the seedlings, planting and marketing; in addition to becoming expert foresters, they also earn a cash income. The Greenbelt Movement is not only restoring the environment, but also enables women to benefit from environmental education, and to practice professional forestry techniques, while at the same time they are developing their status."[59] This kind of organizing not only meets women's practical gender interests but also creates conditions under which women can fight for their strategic gender interests.

This holistic strategy is also evident in such movements as the Calcutta Social Project, started by middle-class Indian women in the 1960s. The Calcutta Social Project was designed to change the lives of the poor who were forced to live on and around the city's massive waste dumps. "They began with literacy and recreational classes for young garbage pickers in an abandoned shed. Then vocational training in carpentry, masonry, and

Women in the landscape

Women as fetchers of water, collectors of firewood, tillers of the land and as mothers are usually the first to feel the effects of environmental degradation in the developing world. They are also in the best position to manage the environment but their role is frequently ignored by policy makers and planners.

In Africa, women are responsible for 75% of all subsistence agriculture and 95% of domestic work.

FIGURE 5.5 Women for the land. This illustration shows how close women's work is to the land and how responsible they are for its preservation. From Jeanne Vickers, *Women and the World Economic Crisis* (London: Zed Books, 1991), p. 92. Originally from "The State of the World's Women 1985." Courtesy of UNFPA.

sewing were added. A primary health care clinic now flourishes."[60] Such projects not only reduce the misery experienced by people living in extreme poverty but also gives them the tools to change their landscape and their work. Once again, however, such projects do not directly counteract the economic, political, and social forces that construct and perpetuate a "throwaway" society.

For Western ecofeminists, the key to confronting systemic forces that despoil the environment is questioning the treatment of both women and nature as resources to be used and abused by men and industries. This orientation gained momentum following the Three Mile Island nuclear power plant accident in Pennsylvania. Shortly afterward, 600 women gathered for a weekend meeting on "Women and Life on Earth: A Conference on Eco-Feminism in the Eighties." Ecofeminist, Ynestra King, opened this conference, proclaiming: "We're here to say the word ECOL-

OGY and announce that for us as feminists it's a political word—that it stands against the economics of the destroyers and the pathology of racist hatred. It's a way of being, which understands that there are connections between all living things and that indeed women are the fact and flesh of connectedness."[61]

In 1980 this U.S. movement spawned a similar one in the UK, which became known as Women for Life on Earth. Ecofeminist activists on both sides of the Atlantic were prominent in the 1980 and 1981 Women's Pentagon Actions and the December 12, 1980, encirclement of the Greenham Common nuclear base. These actions were based on the premise that "we see the devastation of the earth and her beings by the corporate warriors and the threat of nuclear annihilation by the military warriors as feminist concerns."[62]

From this ecofeminist perspective, if patriarchy, capitalism, racism, industrial development, and militarism are the sources of environmental degradation, women are the solution to it. Rather than questioning the gender stereotypes that associate women with nature and stewardship, most ecofeminists insist that women are closer to nature because of the reproductive and productive work they do and, thus, are in the best position to care for the environment. Ecofeminists use this argument in an attempt to counter other gender stereotypes about women and nature as objectified and passive resources, which powerful men may manipulate for their own purposes.

This perspective predominated at the October 1990 four-day meeting of fifty leading environmentalist women from Latin America, Africa, Asia, Europe, and North America. Assembled at the UN Church Center, participants drafted an international plan of action for the next decade with the following major goals:

☐ Full participation by women in environment policy at all levels
☐ Freedom of choice in family planning
☐ Redefinition of development on the principle that investment must not destroy the environment
☐ Increased education and information on the environment and development
☐ Protection of natural resources
☐ Development of a code of earth ethics[63]

The plan of action was created and signed by women from all over the world: Vandana Shiva of India; Wangari Maathai of the Greenbelt Movement in Kenya; Canadian radiation and health specialist Rosalie Bertell; Bella Abzug of the U.S. Women's Foreign Policy Council; Chodchoy Sophonpanich, president of the Thai Environmental and

Community Development Association; Maria Eugenia de Cotter, director of the Arias Foundation of Costa Rica; Tamar Eschel, former member of the Israeli parliament; Rosina Wiltshire of the Caribbean Conservation Association; Gertrude Mongella, a member of the Central Committee of Tanzania's governing party; and Bernadette Vallely of the Women's Environmentalist Network in Britain. It was brought forward to the International Women's Congress on the Environment in Miami in November 1991 and to the UN Conference on Environment and Development (UNCED) in Rio de Janeiro in June 1992.

Although this international plan of action is consistent with the positions of most environmentalist groups, particularly in the North, it is distinguished by its insistence that women can no longer be shut out of environmental policy-making. Rather, it argues that women bear the brunt of environmental degradation and are therefore most likely to seek solutions to it. In addition, the drafters of this document held accountable not just the North but also all the male-dominated power structures—local, national, and international—for the state of the Earth. Nevertheless, the plan of action falls short of more-radical ecofeminist and nonfeminist "deep ecology" positions that draw from Native American traditions and claim that nature, or the Earth, has intrinsic value. In this view, human beings should cease imposing their own values on the Earth and encroach upon natural processes as little as possible.

This "Earth as inviolate" position is problematic to the degree that it celebrates "the primitive" in a way that denies development not only to the South generally but also to women, who have the least access to land, technologies, and resources worldwide. The ecofeminist strategy that maintains the connection of women to nature in order to argue that women and nature should be equally inviolate—safe from rape, abuse, and use as cheap resources—is flawed. It makes women so coterminous with nature that it provides a rationale for continuing to keep them out of decision-making about the use of nature by humans. Here, women's strategic gender interests, which lead to calls for low-technology strategies to protect women and nature, conflict with their practical gender interests in gaining access to the resources necessary for meeting the basic needs of their families. Radical ecofeminist definitions of strategic gender interests also conflict with other strategic gender interests in participating as equals in modern, high-technology, presently male-dominated institutions that control or "manage" resources.

Finally, what is still unchallenged by all types of women's ecology movements is that women are the most "natural" stewards of the environment. Certainly not all women are environmentalists. Middle- and upper-class women in the North and South, by being major consumers, are particularly profligate destroyers of natural resources. Moreover, poor and working-class women often lack the tools and skills necessary to be effective stewards. These contradictions within women's ecology movements once again remind us that there is no simple formula for righting gender wrongs. Ending the gendered division of resources is contingent on ending the assumption that masculinism equals resource ownership and exploitation. It is dependent too on feminism's relinquishing the principle that stewardship is the property and responsibility of women only.

CONCLUSION

The pursuit of practical gender interests often leads activists to discover strategic gender interests, which, in turn, drive the participation of women (and men) in anti- and transstate social movements. The issues raised and actions undertaken have important implications for both how we understand world politics and how we choose to shape our future.

That women's political movements of all types are complicit, to a greater or lesser degree, in gendering processes leads us to some ruminations in our final chapter on what it will take to "ungender" world politics. There, we hope to integrate our findings and our arguments and leave the reader with some sense of the enormity, but also the necessity, of the transformational project to ungender world politics.

SIX

□ □ □

Ungendering World Politics

W orld politics has long been practiced and studied as if it were "ungendered"—that is, either gender neutral or devoid of gender issues. We have argued that world politics is, in fact, a highly gendered enterprise that privileges the interests of one gender over the other. In Chapter 5, we differentiated and drew linkages between practical and strategic gender interests. In this chapter, we connect women's practical gender interests with the largely reformist strategy of increasing the presence of women in world politics. Similarly, we connect women's strategic gender interests with the more transformative strategy of calling attention to the "power of gender" in reformulating world politics. In doing so, we argue that both strategies are necessary to ungender world politics in the interests of all the world's inhabitants.

UNGENDERING POWER AND POLITICS

To ungender power and politics we must alter the gendered division of power that established and has continued to reproduce masculinist politics. The latter privileges an androcentric definition of power—as power-over—and discriminates against women as political actors. As Chapter 3 illustrated, women are un- or underrepresented in elite decision-making power in state governments and international organizations. And women who do hold such positions are either depicted as exceptional or rendered largely invisible as significant actors in world politics. Moreover, when a few "exceptional" women do gain power, particularly as heads of state, they often adopt masculinist leadership styles and eschew gender-sensitive or feminist policy-making.

These observations highlight a two-way interaction between the un-derrepresentation of women in conventional power structures and the in-visibility of gender issues in world politics: too few women and too little awareness of gender hierarchy. Therefore, we need to have more women in leadership positions and greater attention paid to the role of gender in shaping world politics. The former increases the presence of women in in-ternational affairs, whereas the latter alters the power of gender as a hierarchical-ordering principle. Similarly, for large numbers of women to be "present" in positions of conventional power, the power of gender to produce the inequalities that keep women out of conventional power structures must be challenged. In short, the task of ungendering power is twofold—adding women to the existing world politics power structures *and* transforming those very power structures, ideologically and materi-ally.

At the very least, adding more women to existing power structures will put so-called women's issues on policy-making agendas. Evidence for this comes from recent studies in the United States indicating that female legislators tend to focus more than male legislators on such "domestic" is-sues as unemployment, housing, poverty, the homeless, health care, and child care.[1] Moreover, both liberal and conservative female legislators are more likely than either liberal or conservative male legislators to propose and support women's rights legislation.[2] Indeed, women's unprece-dented successes in the 1992 U.S. election are attributable in part to their ability to address domestic and equity problems that have become key political issues since the demise of the cold war. People in the United States now realize the relationship between the costs of that war and the decreased social services and increased social inequalities it not just hid but also exacerbated. Evidence suggests that women are most willing and, perhaps, best able to grapple with these problems.

If these trends were generalized, then increasing women's representa-tional power substantially would make a significant difference in political decision-making by shifting the focus away from short-term gains for the few and toward long-term benefits for the many. This kind of policy-making is required in a world where economic, social, and environmental security rival military security on the world politics agenda of govern-ments and in the minds of citizens. Moreover, as female policymakers ex-amine these issues from a fresh perspective, they will call attention to the disproportionate impact of these problems on women.

In line with this view, increasing the presence of women in formal po-litical representation at all levels serves women's practical gender inter-ests. First, greater attention would be drawn to issues related to women's reproductive roles and work. Second, there would be increased demand for gender-differentiated research to document how such national and global problems as authoritarianism, militarization, poverty, and environmental degradation disadvantage women particularly. Third, this type of gender-differentiated research would serve as a basis to change policy to transfer more public resources to women and other overburdened groups. This would entail reducing subsidies for military and industrial practices that impoverish and/or endanger the lives of women and their families. Instead, more public funds would be directed toward providing adequate food and shelter, clean and accessible water, safe and affordable energy sources, adequate health and child-care services, and sufficient income-generating or employment opportunities in environmentally safe workplaces. This redistribution of funds and resources to meet women's practical gender interests in fulfilling their reproductive tasks is what needs to be done to create the basic conditions for gender justice. It is also necessary for reducing women's vulnerability to military conflicts and economic crises. Moreover, distributive gender justice reduces the likelihood of military conflicts because there would be fewer resources put into war preparation (and thus more respect for international law); it reduces the likelihood of economic crises because resources would no longer be concentrated at the top.

Increasing women's access to public power and resources also serves their strategic gender interests by empowering women to meet their own needs and control their own futures. However, for substantial numbers of women to gain public power and shape the transfer of public resources, a second, more transformative strategy for ungendering power must be pursued along with the reformist strategy of adding women to the ranks of power wielders. This involves undermining the "power of gender" to produce inequalities of all kinds. To do so requires that we think about power in a way that denaturalizes, deglorifies, and delegitimates power-over—coercive power—as it is exercised at all levels—from the interpersonal to the interstate. This rethinking would necessarily alter how we identify power-over as a desirable, masculine, attribute.

Whereas international law has long recognized that the use of force is legitimate only as a last resort, we argue that coercion in general is necessitated only by a hierarchically divided and therefore unjust world order. The use of or threat of coercion to maintain social hierarchies involves the concentration and expenditure of a great deal of power. This power—and the resources it drains—could be employed for more productive and less destructive purposes. In Cynthia Enloe's words, IR commentators

> have put power at the center of their analyses—often to the exclusion of culture and ideas—but they have under-estimated the amount and varieties of power at work. It has taken power to deprive women of land titles and leave them little choice but to sexually service soldiers and banana workers. It has

taken power to keep women out of their countries' diplomatic corps and out of the upper reaches of the World Bank. It has taken power to keep questions of inequity between local men and women off the agendas of many nationalist movements in industrialized as well as agrarian societies. It has taken power to construct popular culture—films, advertisements, books, fairs, fashions—which reinforces, not subverts, global hierarchies.[3]

When we recognize how much coercive power it takes to run this inequitable system, we begin to see why feminists argue that the deployment of coercive power is ultimately destructive of those who rule as well as those who are ruled. Disabling people—especially women—by depriving them of even the most basic needs so that the few can accumulate wealth and weaponry destroys genuinely popular support for states, international organizations, and their leaders. In the absence of popular support and consent as the source of legitimacy for those in power, coercion is the *only* mechanism available to insecure rulers, who must rely on dividing, impoverishing, and degrading people and the planet to maintain their power. Therefore, we must question not only the validity but also the efficacy of coercive power—or, as we have argued, gendered power—as *the* mechanism for organizing world politics or solving world problems.

An alternative to coercive power is the more feminist concept of empowerment, or enabling power. If this model is used, world order looks less like a pyramid, where few are on the top and many are on the bottom, and more like a rotating circle in which no one is always at the top and no one is always at the bottom. Instead, all participate in complex webs of interdependence. Interests, rather than being defined in opposition to each other, are developed through relationships with others. Conflicts are resolved not by force or its threat but in nonviolent interaction and mutual learning.

This model is derived in part from feminist theorizing about the high degree of reciprocity and interconnectedness typifying most social relations even though they take place in contexts of contingency and ambiguity. The model denies neither the need for autonomy nor the complexities of social interaction, but it does deny that a depiction of only hostile and competitive forces at work in the world is accurate or adequate. Christine Sylvester described this model as **"relational autonomy"** and contrasted it with the masculinist ideal of **reactive autonomy** (valuing independence over interdependence and order over justice), which permeates the practice of international relations:

> In liberal theory, the cast of masculine reactive autonomy appears in stories of abstract social contracts entered into, seemingly, by "orphans who have reared themselves, whose desires are situated within and reflect nothing but independently generated movement." Realist international relations theory

follows this mold, even as it focuses on those anarchic spaces that elude social contract; for it depicts states as primitive "individuals" separated from
history and others by loner rights of sovereignty—backed up, for good measure, by military hardware—and involved in international conventions and
institutions only on a voluntary basis.[4]

The reactive autonomy model in effect erases most social reality, especially the webbing that constructs meaning and order. Reactive autonomy
assumes that cooperative relations are virtually impossible without coercion. In contrast, **relational autonomy** assumes that cooperation typifies
human relations when they are relatively equal and is destroyed in the
presence of inequality and coercion. By adopting the lens of reactive autonomy, IR practitioners—even without intending to—reproduce expectations of hostile and competitive behavior, which, in turn, generate unco-
operative and defensive responses. This is how we find ourselves caught
in self-perpetuating, vicious cycles such as arms races. For the model of
relational autonomy to flourish, we must not only alter our lenses but also
make profound changes in our individual and collective practices.

Moving toward a relational autonomy model for world politics would
move us toward ungendering world politics more deeply than we could
simply by adding women to existing power structures. However, this
transformation cannot take the form of a simple reversal that merely privileges feminine "care" over masculine "coercion." Not only gender dichotomies but also features of the feminine concept of care that oppress
women would remain in place in such a reversal. Specifically, because
caring has historically been a demand imposed upon subordinated
groups and is in this sense inextricable from relations of inequality, a care
model may offer insights on, but not solutions to, oppressive social relations. Caring that exclusively takes the form of sacrificing self or group interests is just another framing of inequality. Emphasizing relational autonomy as a model of international relations would assist women in terms
of their practical gender interests, but that is not sufficient. We also need
to facilitate women's autonomy (and sometimes of the reactive sort) so
that women's strategic gender interests can be met. Full equality, not only
between men and women but also *among* women and *among* men cannot be
achieved until men have an equal responsibility for reproductive or relational work and women have an equal say in how the world is organized.

Ungendering power by increasing women's political representation
and reconceiving power as relational autonomy requires a variety of material changes in the organization of world politics. Most important, there
must be proportional representation of women in the governments of all
countries and in international organizations. As indicated earlier, there is
growing evidence that women do bring a relational autonomy perspec-

tive to governing, especially if there are significant numbers of women and if they have commitments to principles of equality. Ideally, proportional representation would mean approximately equal percentages not only of women and men at all levels but also of women (and men) in terms of nationality, race, ethnicity, class, sexual orientation, and so on.

In order for women in power to be truly representative of all women, the paths to power must change. Given the global problems now confronting us, a legal career and military service cannot remain the major prerequisites for public service. Why are human relations skills not deemed crucial for practitioners of international relations? Local grassroots organizing challenges multiple aspects of the global divisions of power, violence, labor, and resources. Why are these skills not considered far more important qualifications for global leadership? In a world of reactive autonomy that shores up global hierarchies, these skills and experiences are seen as trivial, useless, and even dangerous. But trivial, useless, and dangerous for whom and for what? One could hazard that those who are most threatened by such leadership would be those interested in maintaining a world of reactive autonomy. However, those committed to creating a world of relational autonomy where global divisions and inequalities are challenged might find such leadership qualities essential.

As we make the transition, however, from reactive autonomy to relational autonomy, women will need more resources and new laws behind them to seek public office. Some political parties, particularly of the social democratic and green party variety, have adopted rules ensuring that up to 50 percent of the candidates put forward are women, who are then given equal access to party funds and machinery. Similar quotas and practices should be adopted by all political parties in the world. This could be enforced by making a state's UN membership contingent on such measures to create proportional representation. For this to be credible, however, the United Nations, the biggest men's club in the world, must alter its own top-down image by implementing a quota system—for women *and* Third World representation.

To ungender world politics more completely, we require more than quota systems for women leaders. It is also vital that *all* states ratify the UN conventions relevant to the status of women. Table 6.1 identifies a number of such conventions that still lack ratification by many UN member states. The table includes the Convention on the Elimination of All Forms of Discrimination Against Women (CEDAW), which was adopted in the middle of the UN Decade for Women. Equally important, the Nairobi Forward-Looking Strategies for the Advancement of Women (FLS) was adopted by 157 governments on July 27, 1985, at the end of the Decade for Women.[5]

TABLE 6.1 Selected UN Conventions of Concern to Women

Adopted		In Force	Ratification
1949	Convention for the Suppression of Traffic in Persons and the Exploitation of the Prostitution of Others	1951	60[a]
1951	Equal Remuneration for Men and Women Workers for Work of Equal Value (ILO No. 100)	1953	109[b]
1952	Convention on the Political Rights of Women	1954	96[a]
1958	Discrimination in Respect of Employment and Occupation (ILO No. 111)	1960	109[b]
1960	International Convention Against Discrimination in Education (UNESCO)	1962	77[b]
1962	Convention on Consent to Marriage, Minimum Age of Marriage, and Registration of Marriages	1964	36[a]
1979	Convention on the Elimination of All Forms of Discrimination Against Women	1981	110[a]
1981	Convention Concerning Equal Opportunities and Equal Treatment for Men and Women Workers: Workers with Family Responsibilities (ILO No. 156)	1982	13[b]
1985	Nairobi Forward-Looking Strategies for the Advancement of Women (FLS)[c]		

[a]Total as of December 31, 1991.

[b]Total as of end of 1988.

[c]Adopted in 1985 but not a formal convention and therefore not subject to formal ratification.

SOURCES: Hilkka Pietilä and Jeanne Vickers, *Making Women Matter: The Role of the United Nations* (London: Zed Books, 1990), p. 117, and "Multilateral Treaties Deposited with the Secretary-General, Status as of 31 Dec 1991" (New York: United Nations, 1992).

The Decade for Women had three interrelated and mutually reinforcing objectives: equality, development, and peace. Three subthemes— employment, health, and education—represented the concrete basis for achieving the decade's triple objectives. Attaining the multiple goals of the decade and the FLS entails a sharing of responsibility by women and men and society as a whole. It also requires that women play a central role as intellectuals, policymakers, decision-makers, planners, and contributors to and beneficiaries of development.

As summarized in *The World's Women*, the strategies demand that governments:

□ Play key roles in ensuring that both men and women enjoy equal rights in such areas as education, training, and employment.

☐ Act to remove negative stereotypes and perceptions of women.
☐ Disseminate information to women about their rights and entitlements.
☐ Collect timely and accurate statistics on women and monitor their situation.
☐ Encourage the sharing and support of domestic responsibilities.[6]

At present, CEDAW and FLS are the two most comprehensive tools for significantly changing women's roles and positions in the international system. Yet both require greater support from UN member states, including the United States.

Implementation of CEDAW and FLS would obligate states to provide the funds and infrastructures to produce and enforce legislation that would not only end the formal and informal discrimination against women in all sectors but also change development practices, reverse militarization, and ensure equal representation of women in all decision-making bodies. Because this would involve restructuring states and their priorities, neither full ratification nor any serious enforcement after ratification is likely until there are sufficient women (and men) in power who are committed to such restructuring. In this sense, ratification of these conventions is linked to women's proportional representation in state and UN bodies.

As more women gain power through quota mechanisms and eventually reach parity in power structures, the question arises how female leaders will remain accountable not only to women in their own countries but also to women in other countries who may be negatively affected by the domestic policies of foreign governments. A mechanism for ensuring that one woman's "liberation" does not translate into another's oppression would be the ratification and enforcement on both the national and global level of such documents as the FLS. Indeed, relational autonomy cannot be practiced in one state alone, and women's strategic gender interests will not be served so long as women are treated as second-class citizens anywhere. Ungendering national politics entails globalizing relational autonomy in ways that challenge not only the divisions of sex, race, class, and sexuality, but also nationality and state sovereignty. This will produce as-yet-unimagined political communities that do not rely on coercive power for their unity or inequality for their stability.

As two sides of the same coin, rethinking world politics requires rethinking gendered "givens." For women to reach parity in power structures, we must revalue women as leaders, which challenges conventional gender dichotomies. For men to endorse the model of relational autonomy, we must revise divisions of labor that largely exclude men from nurturing activities. For world politics to change, we must relate the gender

THE DECADE FOR WOMEN

2000

1985 AND FORWARD TO THE YEAR 2000!

Looking to the Year 2000. The symbol of the UN Decade for Women (representing equality, development, and peace) flies to the Year 2000 with the FLS document under her wing. The next world meeting to assess the progress of the FLS will be in Beijing, China, in 1995. Courtesy of the International Women's Tribune Centre, Inc. Illustrator: Anne S. Walker.

politics of everyday life and personal experience to their consequences for systemic processes and global crises.

UNGENDERING VIOLENCE

As we pointed out in Chapter 4, women have rarely been the beneficiaries of world politics organized around military security. Women make up a very small portion of the world's armed services, and they and their children tend to suffer most from military priorities that reduce "butter" in order to increase "guns." However, one reformist strategy to make women "count" in military security policy-making, assuming that military security will likely remain a significant aspect of world politics for some time to come, is to increase the presence of women in the world's militaries. As we indicated in Chapter 4, the odds are against reaching female-male parity in the armed services of even the most "democratic," advanced industrial nations. Nevertheless, as long as state militaries continue to control a great deal of national and global wealth and resources, provide paths to power for government leaders, and offer some of the best avenues for employment and benefits for unskilled and semiskilled workers, pressure will continue for greater access to and opportunities in the military for women.

Again, the United Nations could be instrumental in encouraging states to increase their proportion of female soldiers. Since the Gulf war, in which women in the U.S. military were extremely visible, more and more military actions are being coordinated by the United Nations. At the end of 1992, UN-sponsored military actions were undertaken in Somalia to facilitate the flow of international humanitarian aid. Under such conditions, the United Nations could argue that all contributing countries should send a certain percentage of women in their complement of troops. This commitment to nondiscrimination in terms of military participation would be consistent with the emerging goals of UN-sponsored peacekeeping and humanitarian relief efforts.

Increasing the presence of women in state- and UN-sponsored militaries serves women's practical gender interests to the degree that more women will have access to the considerable resources of militaries. Partaking of a (larger) piece of the military pie would mean less poverty for some women and increased wages and health and social security benefits for other women. It would also mean that more women would have access to training in a variety of male-dominated fields, enhancing their job opportunities when and if they return to civilian life. However, as we also indicated in Chapter 4, military preparation and action have sorely compromised women's practical gender interests by extracting health, welfare, and environmental resources from the civilian economy. Beyond impoverishing many women and children through this resource extraction, militarism and wars have contributed to a culture of violence against women, rendering them unsafe in their homes and on the street. Systemic violence—sexual harassment, battering, rape, and torture—is the persistent price women pay for the maintenance of large militaries and the accompanying militarization of national life.

In short, the increase in economic security that some women could achieve if there were a greater presence of women in the military must be measured against the continued economic and physical insecurities experienced by women outside of (and partly as a result of) the armed forces. Indeed, even women inside the military face the physical insecurities of sexual harassment and rape as well as, of course, the possibility of dying in combat along with female noncombatants. Accordingly, increasing the presence of women in the military does not greatly benefit the practical gender interests of most women and only minimally serves their strategic gender interests. Allowing women to join militaries and take combat roles does strike a major blow against the stereotype of femininity and the discrimination that women face in the context of the gendered division of violence. However, it does not necessarily challenge the masculine side of the gendered division of violence, and it does not necessarily contribute to gender equality outside or even inside the military. Finally, increasing the presence of women in militaries does not necessarily call into question the utility and inevitability of violence itself.

Thus, like ungendering power, ungendering violence is a twofold process. Increasing the presence of women in militaries does yield some benefits for some women in the short term. But the reigning power of gender violently divides the human community into unequal and opposed beings who must resort to violence to settle disputes, usually without significantly reducing existing inequalities. As a consequence, merely increasing the presence of women without also analyzing the power of gender will leave most women's practical and strategic gender interests unmet. Such an analysis must take issue with gendered dichotomies in world politics that arise from the gendered division of violence. These include distinctions between domestic and international violence, between structural and direct violence, and between "us" and "them."

The assumption that violence is largely the result of anarchic international relations—in contrast to supposedly "peaceful" domestic communities—obscures the question of the amount of and the way in which violence is deployed from the local to the global level. For example, domestic violence—the euphemism for the wide range of physical and emotional abuse suffered mostly by wives and children in families—is widespread throughout the world.[7] Hence, it makes little sense to argue that the level and frequency of violent conflict is what separates international relations from domestic relations. It makes more sense to see domestic and international violence as intimately connected. Through this lens, international violence is revealed more as an extension of domestic masculinist socialization designed to produce aggressive "men" (including some females). In addition, military security policies and practices can be seen, in part, as the pursuit of masculinist reactive autonomy that can tolerate no interdependent relations.

Similarly, the definition of peace simply as the absence of the direct violence of war obscures the deep, structural inequalities that both give rise to and are the result of violence. Sustaining sexism, racism, classism, heterosexism, and gendered nationalism has heretofore been vital to sustaining militarism and the "us" and "them" mentality that goes along with it. Thus, any serious attempt to end war must involve significant alterations in local, national, and global hierarchies.

One promising strategy that would greatly assist women's practical and strategic gender interests is being implemented by feminists in human rights groups. The Women's Project of Human Rights Watch, for example, has begun monitoring the amount of domestic violence occurring in states around the world. Through this project, Human Rights Watch will be holding "countries responsible for 'complicity' in the actions of private individuals—like husbands—who violate women's human rights."[8] Minimally, this strategy could facilitate the passage and enforcement of domestic violence legislation in all states. But it could also promote critiques of a military "security" that generates a great deal of economic, social, and physical insecurity for women and put into question the right of states to manipulate **sovereignty** (claims to self-determination and nonintervention) to hide and avoid dealing with the abuses of women within their borders. In fact, feminists in human rights groups want to eventually see an overhaul of the UN Charter for Human Rights to make it fully reflect the specific human rights concerns raised by CEDAW. If all states were to abide by such a revised charter, it is doubtful that the use of force could continue to be a justifiable prerogative of states.

In short, ungendering violence may require increasing the presence of women in militaries to begin to uproot their "victim" or "protected beautiful soul" status, but, more important if transformative changes are to occur, it will require undermining the power of gender to victimize vast numbers of women—and all who are vulnerable to structural violence—in the name of military security.

UNGENDERING LABOR

According to the statistics provided in Chapter 4, women are very much "present" in the world's labor force, constituting almost half the paid workers in many countries and continuing to enter the work force in unprecedented numbers worldwide. Yet, as we also pointed out, women tend to be clustered in low-wage jobs in formal and informal labor markets, so the feminization of poverty is increasing despite the growing number of women workers and breadwinners. In order for women to realize their practical gender interest in making a living wage, the presence of women must be increased in particular sectors of the labor market—male-dominated sectors that tend to offer the highest pay and best benefits—and the presence of men must be increased in the caring professions such as nursing and teaching.

As we noted in Chapter 3, women are relatively absent at the top of corporate hierarchies. In fact, they are less represented there than in governments. This is not surprising, given that TNCs rival and even surpass states as powers in the global political economy. Transnational capital depends on women's cheap labor to exert its power. Because there have been so few women at the top of TNC and finance hierarchies, there is little way of telling if female executives would make a difference—that is, would be less willing than men to exploit other women to make a profit. However, there is some evidence that women employ a management style that is more interpersonal, less hierarchical, less individualistic, and more group oriented than men's.[9] Female managers are also more sensitive to the dual demands of work and family that affect women far more than men. It thus seems likely that women, in sufficient numbers, might be more supportive of corporate and national day-care policies.

Although increasing women's presence at the top of corporate hierarchies might translate into more-humane and gender-sensitive work policies, the fact remains that few women and few men can actually be at the top of pyramidal hierarchies. Increasing the number of women in higher-paying, male-dominated occupations may increase some women's wages and status. But that would not necessarily lead to challenging the global gendered dichotomy between productive and reproductive labor, which renders the latter "nonwork." Nor would it necessarily lead to questioning what is produced, why, and under what circumstances. These more-fundamental problems lie at the heart of the international gendered division of labor and disadvantage women in the global political economy. To get at these problems and completely ungender labor, we need transformative strategies.

To begin with, we must continue efforts to include women's reproductive labor and their work in the informal and extralegal labor force in the UN System of National Accounts (UNSNA). These activities were previously deemed "externalities" in national accounting systems. Including statistics on such activities to determine GDP and guide policy-making would significantly reorient the way that states generate wealth because the costs of generating that wealth would seem much greater. As Marilyn Waring pointed out:

> Can you imagine a nation's annual budget becoming a realistic description of the well-being of the community and its environment, a reflection of real wealth and different values? The budget would answer all of the following: Who does what work and where—paid and unpaid? What is the position of the nation's children and the aged? Who is not housed adequately? Who has the poorest health? What changes have occurred in water and air quality levels and why? What is the nature, cause, and region of pollution, and what are the health costs? What national resources have been harvested or conserved? Who relieves the state of the burden of care and dependency of others? What is the scope of subsistence production, and what are the nutritional results? At what price does the nation currently value war?[10]

By making the costs of current economic priorities visible and making visible who (women) and what (the environment) bear the brunt of these costs, states and corporations would find it hard to justify a great deal of what they claim is wealth-generating activity. Indeed, a state budget reflecting such statistics would reveal that only a few are benefiting from the wealth that many workers are producing. In fact, such a budget would demystify the current assumption that reproductive work and informal labor is of little or no value. It would show that the formal sector of so-called productive work is dependent on the reproductive and informal sectors rather than the reverse. Keeping the reproductive and informal sectors undervalued is only "functional" for those few at the top who reap greater profits as a result of this under- or devaluation.

Although valuing women's reproductive work and informal labor would better protect and enhance women's practical gender interests, additional strategies will be needed to fully meet women's strategic gender interests. These include legislation in every country to institute equal pay for equal or comparable work (which would aid in "degendering" jobs); national child-care policies as well as legislative and educational programs to encourage shared parenting and an ethic of responsibility for all the nation's and the world's children; and the guarantee of full reproductive rights to every woman in every country to ensure that women can participate equally in the work force, whether or not they *choose* to have children.

It will also be necessary to undermine the gendered dichotomy of "traditional" versus "modern" that pervades the thinking and practices of international development agencies. The power of gender creates an association between "women's work" and "primitive" economic and technological practices found in traditional societies, which acts to marginalize women in modernization processes. But it also acts to devalue the quite complex, self-sufficient, and ecologically sustainable economic activities and technological developments in which many women engage in traditional societies. Undermining this association and the devaluation of both women and traditional cultures requires questioning the kind of progress that men and modernity have brought to us.

These proposals may seem utopian at the present time. However, if the UNSNA accurately reflected the costs—not just to women, but also to national and global economies—of keeping women impoverished, overworked by the double and even triple day, and discriminated against in the workplace, then such equity-based measures would have a much greater chance of being instituted worldwide. Moreover, there are specific actions that developed country governments, which may be in the best position to take and to encourage, can engage in right now. For example, the United States could lift *all* restrictions on funding family-planning clinics at home and abroad that offer abortion services; ratify the UN Convention concerning Equal Opportunities and Equal Treatment for Men and Women Workers,[11] CEDAW, and the FLS; refuse to sign the

North American Free Trade Agreement (NAFTA) until it has adequate provisions to protect workers, their wages, their jobs, and the environment; and enforce and extend the UN Convention for the Suppression of the Traffic in Persons and the Exploitation of the Prostitution of Others in order to protect women forced into prostitution and exploitive domestic service at home and abroad.[12]

Individual women, too (particularly middle- and upper-class women in advanced industrial societies), have a responsibility to change and curb their consumption patterns. These women benefit—in the form of cheap consumer goods—from the cheap labor of primarily poor, Third World women. However, they do so at the expense of creating international solidarity among women to struggle against the global gendered division of labor. Ultimately, ungendering labor will involve increasing not only the presence of women in male-dominated occupations but also the presence of all women (and supportive men) in struggles against the power of gender to divide, devalue, impoverish, and unequalize women (and many men).

UNGENDERING RESOURCES

As enumerated in Chapter 4, the sum of the effects of the gendered divisions of power, violence, and labor denies women any significant access to or control over the world's resources. Women have lost land rights to men, states, and corporations the world over and have been generally kept out of the decision-making within families, states, and corporations about how to use resources and for what purposes.

Instead of having an equal say in what and how resources are to be used, women are treated as resources themselves. Noting that "added resources" give added power to "states to do things that they could not have done previously," Christine Sylvester argued that "women are nonrecognized resources for realist states, occupying positions ranking with oil, geography, industrial capacity, and military preparedness as contributions to power."[13] In fact, all states appropriate women's bodies and labor to extend their resource base and thus their power within and outside their borders. Yet this fact is concealed by the gendered division of resources. However, when a gender-sensitive lens is used to view world politics, the positions of women in a state's resource base are revealed, permitting women to specify strategies of resistance against the appropriation of their bodies and labor by states.

Those most likely to see that states and corporations turn women into resources to expand state and corporate power are women themselves. Therefore, it is crucial that the presence of women be increased in a variety of decision-making bodies, from the local to the global level, that determine which resources are expendable in order to create other resources. In Chapter 5 we described a transnational coalition of female leaders of environmental, health, and social justice movements who are demanding the equal representation of women in all environmental policy-making bodies. These leaders believe that women can see more clearly than men how women as well as nature and the environment are reduced to resources for the enhancement of state and corporate power. Moreover, these leaders suggest that women would be more likely than men to question both the process of state and corporate resource expropriation and the goal of such resource expropriation—that is, the expansion of state and corporate power. Making women and nature expendable by sacrificing them on the altar of elite male power serves neither women's practical nor their strategic gender interests.

It is in women's practical gender interests to have the presence of women as state resources exposed and in women's strategic gender interests to increase the presence of women in decision-making bodies that control resource use and allocation. However, in order for women to cease being used as resources and to avoid abusing resources that come into their hands, the human community—perhaps led by individuals with ecofeminist analyses and sensibilities—will have to develop a different relationship with "nature." That is, we must undermine the global gendered dichotomy of culture (or man) versus nature that leads to the growth imperative (at any cost) in the world economy.

Worldwide ratification of the Earth Charter adopted at the UN Conference on Environment and Development (UNCED) in June 1992 represents a start in this direction.[14] But we must go beyond this to challenge the power of gender that permits corporate and state elites to rest their networks of transnational production and capital and their military conflicts on the back of nature as well as on the backs of women. We must begin to see nature as part of, not distanced from or beneath, "our" world community. Using an ecofeminist lens, we are more likely than before to respect the ecosystems of which we, as humans, are only a part.

Respect for nature as a partner in, not a slave to, the world community must be accompanied by respect for the needs of women and Third World peoples to enjoy a much greater share of the world's resources. At the same time, it is incumbent on those who struggle for equity in parenting, work, consuming, soldiering, officeholding, decision-making, and property-owning to concern themselves with transforming these activities in ways that are not ecologically harmful.

CONCLUSION

Looking at world politics through a gender-sensitive lens affords a different view of "reality." What we see is in many ways harsher than the realist image of warring states. Indeed, conventional IR lenses show us an iceberg as it emerges from the sea. Feminist lenses take us below the surface to see the deep inequalities that shape international hierarchies and erupt into international conflict on the surface.

If we were interested only in the surface problems that women face as a result of international hierarchies and conflict, we would recommend that women be given more resources—more land, food, clean water, health care, education, jobs, child care, reproductive rights, money, and formal political power. However, transferring resources to meet women's practical gender interests represents only a small part of what needs to be done. We must also deal with what forms the iceberg largely below the surface. As argued in this text, the production of gender dichotomies and inequalities significantly contributes to the chilly climate that freezes international hierarchies in place. These hierarchies generate the conflicts and crises of world politics.

The global gender dichotomy of masculine-feminine fuels the production of other dichotomies that shape world politics: from war-peace and us-them to modern-traditional, production-reproduction, and culture-nature. The value of the "feminine" sides of these dichotomies is consistently denigrated, whereas the value of the "masculine" side is overinflated. Clearly, gender divisions of power, violence, labor, and resources present an oppressive image. Although a gender-sensitive lens reveals the pervasiveness of gender hierarchy, it also offers hope. Through this lens, those with the most conventional power in world politics appear surprisingly dependent because their power-over relies on sustaining the dichotomies that reproduce gender and other inequalities. According to this view, those in power are remarkably insecure and their power remarkably unstable. If we expose how world politics depends on artificial notions of masculinity and femininity, we can see that "this seemingly overwhelming world system may be more fragile and open to radical change than we have been led to imagine."[15]

A great deal must change before world politics is ungendered. Toward that end we have identified a number of policy options, but these are only a beginning. Ungendering world politics requires a serious rethinking of what it means to be human and how we might organize ourselves in more cooperative, mutually respectful ways. We would have to reject gendered dichotomies: male versus female, us versus them, culture versus nature. Ungendering world politics also requires a reconceptualization of politics and a shift from power-over to power-to. We would have to recognize power in its multiple forms and be willing to imagine other worlds. Overall, these changes are less a matter of top-down policy and more a matter of individually and collectively remaking human society by reconstructing our beliefs, expectations, and institutions. This is the most difficult and complex of human projects, but history shows we are capable of such revolutionary transformations.

In one sense, we have no choice. Contemporary global processes force us to develop new understandings of who "we," as humans, are and how we, as global citizens and planetary stewards, must act. In another sense, we willingly seek systemic transformations because we desire more than the absence of war: We demand the actualization of justice. And whatever our commitments to justice, we cannot pursue them if we remain blind to gender hierarchy and the (re)production of other hierarchies that it fuels. There is no single enemy to fight or simple strategy to follow—but there is much that we can do.

By acting in concert around particular issues in particular contexts to advance practical and strategic gender interests all over the world, women *and* men alter existing power structures. Although the goals of the struggles may vary, the most important point is that each struggle contributes to a global climate that nourishes equity and social justice. Such a climate will melt the iceberg of international hierarchies that deprives many women, men, and children of resources they need and deprives the planet of the care it requires to support those lives. Nothing less than the elimination of structural violence will ungender world politics.

□ □ □

Discussion Questions

CHAPTER ONE

1. How does the metaphor of a lens permit us to see world politics—or other topics—from varying perspectives?

2. How are the terms *global, gender,* and *issues* used in this text?

3. What do the "presence of women" and the "power of gender" refer to? How are they related, and what is their relevance to world politics? Apply this gender-sensitive lens to an institution you are familiar with (e.g., school, church, organization) and give examples of the presence of women and the power of gender.

4. Why is gender hierarchy an issue now? In what ways is it relevant to the study of world politics? How is it relevant in your own life? What activities do you engage in that reinforce or resist gender heirarchy?

CHAPTER TWO

1. How is gender distinguished from sex? What does gender hierarchy refer to, and how is it related to other social inequalities?

2. What do stereotypes, dichotomies, and ideology refer to? How do they interact in the construction of gender hierarchy? Provide examples from your own life (consider family history, educational opportunities, career decisions, etc.) of how stereotypes, dichotomies, and ideologies interact.

3. If gender is so pervasive, why is it so invisible? What are the ways in which gender is obscured in the study of world politics? Look at a reading assignment in this or another course: How visible is gender? Is the argumentation altered by recognition of gender biases?

4. How are gendered divisions of power, violence, labor, and resources related to issues of world politics, world security, global political economy, and global ecology? Provide examples that demonstrate how these divisions in one country are linked to divisions in another country.

5. How does the study of gender and the examination of gender dichotomies inform our understanding of world politics? What do they enable us to "see" that was "invisible" in conventional accounts of international relations?

CHAPTER THREE

1. What does the gendered division of power refer to? In what ways does it privilege men and masculinist ideologies?

2. In which decision-making bodies have women been increasing their representation and, therefore, power? What patterns are emerging in terms of where women and men are located as state actors?

3. How are women in power rendered invisible, insignificant, or viewed as "honorary males"? Collect news accounts of a female head of state in the past or present and look for the images/stereotypes that are used to describe her and her actions.

4. How do gender socialization, situational constraints, and structural obstacles shape the proportion of women and men as state actors and position women and men in different locations of state power?

5. What are typical paths to power for women? For men? How do women and men in office differ in terms of gender issues? What variables affect the amount of attention political actors pay to gender issues? Choose a current woman leader and track how she rose to power, what issues she has been associated with, and what she has done for women's rights.

CHAPTER FOUR

1. Find a traditional definition of power in conventional international relations (IR) literature and explore how this concept of power is gendered. What are the world political consequences of this for women? For men?

2. Compare a traditional IR description of militarism with a gender-sensitive analysis of it. How does a gender-sensitive analysis affect our understanding and pursuit of "security" in international relations?

3. Look for traditional IR explanations (liberal, realist, Marxist) of the global political economy and identify in what ways women and gender relations are absent from or rendered invisible by these accounts. In what ways would making women and gender dynamics visible in discussions of the international political economy alter our understanding of how states and transnational corporations amass wealth, how international trade works, and how Western development strategies do and do not work?

4.Choose an environmental problem and explain how the sources and proposed solutions to the problem may be gendered. What does such an inquiry tell you about the causes of and the (lack of) solutions to the global ecological crisis?

5. Find an example in the United States and in one other country of how the global gendered divisions of violence, labor, and resources interact to reduce women's power and influence in international politics.

CHAPTER FIVE

1. How do different feminist perspectives challenge and/or reinforce conventional definitions of power in international relations? What are the differences between practical and strategic gender interests?

2. How have practical gender interests motivated women to protest war? What strategic gender interests do women have in promoting peace? What might be a feminist definition of peace? How might different feminist perspectives/movements analyze and respond to the Gulf war?

3. How might socialist and democratizing revolutions serve women's practical gender interests? Why have socialist and democratizing revolutionary movements failed to meet women's strategic gender interests? How might our views on terrorism change if we looked at it through a gender-sensitive lens? For example, look for accounts of women's participation in the Palestinian "intifada" (uprising) and determine if you would label these women "terrorists."

4. What factors unique to women's roles and responsibilities in the family and the world economy hinder and/or facilitate women's organizing against economic exploitation? How might transnational movements against economic exploitation be strengthened by their paying attention to women's practical and strategic gender interests? Look for feminist critiques of the North American Free Trade Agreement (NAFTA) and determine what changes may need to be made to the agreement to protect women workers.

5. How is women's activism in environmental movements connected to their practical and strategic gender interests? How might women's environmentalist movements intersect with other women's movements? On what bases can women (and supportive men) form transnational coalitions to confront the gendered divisions of power, violence, labor, and resources simultaneously? Can you find any contemporary examples of such coalitions?

CHAPTER SIX

1. How is increasing the presence of women in all aspects of world politics related to women's practical gender interests? To women's strategic interests?

2. How does the power of gender operate to decrease the presence of women in world politics? How is undermining the power of gender related to women's strategic gender interests? Why is it important to consider the power of gender when we analyze world politics?

3. What might a world based on the model of relational autonomy look like? How would it be different from the world of reactive autonomy for women? For men? For children?

4. What strategies would you recommend to ungender violence, labor, and resources in world politics? How would you interrelate these projects?

5. Do you think it is important to ungender world politics? Why or why not?

6. As an exercise, participate in the feminist-IR computer network FEMISA (to subscribe, see information in "Suggested Readings") for a brief period. What are the issues being discussed? How do they relate to your own studies and international understanding?

□ □ □

Notes

CHAPTER ONE

1. Paul R. Viotti and Mark V. Kauppi, *International Relations Theory* (New York: Macmillan, 1987), pp. 2–3.

2. Patrick M. Morgan, *Theories and Approaches to International Politics*, 4th ed. (New Brunswick: Transaction Books, 1987), p. 2.

3. Jessie Bernard, "Women," in Sheila Ruth, *Issues in Feminism* (Boston: Houghton Mifflin, 1980), pp. 32–35.

4. It is worth noting that recorded history constitutes approximately the past six thousand years, which is only 1 percent of human "history."

5. "The average gap is between 30 percent and 40 percent and there is no sign that it is substantially narrowing." United Nations, *The World's Women: 1970–1990 Trends and Statistics* (New York: United Nations, 1991), p. 5.

6. On feminist IR theory, see Rebecca Grant and Kathleen Newland, eds., *Gender and International Relations* (Bloomington: Indiana University Press, 1991); V. Spike Peterson, ed., *Gendered States: Feminist (Re)Visions of International Relations Theory* (Boulder, Colo.: Lynne Rienner Publishers, 1992); Christine Sylvester, *Feminist Theory and International Relations in a Postmodern Era* (Cambridge: Cambridge University Press, forthcoming); J. Ann Tickner, *Gender in International Relations: Feminist Perspectives on Achieving Global Security* (New York: Columbia University Press, 1992).

7. Hilary Lips, *Women, Men, and Power* (Mountain View, Calif.: Mayfield, 1991), p. 11.

CHAPTER TWO

1. Sheila Ruth, *Issues in Feminism* (Dallas: Houghton Mifflin, 1980), p. 17. In this chapter, our discussion focuses on U.S. culture because it is the most appropriate for our readers.

2. Arthur Brittan, *Masculinity and Power* (New York: Blackwell, 1989), p. 4.

3. Laurel W. Richardson and Verta A. Taylor, eds., *Feminist Frontiers: Rethinking Sex, Gender, and Society* (Reading, Mass.: Addison-Wesley), p. 1.

4. Hilary Lips, *Women, Men, and Power* (Mountain View, Calif.: Mayfield, 1991), p. 19.

5. Cynthia Fuchs Epstein, *Deceptive Distinctions* (New Haven: Yale University Press, 1988), p. 232.

6. English-language training exacerbates this tendency by teaching word meanings as opposites. Learning antonyms forces us to think in apparently unchanging oppositions: right-wrong, hot-cold, friend-foe, boy-girl, night-day. Dichotomized or dualistic thinking is criticized from diverse perspectives but especially those identified as postmodernism, poststructuralism, or postpositivism.

7. A vast feminist literature supports these claims but cannot be elaborated here. See, for example, Sandra Harding and Merrill Hintikka, eds., *Discovering Reality* (Dordrecht, Netherlands: Reidel Publishing, 1983); Evelyn Keller, *Reflections on Gender and Science* (New Haven: Yale University Press, 1985); Susan Hekman, *Gender and Knowledge* (Cambridge: Polity Press, 1990).

8. Consider how cultural media and academic studies highlight issues and activities that are masculinist or male-dominated: making money, competitive sports, crime, spying, fighting, killing, war, death, sexual pursuits and conquests, male bonding, public figures and events, diplomacy, national and international politics. In comparison, media and academic studies rarely focus on issues and activities associated with women's lives: poverty and physical victimization (assault, rape, homicide), care-taking activities (of children and other dependents), building cooperative interpersonal and community relations, reproducing everyday life and activities—in the home, family, workplace, public forums—and, especially, reproductive issues involving women's mental and physical health and when, whether, and under what circumstances to bear children.

9. Margaret L. Andersen, *Thinking About Women: Sociological and Feminist Perspectives* (New York: Macmillan, 1983), p. 213.

10. Ibid., p. 39.

11. Ibid.

12. Fred Halliday, "Hidden from International Relations: Women and the International Arena," *Millennium* 17 (Winter 1988): 419.

13. Sarah Brown, "Feminism, International Theory, and International Relations of Gender Inequality," *Millennium* 17 (Winter 1988): 461.

14. Wendy Brown, *Manhood and Politics* (Totowa, N.J.: Rowman and Littlefield, 1988), p. 4.

15. Ashley Montagu, *The Natural Superiority of Women* (New York: Collier Books, 1974), pp. 61–62.

16. W. Brown, *Manhood*, p. 182.

17. See Simon Dalby, "Security, Modernity, Ecology: The Dilemmas of Post Cold War Security Discourse," *Alternatives* 17 (1992): 95–133; V. Spike Peterson, "Security and Sovereign States: What Is at Stake in Taking Feminism Seriously?" in *Gendered States*, ed. V. Spike Peterson (Boulder, Colo.: Lynne Rienner Publishers, 1992), pp. 31–64.

18. For example, see Charles Tilly, "War Making and State Making as Organized Crime," in *Bringing the State Back In*, ed. Peter Evans, Dietrich Rueschemeyer, and Theda Skocpol (New York: Cambridge University Press, 1985).

19. Peterson, "Security and Sovereign States."

20. Historically, moralities generated from women's lives and experiences have been silenced or subordinated. In regard to facing difficult moral choices, Carol Gilligan argued that women are more likely to emphasize responsibility and care,

whereas men are more likely to emphasize a weighing of rights. See Gilligan, *In a Different Voice* (Cambridge: Harvard University Press, 1982). Important feminist treatments of justice include Susan Moller Okin, *Justice, Gender, and the Family* (New York: Basic Books, 1989); Iris Marion Young, *Justice and the Politics of Difference* (Princeton: Princeton University Press, 1990).

21. Richardson and Taylor, *Feminist Frontiers*, p. 2.

22. For a discussion of the implications for international relations of postpositivist and feminist critiques, see V. Spike Peterson, "Transgressing Boundaries: Theories of Knowledge, Gender, and International Relations," *Millennium* 21 (Summer 1992): 183–206.

CHAPTER THREE

1. World Commission on Environment and Development, *Our Common Future* (Oxford: Oxford University Press, 1987).

2. Special Issue, *Time* 136 (Fall 1990): 34.

3. Gayle Kirshenbaum and Shazia Rafi, "Inside the World's Largest Men's Club," *Ms.*, September/October 1992, pp. 16–19.

4. From B. Hunter, ed., *The Statesman Yearbook,* 129th ed. (New York: St. Martin's Press, 1992–1993); Jacques Lafitte, ed., *Who's Who in France 1991/92,* 23d ed. (Paris: Dictionnaire Bibliographique, 1991); U.S. Government Manual 1991/92, Office of the Federal Register, National Archives and Records Administration, *U.S. Department of State—Diplomatic List 1992* (May) (Lanham, Md.: Bernan Press, 1992).

5. United Nations, *The World's Women: 1970–1990 Trends and Statistics* (New York: United Nations, 1991), p. 32.

6. From Yolanda Dolling and Polly Cooper, eds., *Who's Who of Women in World Politics* (London: Bowker-Saur, 1991).

7. Janet M. Martin, "The Recruitment of Women to Cabinet and Subcabinet Posts," *Western Political Quarterly* 142 (March 1989): 164–165.

8. David W. Dent, "Women's Political Power," *Christian Science Monitor* 84, 145 (June 22, 1992): 19.

9. Carolyn H. Becraft, "Military Women: Policies and Politics," *Bureaucrat* 20, 3 (Fall 1991): 10.

10. Ibid., p. 12.

11. United Nations, *World's Women*, p. 31.

12. Vicky Randall, *Women and Politics: An International Perspective,* 2d ed. (Chicago: University of Chicago Press, 1987), p. 96; United Nations, Division for the Advancement of Women, "Women and Decision-Making," EGM/EPPDM/1989/WP.1/Rev.1 (Vienna: United Nations, 1989), p. 8.

13. United Nations, *World's Women*, p. 34.

14. United Nations, "Women and Decision-Making," p. 20.

15. Randall, *Women and Politics*, pp. 112–115.

16. United Nations, "Women and Decision-Making," pp. 8–10.

17. Cynthia Fuchs Epstein and Rose Laub Coser, eds., *Access to Power: Cross-National Studies of Women and Elites* (London: George Allen and Unwin, 1981), p. 7.

18. Randall, *Women and Politics*, pp. 112–114.

19. Reported in *National NOW Times,* April 1992, p. 12.

20. United Nations, *World's Women,* p. 35.

21. Ibid.

22. Randall, *Women and Politics,* p. 115.

23. Hilary Lips, *Women, Men, and Power* (Mountain View, Calif.: Mayfield, 1991), p. 191.

24. Randall, *Women and Politics,* pp. 83–94.

25. Eschel M. Rhoodie, *Discrimination Against Women: A Global Survey of the Economic, Educational, Social and Political Status of Women* (Jefferson, N.C.: McFarland, 1989), p. 28.

26. Randall, *Women and Politics,* p. 125.

27. Kathleen Staudt, "Women in High-Level Political Decision Making: A Global Analysis," EGM/EPPDM/1989/WP.2 (Vienna: United Nations, 1989), p. 11.

28. Reported in ibid., p. 11 and p. 32 n. 36.

29. Shirley Nuss, "Women and Political Life: Variations at the Global Level," *Women & Politics* 5, 2/3 (Summer/Fall 1985): 67.

30. United Nations, "Women and Decision-Making," p. 13.

31. Lips, *Women,* p. 159.

32. Laura Balbo, "The Servicing Work of Women and the Capitalist State," in *Political Power and Social Theory,* vol. 3, ed. Maurice Zeitlin (Greenwich, Conn.: JAI Press, 1982).

33. Virginia Sapiro, *The Political Integration of Women: Roles, Socialization, and Politics* (Urbana: University of Illinois Press, 1983).

34. Equal suffrage with men was not granted until 1928, but women over thirty years of age were permitted to vote in 1918.

35. Lips, *Women,* p. 179.

36. Ruth Leger Sivard, *Women … A World Survey* (Washington, D.C.: World Priorities, 1985), p. 19.

37. Judith Stiehm and Michelle Saint-Germain, *Men, Women and State Violence: Government and the Military* (Washington, D.C.: American Political Science Association, 1983), p. 15. According to *US News and World Report* 111, 7 (August 12, 1991), former military personnel serving in the Senate numbered 62 (of 100) and in the House, 219 (of 435).

38. Sheila Tobias, "Shifting Heroisms: The Uses of Military Service in Politics," in *Women, Militarism, and War,* ed. Jean Bethke Elshtain and Sheila Tobias (Savage, Md.: Rowman and Littlefield, 1990), pp. 163–185.

39. *Newsweek* (April 1, 1991, p. 24) acknowledged that his "politics are a mystery" but predicted that "Schwarzkopf could probably win the Democratic nomination if he wanted it and systematically set out to get it."

40. For a fascinating discussion of the role of "warrior queens" throughout history and of contemporary female leaders specifically, see Antonia Fraser, *Boadicea's Chariot: The Warrior Queens* (London: Weidenfeld and Nicholson, 1988).

41. Randall, *Women and Politics,* pp. 92–94.

42. Ibid., p. 93. The "men's club" atmosphere of the U.S. Senate was vividly revealed in televised hearings on the Clarence Thomas nomination for the Supreme Court. The Senate stands out as a bastion of male dominance: Including the four

women elected in 1992, only nineteen women have served in the Senate during its entire history.

43. Randall, *Women and Politics*, p. 132.

44. A May 1991 *New York Times* piece described Bush's presidency as an "all-male club" and characterized the inner sanctum as "what one top Republican calls 'a male prep school, locker room atmosphere,'" including "racy jokes" within the exclusively male group (May 20, 1991, pp. A1, B6). Paternalistic discrimination continues to shape women's participation in international politics: Cynthia Enloe (*Bananas, Beaches and Bases* [Berkeley: University of California Press, 1990], p. 113) reported that the Chinese government considers unmarried women (but not men!) too vulnerable and "open to temptations" to be posted abroad. And the UN has been faulted for continuing to let cultural stereotypes deter it from assigning women to particular countries. See Kirshenbaum and Rafi, "Inside," p. 19.

45. Staudt, "Women," pp. 5–8.

46. Daughter of Jawaharlal Nehru, Indira Gandhi rose through the ranks of the Congress party, serving briefly as president in 1959. She became prime minister after the sudden death of Prime Minister Shastri and quickly established her own formidable style. A cover story, "The Changing Woman," in *India Today* (July 15, 1992, pp. 36–43), argued that Gandhi "inspired scores of women politicians" who are now "coming in on their own steam, not as daughters, wives and widows of politicians. ... [They] are an altogether different breed of politician" (p. 39).

47. Randall, *Women and Politics*, p. 151; Staudt, *Women*, pp. 2–4.

48. Randall, *Women and Politics*, p. 152; Fraser, *Warrior Queens*, pp. 305–322.

49. Betsy Thom, "Women in International Organizations: Room at the Top," in *Access to Power: Cross-National Studies of Women and Elites*, ed. Cynthia F. Epstein and Rose L. Coser (London: George Allen and Unwin, 1981), p. 179.

50. Cynthia Enloe, "Womanandchildren: Making Feminist Sense of the Persian Gulf Crisis," *Village Voice*, September 25, 1990, pp. 29ff.

51. Helen Callaway, "Survival and Support: Women's Forms of Political Action," in *Caught Up in Conflict: Women's Responses to Political Strife*, ed. Rosemary Ridd and Helen Callaway (London: Macmillan, 1986), p. 228.

52. United Nations, *World's Women*, p. 31; Staudt, "Women," p. 8.

53. Randall, *Women and Politics*, p. 141; Dent, "Women's Political Power," p. 19.

54. United Nations, "Women and Decision-Making, " p. 11.

55. Ibid., p. 12.

56. United Nations, *World's Women*, pp. 39–42.

57. Nuss, "Women and Political Life," p. 67.

58. *Ms.*, January/February 1991, p. 12.

CHAPTER FOUR

1. See Jean Bethke Elshtain, *Women and War* (New York: Basic Books, 1987).

2. Cynthia Enloe, *Does Khaki Become You?* (Boston: South End Press, 1983), p. 212.

3. Ruth Leger Sivard, *World Military and Social Expenditures, 1991*, 14th ed. (Washington, D. C.: World Priorities, 1991), p. 11.

4. Ibid.

5. Ibid., p. 6.

6. Francine D'Amico, "Women as Warriors: Feminist Perspectives." Paper presented at 32nd Annual Convention of the International Studies Association, Vancouver, British Columbia, March 20–23, 1992, p. 29.

7. Ibid., p. 16.

8. As wives of soldiers, women may receive part of their husband's military salary and other "benefits" militaries may provide to military families.

9. D'Amico, "Women as Warriors," p. 27.

10. Susan Faludi, *Backlash: The Undeclared War Against American Women* (New York: Crown Publishers, 1991).

11. Ibid., pp. xiii–xvi.

12. Jane Midgley, *The Women's Budget* (Philadelphia: Women's International League for Peace and Freedom/The Jane Addams Peace Association, 1985), p. 29.

13. Jill Smolowe, "An Officer, Not a Gentleman, " *Time*, July 13, 1992, p. 36.

14. Enloe, *Does Khaki Become You?* p. 87.

15. D'Amico, "Women as Warriors," p. 31.

16. United Nations, *The World's Women: 1970–1990 Trends and Statistics* (New York: United Nations, 1991).

17. Amnesty International, *Women in the Front Line: Human Rights Violations Against Women* (New York: Amnesty International Publications, 1990).

18. The "International News" section of *Ms.* cited an Amnesty International report documenting the use of rape as a method of torture in Uganda and quoted a Serbian soldier saying, "We have orders to rape the girls." See *Ms.*, November/December 1992, pp. 10–11.

19. Cynthia Enloe, *Bananas, Beaches and Bases* (Berkeley: University of California Press, 1990), p. 66.

20. Ibid., pp. 86–87.

21. Ruth Leger Sivard, *World Military and Social Expenditures, 1987–88* (Washington, D.C.: World Priorities, 1987), p. 6.

22. Robin Morgan, *The Demon Lover: On the Sexuality of Terrorism* (New York: W. W. Norton, 1989), p. 45.

23. In 1990, of the estimated 20 million refugees in the world, approximately 80 percent were women and children. See Susan Forbes Martin, *Refugee Women* (London: ZED Books, 1991).

24. Ibid., p. 19.

25. Judith Hicks Stiehm, *Arms and the Enlisted Woman* (Philadelphia: Temple University Press, 1989).

26. D'Amico, "Women as Warriors," p. 27.

27. Enloe, *Does Khaki Become You?* p. 200.

28. Ibid., p. 195.

29. Stiehm, *Arms*, p. 273.

30. Elshtain, *Women and War*.

31. See, for example, Ifi Amadiume, *Male Daughters, Female Husbands* (London: Zed Books, 1987); Jocelyn Linniken, *Sacred Queens and Women of Consequence* (Ann Arbor: University of Michigan Press, 1990); and Harriet Whitehead, "The Bow and the Burden Strap: A New Look at Institutionalized Homosexuality in Native North

America," in *Sexual Meanings,* ed. Sherry B. Ortner and Harriet Whitehead (Cambridge: Cambridge University Press, 1981), pp. 80–115.

32. Ester Boserup, *Woman's Role in Economic Development* (New York: St. Martin's Press, 1970), p. 19.

33. Ibid.

34. See ibid., chap. 3.

35. Gita Sen and Caren Grown, *Development, Crises, and Alternative Visions: Third World Women's Perspectives* (New York: Monthly Review Press, 1987), p. 24.

36. Sue Ellen Charlton, *Women in Third World Development* (Boulder, Colo.: Westview Press, 1984), p. 61.

37. See ibid.

38. Eschel M. Rhoodie, *Discrimination Against Women* (Jefferson, N.C.: McFarland, 1989), p. 29.

39. Nuket Kardam, *Bringing Women In: Women's Issues in International Development Programs* (Boulder, Colo.: Lynne Rienner Publishers, 1991), p. 91.

40. Ibid., pp. 94, 56–57.

41. Ibid., pp. 23–24.

42. Ibid., p. 25.

43. Ibid.

44. Ibid., p. 54.

45. Ibid., p. 119.

46. For example, the July 1991 report of the International Fund for Agricultural Development (IFAD; a UN agency) indicated that the number of Third World rural women living in poverty had actually increased by 50 percent in the past twenty years; approximately "550 million women—who represent 67% of the agricultural labor force and produce up to 70% of their family's food supply—remain impoverished." From "International News: Rural Women Worldwide," *Ms.,* November/December 1991, p. 11.

47. Enloe, *Bananas, Beaches,* p. 1.

48. Thanh-Dam Truong, *Sex, Money and Morality: Prostitution and Tourism in South-East Asia* (London: Zed Books, 1990), p. 167.

49. Ibid., p. 173.

50. Ibid., p. 185.

51. Ibid., p. 182.

52. Enloe, *Bananas, Beaches,* p. 192.

53. Ibid., p. 188.

54. For example, an August 1992 report by the Women's Rights Project and Middle East Watch documented a pattern of physical abuse and mistreatment of Asian women working as maids in Kuwait. Since March 1991, "nearly 2,000 domestic servants have sought refuge from abusive employers." See "International News: Kuwait," *Ms.,* November/December 1992, p. 10.

55. ISIS: Women's International Information and Communication Service, *Women in Development* (Philadelphia: New Society Publishers, 1984), pp. 98–99.

56. Marilyn Waring, *If Women Counted* (San Francisco: Harper, 1988), p. 33.

57. United Nations, *The World's Women,* chap. 6.

58. Rachael Kamel, *The Global Factory: Analysis and Action for a New Economic Era* (Philadelphia: American Friends Service Committee, 1990), pp. 10–11.

59. Ibid., p. 35.

60. Ibid., p. 10.

61. Ibid., p. 37.

62. Ibid., p. 6.

63. Rhoodie, *Discrimination Against Women*, p. 30; and "Single-Parent Families: On the Rise, " *New York Times,* October 5, 1992, p. A16 (based on Census Bureau data).

64. See Jeanne Vickers, *Women and the World Economic Crisis* (London: ZED Books, 1991).

65. June Nash, "Global Integration and Subsistence Insecurity: Comparative Perspectives and Strategies," a presentation made at the Gender, Justice and Development Curriculum Institute, University of Massachusetts at Amherst, January 16, 1993.

66. Vandana Shiva, *Staying Alive: Women, Ecology, and Development* (London: Zed Books, 1989).

67. See Carolyn Merchant, *The Death of Nature: Women, Ecology and the Scientific Revolution* (New York: Harper & Row, 1980).

68. Sen and Grown, *Development, Crises,* pp. 44–52. The specter of ecological crisis appears in the First World as well. For example, oil spills, fuel shortages, and unreliable and/or unsafe water supplies are threats increasingly experienced worldwide.

69. Annabel Rodda, *Women and the Environment* (London: Zed Books, 1991).

70. In Mali, for example, certain trees are designated as "women" trees. This means that they are reserved for firewood, which is typically harvested from dead branches, and thus, the trees are not to be cut down. Ibid., p. 75.

71. Kamel, *The Global Factory,* p. 35.

72. Sivard, *World Military ... 1991,* p. 37.

73. Lin Nelson, "The Place of Women in Polluted Places," in *Reweaving the World: The Emergence of Ecofeminism,* ed. Irene Diamond and Gloria Feman Orenstein (San Francisco: Sierra Club Books, 1990), pp. 177–179.

74. Ibid., p. 179.

75. See Rosalie Bertell, *No Immediate Danger* (London: Women's Press, 1985).

76. Sivard, *World Military ... 1991,* p. 37.

77. Jodi L. Jacobson, "Coming to Grips with Abortion," in *State of the World 1991,* ed. Lester R. Brown (New York: W. W. Norton, 1991), p. 116.

78. Ibid., p. 128.

79. Ibid., p. 130.

80. Marcia Ann Gillespie, "HIV: The Global Crisis," *Ms.,* January/February 1991, p. 20.

CHAPTER FIVE

1. There are many feminisms. Readers should note that our brief survey cannot address all the varieties of feminism or the extensive overlap among them, which is

obscured by the simplifying labels we adopt here. We present characterizations of several feminisms in order to familiarize readers with a range of feminist issues and positions. In fact, most feminists identify with positions appearing in several of our characterizations.

2. For a discussion of the implications of postmodernist and feminist perspectives on IR, see V. Spike Peterson, "Transgressing Boundaries: Theories of Knowledge, Gender, and International Relations," *Millennium* (Summer 1992): 183–206.

3. See Maxine Molyneux, "Mobilization Without Emancipation? Women's Interests, the State, and Revolution in Nicaragua," *Feminist Studies* 11 (Summer 1985): 227–254.

4. Ibid., p. 233.

5. Strategic objectives include: "the abolition of the sexual division of labor, the alleviation of the burden of domestic labor and childcare, the removal of institutionalized forms of discrimination, the attainment of political equality, the establishment of freedom of choice over childbearing, and the adoption of adequate measures against male violence and control over women." Ibid., pp. 232–233.

6. See Sandi E. Cooper, "Women's Participation in European Peace Movements: The Struggle to Prevent World War I," in *Women and Peace: Theoretical, Historical, and Practical Perspectives*, ed. Ruth Roach Pierson (London: Croom Helm, 1987), pp. 51–75.

7. Ibid., pp. 63–65.

8. Ursula Herrmann, "Social Democratic Women in Germany and the Struggle for Peace Before and During the First World War," in *Women and Peace*, ed. Pierson, pp. 91–92.

9. See Lela B. Costin, "Feminism, Pacifism, Internationalism and the 1915 International Congress of Women," in *Women and Men's Wars*, ed. Judith Stiehm (Oxford: Pergamon Press, 1983), pp. 301–316.

10. See Yvonne Aleksandra Bennett, "Vera Brittain and the Peace Pledge Union: Women and Peace," in *Women and Peace*, ed. Pierson, pp. 192–213.

11. See Ruth Roach Pierson, *"They're Still Women After All": The Second World War and Canadian Womanhood* (Toronto: McClelland and Stewart, 1986); Maureen Honey, *Creating Rosie the Riveter: Class, Gender, and Propaganda During World War II* (Amherst: University of Massachusetts Press, 1984).

12. See D'Ann Campbell, *Women at War with America* (Cambridge: Harvard University Press, 1985).

13. Karen Beck Skold, "'The Job He Left Behind': American Women in the Shipyards During World War II," in *Women, War and Revolution*, ed. Carol R. Berkin and Clara M. Lovett (New York: Holmes and Meier Pub., 1980), p. 69.

14. James J. Kenneally, "Women in the United States and Trade Unionism," in *The World of Women's Trade Unionism*, ed. Norbert C. Soldon (Westport, Conn.: Greenwood Press, 1985), p. 80.

15. Campbell, *Women at War*, p. 216.

16. Carolyn Strange, "Mothers on the March: Maternalism in Women's Protest for Peace in North America and Western Europe, 1900–1985," in *Women and Social*

Protest, ed. Guida West and Rhoda Lois Blumberg (New York: Oxford University Press, 1990), p. 215.

17. Ibid., p. 216.

18. Berenice Carroll, "Women Take Action! Women's Direct Action and Social Change," *Women's Studies International Forum* 12, 1 (1989): 17.

19. See Anne Sisson Runyan, "Feminism, Peace, and International Politics: An Examination of Women Organizing Internationally for Peace and Security," (Ph.D. Dissertation, American University, Washington, D. C., 1988).

20. See ibid.

21. See, for example, Lynne Segal, *Is the Future Female?* (New York: Peter Bedwick Books, 1987); Jean Bethke Elshtain, *Women and War* (New York: Basic Books, 1987); Christine Sylvester, "Some Dangers in Merging Feminist and Peace Projects," *Alternatives* 12 (October 1987): 493–510.

22. See, for example, Berkin and Lovett, eds., *Women, War, and Revolution;* Miranda Davies, comp., *Third World—Second Sex: Women's Struggles and National Liberation* (London: Zed Books, 1983); and Linda Labao, "Women in Revolutionary Movements: Changing Patterns of Latin American Guerrilla Struggle, " in *Women and Social Protest,* ed. West and Blumberg, pp. 180–204.

23. Margaret Randall, *Sandino's Daughters: Testimonies of Nicaraguan Women in the Struggle* (Vancouver/Toronto: New Star Books, 1981), p. 10.

24. Ibid., p. 16.

25. Ibid., p. 66.

26. Jane Deighton, Rossana Horsley, Sarah Stewart, and Cathy Cain, *Sweet Ramparts: Women in Revolutionary Nicaragua* (London: War on Want and the Nicaraguan Solidarity Campaign, 1983), p. 50.

27. Ibid., p. 55.

28. Davies, *Third World—Second Sex,* p. 105.

29. Ibid.

30. Ibid., p. 119.

31. Ibid.

32. See Margaret E. Leahy, *Development Strategies and the Status of Women: A Comparative Study of the United States, Mexico, the Soviet Union, and Cuba* (Boulder, Colo.: Lynne Rienner Publishers, 1986).

33. Deighton et al., *Sweet Ramparts,* p. 45.

34. Ibid., p. 154.

35. Cynthia Enloe, *Bananas, Beaches and Bases* (Berkeley: University of California Press, 1990), p. 63.

36. See, for example, Minoll Reeves, *Female Warriors of Allah: Women and the Islamic Revolution* (New York: E. P. Dutton, 1989).

37. Elshtain, *Women and War,* p. 170.

38. See Robin Morgan, *The Demon Lover: On the Sexuality of Terrorism* (New York: W. W. Norton, 1989).

39. This does not mean, however, that women in such struggles are unaware of the ways that they are marginalized and stereotyped in the nation- and state-building process. For example, see Suha Sabbagh and Ghada Talhami, *Images and*

Reality: Palestinian Women Under Occupation and in the Diaspora (Washington, D.C.: Institute for Arab Women's Studies, 1990).

40. Cynthia A. Bouton, "Gendered Behavior in Subsistence Riots," *Journal of Social History* 23, 4 (Summer 1990); Carroll, "Women Take Action!" pp. 3–24.

41. Bouton, "Gendered Behavior," p. 743.

42. Carroll, "Women Take Action!" p. 8

43. Ibid.

44. Jackie Pope, "Women in the Welfare Rights Struggle: The Brooklyn Welfare Action Council," in *Women and Social Protest*, ed. West and Blumberg, p. 66.

45. United Nations, *The World's Women: 1970–1990 Trends and Statistics* (New York: United Nations, 1991), p. 90.

46. Debbie Taylor, "Women: An Analysis," in *Women: A World Report* (New York: Oxford University Press, 1985), p. 81.

47. Ibid., p. 26.

48. Marilyn Waring, "A Woman's Reckoning: Update on Unwaged Labor," *Ms.*, July/August 1991, p. 15.

49. Quoted in ibid. [no citation for original Lees remarks included in Waring article].

50. Carroll, "Women Take Action!"

51. Enloe, *Bananas, Beaches*, pp. 144–146.

52. Ibid., p. 39.

53. See ISIS: Women's International Information and Communication Service, *Women in Development* (Philadelphia: New Society Publishers, 1984).

54. See Rachael Kamel, *The Global Factory: Analysis and Action for a New Economic Era* (Philadelphia: American Friends Service Committee, 1990).

55. See Gita Sen and Caren Grown, *Development, Crises, and Alternative Visions: Third World Women's Perspectives* (New York: Monthly Review Press, 1987).

56. Jeanne Vickers, *Women and the World Economic Crisis* (London: Zed Books, 1991), p. 112.

57. Ibid.

58. Annabel Rodda, *Women and the Environment* (London: Zed Books, 1991), p. 110.

59. Ibid., p. 111.

60. Ibid., p. 116.

61. Quoted in Leonie Caldecott and Stephanie Leland, eds., *Reclaim the Earth: Women Speak Out for Life on Earth* (London: Women's Press, 1983), p. 6.

62. Ibid., p. 7.

63. Marvine Howe, "Women's Group Seeks Environmental Role," *New York Times*, October 28, 1990, p. 16.

CHAPTER SIX

1. Sandy Hill, "Survey: Women Officeholders Make a Difference," *Watertown Times*, October 7, 1992, citing recent studies by the Center for Research on Women in American Politics at Rutgers University.

2. Ibid.

3. Cynthia Enloe, *Bananas, Beaches and Bases* (Berkeley: University of California Press, 1990), pp. 197–198.

4. Christine Sylvester, "Feminists and Realists View Autonomy and Obligation in International Relations," in *Gendered States: Feminist (Re)Visions of International Relations Theory,* ed. V. Spike Peterson (Boulder, Colo.: Lynne Rienner Publishers, 1992), p. 157.

5. For the full text of CEDAW, see Hilkka Pietila and Jeanne Vickers, *Making Women Matter: The Role of the United Nations* (London: Zed Books, 1990). For the full text of the FLS, see Arvonne S. Fraser, *The U.N. Decade for Women: Documents and Dialogue* (Boulder, Colo.: Westview Press, 1987). See also the comprehensive report, United Nations, Division for the Advancement of Women, "Equality in Political Participation and Decision-Making," EGM/EPPDM/1989/1 (Vienna: United Nations, 1989).

6. United Nations, *The World's Women: 1970–1990 Trends and Statistics* (New York, 1991), p. 7; see also Women, Public Policy and Development Project of the Hubert H. Humphrey Institute of Public Affairs, *Forward Looking Strategies for the Advancement of Women to the Year 2000* (Minneapolis: University of Minnesota, 1985).

7. See Lori Heise, "Crimes of Gender," *Worldwatch,* March–April, 1989; Marilyn French, *The War Against Women* (New York: Simon & Schuster, 1992).

8. Gayle Kirshenbaum, "Why Aren't Human Rights Women's Rights?" *Ms.,* July/August 1991, p. 12. Also Natalie Kaufman Hevener, *International Law and the Status of Women* (Boulder, Colo.: Westview Press, 1983); V. Spike Peterson, "Whose Rights? A Critique of the 'Givens' in Human Rights Discourse," *Alternatives* (Summer 1990): 303–344.

9. See, for example, Patricia Lunneborg, *Women Changing Work* (New York: Bergin and Garvey, 1990).

10. Marilyn Waring, *If Women Counted* (San Francisco: Harper, 1988), p. 314.

11. For more background on this convention and other labor conventions relevant to women, see Carol Riegelman Lubin and Anne Winslow, *Social Justice for Women: The International Labor Organization and Women* (Durham, N.C.: Duke University Press, 1990).

12. For the full text of this convention, see Kathleen Barry, Charlotte Bunch, and Shirley Castley, eds., *International Feminism: Networking Against Female Sexual Slavery* (New York: International Women's Tribune Center, 1984).

13. Sylvester, "Feminists and Realists View Autonomy," p. 169.

14. For background on the Earth Charter and UNCED, see Jim McNeil, Peter Winsemius, and Taizo Yakushiji, *Beyond Interdependence: The Meshing of the World's Economy and the World's Ecology* (New York: Oxford University Press, 1991).

15. Enloe, *Bananas, Beaches,* p. 17.

□ □ □

Suggested Readings

Unpublished material is increasingly important. FEMISA is a new email network for people working on or thinking about women/gender/feminism in relation to world politics. To subscribe, send the following one-line message to listserv@csf.colorado.edu:

sub femisa yourname

Amnesty International. 1990. *Women in the Front Line: Human Rights Violations Against Women.* New York: Amnesty International Publications.

Ballara, Marcela. 1991. *Women and Literacy.* London: Zed Books.

Barry, Kathleen. 1979. *Female Sexual Slavery.* New York: Avon.

Beneria, Lourdes, ed. 1982. *Women and Development: The Sexual Division of Labor in Rural Societies.* New York: Praeger.

Bernard, Jessie. 1987. *The Female World from a Global Perspective.* Bloomington: Indiana University Press.

Blumberg, Rae Lesser. 1992. *Women, Development, and the Wealth of Nations: Making the Case for the Gender Variable.* Boulder, Colo.: Westview Press.

Bookman, Ann, and Sandra Morgen, eds. 1988. *Women and the Politics of Empowerment.* Philadelphia: Temple University Press.

Boulding, Elise. 1992. *The Underside of History: A View of Women Through Time.* 2 vols. Boulder, Colo.: Westview Press.

Boylan, Esther. 1991. *Women and Disability.* London: Zed Books.

Brittan, Arthur, and Mary Maynard. 1984. *Sexism, Racism and Oppression.* Oxford: Basil Blackwell.

Brocke-Utne, Birgit. 1985. *Educating for Peace.* Oxford: Pergamon Press.

_____. 1989. *Feminist Perspectives on Peace and Peace Education.* New York: Pergamon Press.

Brown, Wendy. 1988. *Manhood and Politics.* Totowa, N.J.: Rowman and Littlefield.

Bunch, Charlotte. 1988. *Passionate Politics.* New York: St. Martin's Press.

Burton, Clare. 1985. *Subordination: Feminism and Social Theory.* Sydney: Allen and Unwin.

Buvinic, Mayra, Margaret Lycette, and William McGreevey, eds. 1983. *Woman and Poverty in the Third World.* Baltimore: Johns Hopkins University Press.

Callaway, Helen. 1986. "Survival and Support: Women's Forms of Political Action." In *Caught Up in Conflict: Women's Responses to Political Strife,* ed. Rosemary Ridd and Helen Callaway. London: Macmillan.

Center for Political Leadership. 1992. *International Directory of Women's Political Leadership 1992.* College Park, Md.: Center for Political Leadership and Participation.

Charlton, Sue Ellen M. 1984. *Women in Third World Development.* Boulder, Colo.: Westview Press.

Charlton, Sue Ellen, Jane Everett, and Kathleen Staudt, eds. 1989. *Women, the State and Development.* Albany: State University of New York Press.

Clark, Lorenne M.G., and Lynda Lange, eds. 1979. *The Sexism of Social and Political Theory: Women and Reproduction from Plato to Nietzsche.* Toronto: University of Toronto Press.

Clatterbaugh, Kenneth. 1990. *Contemporary Perspectives on Masculinity: Men, Women, and Politics in Modern Society.* Boulder, Colo.: Westview Press.

Cohn, Carol. 1987. "Sex and Death in the Rational World of Defense Intellectuals." *Signs* 12 (Summer): 687–718.

Connell, R. W. 1987. *Gender and Power.* Cambridge: Polity Press.

Coole, Diana H. 1988. *Women in Political Theory: From Ancient Misogyny to Contemporary Feminism.* Boulder, Colo.: Lynne Rienner Publishers.

D'Amico, Francine, and Peter Beckman. Forthcoming. *Women and World Politics.* New York: Bergin and Garvey.

Davies, Miranda, comp. 1983. *Third World—Second Sex: Women's Struggles and National Liberation.* London: Zed Books.

———. 1987. *Third World—Second Sex.* Vol. 2. London: Zed Books.

Diamond, Irene, and Gloria Feman Orenstein, eds. 1990. *Reweaving the World: The Emergence of Ecofeminism.* San Francisco: Sierra Club Books.

Di Stefano, Christine. 1991. *Configurations of Masculinity: A Feminist Perspective on Modern Political Theory.* Ithaca: Cornell University Press.

Dolling, Yolanda, and Polly Cooper, eds. 1991. *Who's Who of Women in World Politics.* 1st ed. London: Bowker-Saur.

Duley, Margot I., and Mary I. Edwards, eds. 1986. *The Cross-Cultural Study of Women.* New York: Feminist Press.

Easlea, Brian. 1981. *Science and Sexual Oppression: Patriarchy's Confrontation with Woman and Nature.* London: Weidenfeld and Nicholson.

Eisenstein, Zillah R. 1981. *The Radical Future of Liberal Feminism.* Boston: Northeastern University Press.

Elshtain, Jean Bethke. 1987. *Women and War.* New York: Basic Books.

Elshtain, Jean Bethke, and Sheila Tobias. 1990. *Women, Militarism, and War.* Savage, Md.: Rowman and Littlefield.

Enloe, Cynthia. 1983. *Does Khaki Become You?* Boston: South End Press.

———. 1990. *Bananas, Beaches and Bases: Making Feminist Sense of International Politics.* Berkeley: University of California Press.

Epstein, Cynthia Fuchs, and Rose Laub Coser, eds. 1981. *Access to Power: Cross-National Studies of Women and Elites.* London: George Allen and Unwin.

Etienne, Mona, and Eleanor Leacock, eds. 1980. *Women and Colonization.* New York: Praeger.

Fenton, Thomas P., and Mary J. Heffron, eds. 1987. *Women in the Third World: A Directory of Resources.* New York: Orbis Books.

Fraser, Arvonne S. 1987. *The U.N. Decade for Women: Documents and Dialogue.* Boulder, Colo.: Westview Press.

French, Marilyn. 1992. *The War Against Women.* New York: Simon & Schuster.

Frye, Marilyn. 1983. *The Politics of Reality: Essays in Feminist Theory.* Trumansburg, N.Y.: Crossing Press.

Gonick, Lev S., and Edward Weisband, eds. 1992. *Teaching World Politics: Contending Pedagogies for a New World Order.* Boulder, Colo.: Westview Press.

Grant, Rebecca, and Kathleen Newland, eds. 1991. *Gender and International Relations.* Bloomington: Indiana University Press.

Hamilton, Roberta, and Michele Barrett, eds. 1986. *The Politics of Diversity: Feminism, Marxism, and Nationalism.* London: Verso.

Hanmer, Jalna, and Mary Maynard, eds. 1987. *Women, Violence and Social Control.* Atlantic Highlands, N.J.: Humanities Press.

Haraway, Donna. 1988. "Situated Knowledges: The Science Question in Feminism and the Privilege of Partial Perspective." *Feminist Studies* 14: 575–599.

Harding, Sandra. 1991. *Whose Science? Whose Knowledge?* Ithaca: Cornell University Press.

Harris, Adrienne, and Ynestra King, eds. 1989. *Rocking the Ship of State: Toward a Feminist Peace Politics.* Boulder, Colo.: Westview Press.

Hartsock, Nancy. 1983. *Money, Sex, and Power.* New York: Longman.

Hess, Beth B., and Myra Marx Ferree, eds. 1987. *Analyzing Gender: A Handbook of Social Science.* Newbury Park, Calif.: Sage.

Hevener, Natalie Kaufman. 1983. *International Law and the Status of Women.* Boulder, Colo.: Westview Press.

Hooks, Bell. 1984. *Feminist Theory: From Margin to Center.* Boston: South End Press.

ISIS: Women's International Information and Communication Service. 1984. *Women in Development.* Philadelphia: New Society Publishers.

_____. 1986. *Women, Struggles and Strategies: Third World Perspectives.* Rome: ISIS International.

Jaggar, Alison. 1983. *Feminist Politics and Human Nature.* Totowa, N.J.: Rowman and Allanheld.

Jaquette, Jane S. 1982. Review Essay: "Women and Modernization Theory: A Decade of Feminist Criticism." *World Politics* 34 (January): 267–284.

Jayawardena, Kumari. 1986. *Feminism and Nationalism in the Third World.* London: ZED Books.

Joekes, Susan P., comp. 1987. *Women in the World Economy.* New York: Oxford University Press.

Kamel, Rachael. 1990. *The Global Factory: Analysis and Action for a New Economic Era.* Philadelphia: American Friends Service Committee.

Kardam, Nuket. 1991. *Bringing Women In: Women's Issues in International Development Programs.* Boulder, Colo.: Lynne Rienner Publishers.

Lerner, Gerda. 1986. *The Creation of Patriarchy.* New York: Oxford University Press.

Lips, Hilary. 1991. *Women, Men, and Power.* Mountain View, Calif.: Mayfield.

Lubin, Carol Riegelman, and Anne Winslow. 1990. *Social Justice for Women: The International Labor Organization and Women.* Durham, N.C.: Duke University Press.

Macdonald, Sharon, Pat Holden, and Shirley Ardener, eds. 1987. *Images of Women in Peace and War: Cross-Cultural and Historical Perspectives.* London: Macmillan.

Martin, Susan Forbes. 1991. *Refugee Women.* London: Zed Books.

Mies, Maria. 1986. *Patriarchy and Accumulation on a World Scale: Women and the International Division of Labour.* London: Zed Books.

Mies, Maria, Veronika Bennholdt-Thomsen, and Claudia von Werlhof. 1988. *Women: The Last Colony.* London: Zed Books.

Mitter, Swasti. 1986. *Common Fate, Common Bond: Women in the Global Economy.* London: Pluto Press.

Mohanty, Chandra Talpade, Anne Russo, and Lourdes Torres, eds. 1991. *Third World Women and the Politics of Feminism.* Bloomington: Indiana University Press.

Molyneux, Maxine. 1985. "Mobilization Without Emancipation? Women's Interests, the State, and Revolution in Nicaragua." *Feminist Studies* 11 (Summer): 227–254.

Morgan, Robin. 1989. *The Demon Lover: The Sexuality of Terrorism.* New York: W. W. Norton.

Nash, June, and Maria Fernandez-Kelly, eds. 1983. *Women, Men, and the International Division of Labor.* Albany: State University of New York Press.

Nuss, Shirley. 1985. "Women and Political Life: Variations at the Global Level." *Women & Politics* 5, 2/3 (Summer/Fall): 65–78.

Pateman, Carole, and Elizabeth Gross, eds. 1986. *Feminist Challenges: Social and Political Theory.* Boston: Northeastern University Press.

Peterson, V. Spike. 1990. "Whose Rights? A Critique of the 'Givens' in Human Rights Discourse." *Alternatives* (Summer): 303–344.

——— . 1992. "Transgressing Boundaries: Theories of Knowledge, Gender, and International Relations." *Millennium* (Summer): 183–206.

——— , ed. 1992. *Gendered States: Feminist (Re)Visions of International Relations Theory.* Boulder, Colo.: Lynne Rienner Publishers.

Pettman, Ralph. 1991. *International Politics: Balance of Power, Balance of Productivity, Balance of Ideologies.* Boulder, Colo.: Lynne Rienner Publishers.

Pierson, Ruth Roach, ed. 1987. *Women and Peace: Theoretical, Historical, and Practical Perspectives.* London: Croom Helm.

Pietila, Hilkka, and Jeanne Vickers. 1990. *Making Women Matter: The Role of the United Nations.* London: Zed Books.

Randall, Vicky. 1987. *Women and Politics: An International Perspective.* 2d ed. Chicago: University of Chicago Press.

Reardon, Betty. 1985. *Sexism and the War System.* New York: Teachers College Press.

——— . 1988. *Comprehensive Peace Education: Educating for Global Responsibility.* New York: Teachers College Press.

Rhoodie, Eschel M. 1989. *Discrimination Against Women: A Global Survey of the Economic, Educational, Social and Political Status of Women.* Jefferson, N.C.: McFarland.

Rodda, Annabel. 1991. *Women and the Environment.* London: Zed Books.

Rothenberg, Paula S., ed. 1988. *Racism and Sexism: An Integrated Study.* New York: St. Martin's Press.

Runyan, Anne Sisson, and V. Spike Peterson. 1991. "The Radical Future of Realism: Feminist Subversions of IR Theory." *Alternatives* 16 (Winter): 67–106.

Russell, Diana E. H., ed. 1989. *Exposing Nuclear Phallacies*. New York: Pergamon Press.

Schmiltroch, Linda, ed. 1991. *Statistical Record of Women Worldwide*. Detroit: Gare Research.

Seager, Joni. 1990. *The State of the Earth Atlas*. New York: Simon and Schuster.

Seager, Joni, and Ann Olson. 1986. *Women in the World: An International Atlas*. New York: Simon & Schuster.

Sen, Gita, and Caren Grown. 1987. *Development, Crises, and Alternative Visions: Third World Women's Perspectives*. New York: Monthly Review Press.

Shiva, Vandana. 1988. *Staying Alive: Women, Ecology and Development*. London: Zed Press.

Sivard, Ruth Leger. 1985. *Women ... A World Survey*. Washington, D.C.: World Priorities.

Smith, Joan, Immanuel Wallerstein, and Hans-Dieter Evers, eds. 1984. *Households and the World-Economy*. Beverly Hills: Sage.

Smith, Joan, Jane Collins, Terence K. Hopkins, and Akbar Muhammad, eds. 1988. *Racism, Sexism, and the World-System*. New York: Greenwood Press.

Staudt, Kathleen, and Jane Jaquette, eds. 1983. *Women in Developing Countries: A Policy Focus*. New York: Haworth.

Stiehm, Judith. 1989. *Arms and the Enlisted Woman*. Philadelphia: Temple University Press.

———, ed. 1983. *Women and Men's Wars*. Oxford: Pergamon Press.

———, ed. 1984. *Women's Views of the Political World of Men*. Dobbs Ferry, N.Y.: Transnational Publishers.

Sylvester, Christine. 1987. "Some Dangers in Merging Feminist and Peace Projects." *Alternatives* 12 (October): 493–510.

———. 1988. "The Emperors' Theories and Transformations: Looking at the Field Through Feminist Lenses." In *Transformations in the Global Political Economy*, ed. Dennis Pirages and Christine Sylvester. London: Macmillan.

———. Forthcoming. *Feminist Theory and International Relations in a Postmodern Era*. Cambridge University Press.

Taylor, Debbie. 1985. *Women: A World Report*. New York: Oxford University Press.

Tetreault, Mary Ann, ed. Forthcoming. *Women and Revolution in Africa, Asia, and the New World*. Columbia: University of South Carolina Press.

Tickner, J. Ann. 1992. *Gender in International Relations: Feminist Perspectives on Achieving Global Security*. New York: Columbia University Press.

Tinker, Irene, ed. 1990. *Persistent Inequalities*. New York: Oxford University Press.

Tong, Rosemarie. 1989. *Feminist Thought*. Boulder, Colo.: Westview Press.

Truong, Thanh-Dam. 1990. *Sex, Money and Morality: Prostitution and Tourism in South-East Asia*. London: Zed Books.

United Nations. 1991. *The World's Women: 1970–1990 Trends and Statistics*. New York: United Nations.

Vickers, Jeanne. 1991. *Women and the World Economic Crisis*. London: Zed Books.

Walker, R.B.J. 1988. *One World, Many Worlds: Struggles for a Just World Peace.* Boulder, Colo.: Lynne Rienner Publishers.

Waring, Marilyn. 1988. *If Women Counted: A New Feminist Economics.* San Francisco: Harper.

West, Guida, and Rhoda Lois Blumberg, eds. 1990. *Women and Social Protest.* New York: Oxford University Press.

"Women, Men and the State." 1990. *Peace Review* 2 (Fall, Special Issue).

Young, Kate, Carol Wolkowitz, and Roslyn McCullagh, eds. 1984. *Of Marriage and the Market: Women's Subordination Internationally and Its Lessons.* London: Routledge and Kegan Paul.

□   □   □

Glossary

An **androcentric** (male-centered or male-as-norm) orientation treats men's ways of being and knowing as the norm or standard for *all* people (men and women), thus obscuring or denying alternative vantage points.

Colonization, or **colonialism,** is a practice that dates back to the early 1500s when European powers conquered and then ruled peoples throughout the Americas, Africa, and Asia. European monarchies extracted wealth and resources from the colonies through various means, including the use of slave labor; later, colonial empires helped fuel European industrial development. Although most direct colonial rule ended in the first two decades after World War II, it was replaced by neocolonialism, or imperialism, through which Western powers continued to indirectly control the economies and policies of politically independent Third World states.

The **debt crisis** that began in the 1980s was set in motion by the oil crisis in the 1970s when oil-producing nations deposited their windfall profits in the Western banking system. Western banks, in turn, encouraged many Third World countries to borrow money at low interest rates for development purposes. The worldwide recession during the late 1970s and early 1980s led to a reduction in the price of commodities that Third World countries typically export and a rise in interest rates. This combination of factors made it impossible for Third World borrowers to pay back their loans, threatening the stability of the Western banking system.

Dependent development, or **underdevelopment,** occurs when countries in the South are expected to provide cheap raw materials and agricultural commodities to meet the needs of industries and consumers in the North. The North is enriched and the South, which becomes dependent on the North for food and manufactured goods, becomes impoverished.

Development is usually measured by a country's GDP and its degree of industrialization, urbanization, technological advancement, export capability, and consumer orientation. Based on these economic measurements, developed countries are mostly those in the North (or the First World) and developing countries are mostly those in the South (or the Third World).

Dichotomy, as used herein, refers to a binary, oppositional contrast that privileges the first term over the second and obscures the historical and therefore changing meaning of the terms. This usage derives from contemporary critiques of Western philosophy.

Double workday refers to the dual labor women typically perform in the home and in the workplace. Many women in the Third World experience a triple day—

doing reproductive labor in the home, working for wages in the formal or informal economy, and growing subsistence crops to feed their families when their wages do not cover the price of food.

Empowerment, which means "enabling power" or "power to," is in contrast to "power-over." It refers to enhancing the capacity of people to live and work together productively and effectively rather than coercively dividing and controlling people in a way that reduces their abilities to act individually or collectively.

Export-processing zones (EPZs) (sometimes referred to as free trade zones or, in the case of Mexico, *maquiladoras*) are special areas created by governments, especially in the Third World, to attract TNCs to assemble products for export. Host governments promise cheap labor, minimal environmental or workplace regulation, and tax incentives.

The **feminine principle** refers to the basis on which many nonindustrialized people related to the land as a source of sustenance that could be used, but not abused. Central to this understanding was a reverance for the land as a mother and a recognition of women's stewardship of the land.

Feminism is an orientation that views gender as a fundamental ordering principle in today's world, that values women's diverse ways of being and knowing, and that promotes the transformation of gender and related hierarchies. There are many forms of feminism, including liberal, radical, cultural, socialist, postmodern, and ecofeminism.

Feminist describes individuals, perspectives, practices, and institutions that reflectively embody—and thereby promote—feminism.

The **food-fuel-water crises** result from deforestation and desertification brought on by "man-made" development practices and military operations. These crises threaten the ability of people in subsistence economies to meet their daily needs for food, water, and shelter.

Gender is not a physiological but a social concept that refers to sets of culturally defined character traits labeled masculinity and femininity.

Gender hierarchy describes a system of power that privileges men and that which is associated with masculinity over women and that which is associated with femininity. This "privileging" includes men's appropriation of women's productive and reproductive labor, men's control over women's bodies and regulation of women's activities, and the promotion of masculinism to "naturalize" (depoliticize) this hierarchy.

Gendered nationalism refers to the construction of a national identity and solidarity based on masculinist notions of self-determination and autonomy, which is at the expense of women's self-definitions and solidarity. Historically, gendered symbols, identities, and divisions of power, labor, and resources have been central features of nationalism.

A **gender-sensitive lens** is a way of looking at the world that enables us to see the extent and structure of gender hierarchy. It permits us to examine both how social constructions of masculinity and femininity shape our ways of thinking and knowing and how women's and men's lives are patterned differently as a consequence of gendered practices.

The **green revolution** refers to attempts to combat hunger and famine in the Third World by increasing crop yields through the introduction of highly mechanized, large-scale farming techniques developed in the First World.

The **gross domestic product** (GDP) is the total final output of goods and services produced by a nation within its borders. (The United States recently switched from using as its standard measure the gross national product [GNP], which includes U.S. income produced abroad, to the GDP.)

Heterosexism is an ideology that insists heterosexuality is the only "normal" and therefore legitimate mode of sexual and social relations. It presupposes a rigid and hierarchical gender dichotomy that is employed, especially, to "naturalize" gendered divisions of labor and power.

Ideology refers to a system of beliefs and expectations about human nature and social life that seems to justify the status quo by "naturalizing" (depoliticizing) existing arrangements.

Informal work (or **informal sector**) covers activities that earn money but are outside of formal agreements between workers and employers and are not regulated by the state; e.g., street vending, working in the home, underground drug selling.

Internal security refers to the steps taken typically by military regimes to quell revolts by their own people against their authority.

The **interstate system** comprises (formally) equal, sovereign states that are not controlled by a supranational authority and thus are presumed to exist in a state of anarchy where power politics reigns. States, however, do cooperate in various ways through international regimes or organizations, constituting regional and global systems that regulate to some degree the behavior of states.

Masculinism is the ideology that justifies and "naturalizes" gender hierarchy by not questioning the elevation of ways of being and knowing associated with men and masculinity over those associated with women and femininity.

Masculinist describes individuals, perspectives, practices, and institutions that unreflectively embody—and thereby reproduce—masculinism.

Militarization refers to processes by which characteristically military practices are extended into the civilian arena: for example, when businesses become dependent on military contracts, clothing fashions celebrate military styles, or toys and games embody military activities.

The **military-industrial complex** refers to the close association between government defense establishments and corporate defense contractors. This association can lead to a permanent war economy, in which productive resources are disproportionately channeled into the creation of weapons of mass destruction.

Modernization refers to Western or Eurocentric development strategies designed to increase a Third World country's GDP by stimulating industrialization and urbanization to produce an export-led economy. Critics of this kind of economic development argue that it is pursued at the expense of human development because it does not focus on meeting basic human needs.

Power-over systems are those that rely on coercion deployed from the top down in order to control those on the bottom of social, economic, and political hierarchies in the name of order and stability.

Power politics is a realist concept in IR that holds that in the absence of a supranational authority, states will pursue their own self-interests by amassing and deploying military and economic resources in order to gain power over other states or at least maintain a balance of power among competing states.

Practical gender interests, in contrast to strategic gender interests, are local and short term; addressing them requires a change in particular gender-based conditions but need not involve a transformation of gender hierarchy.

Productive labor, or **production,** usually covers work done for wages in the so-called public sector of the formal economy to produce surplus (nonsubsistence) goods and services that can be sold on the open market.

Proportional representation is an electoral system that allots parliamentary seats according to the proportion of votes received for a slate of candidates (e.g., in Norway), in contrast to single-member legislative districts (e.g., United States), where only the candidate with the most votes is seated.

The **public-private** separation or dichotomy refers to the (artificial) distinction between the private sphere of the home, to which women are assigned, and the public sphere of the workplace and government, to which men are assigned.

Reactive autonomy refers to an ideology that values independence over interdependence, separation over connection, and order over justice. It is most associated with realist thinking in IR.

Relational autonomy refers to an ideology that values interdependence over independence, connection over separation, and justice over order. It is most associated with feminist thinking in IR.

Reproductive labor, or **reproduction,** commonly implies activities (rarely referred to as work) undertaken in the the so-called private sphere (the home) that are necessary to meet the daily needs of household members and perpetuate human life. These activities include childbearing, child care, elderly care, housework, subsistence food production, and food preparation and are typically performed by women.

Sex refers to the categorization of persons as male or female based on chromosomal and/or anatomical characteristics.

Socialization is the process by which individuals learn the rules, roles, and relationships deemed appropriate within their culture; people "fit in" to the extent that they adopt and internalize these prescribed behavior patterns.

Sovereignty refers to a state's claim to self-determination and noninterference by other states. In this sense, it is an example of reactive autonomy.

A **stereotype** is an overgeneralized and rigid preconception of traits and behaviors attributed to a particular social group; such fixed images filter people's perceptions and shape their expectations.

Strategic gender interests, in contrast to practical gender interests, are large scale and long term; achieving them requires fundamental transformations constituting the elimination of gender hierarchy.

Structural adjustment refers to austerity programs imposed by the International Monetary Fund on Third World debtor countries amidst the debt crisis. These programs essentially required that debtor countries reduce government expenditure on social services and step up production for export to make more foreign exchange to pay back their loans.

Structural violence, in contrast to direct physical violence, arises from social, economic, and political structures that increase the vulnerability of various groupings of people (women, minorities, children, the aged, the disabled, gays and lesbians, and so forth) to many forms of harm (such as poverty, hunger, infant mortality, disease, isolation).

Terrorism usually refers to semirandom acts of violence perpetrated against innocent civilians by nonstate or antistate groups to bring (media and state) attention to their grievances, legitimate or illegitimate. However, states have also been known to engage in terrorism through the deployment of death squads or even nuclear weapons, which hold ordinary people hostage to the threat of nuclear annihilation.

The **United Nations System of National Accounts** (UNSNA) is supposedly an accounting of everything of value in or to the market in every country, but it fails to take into account such things as the value of reproductive labor and the costs of environmental degradation.

□ □ □

About the Book
and Authors

When we look at world politics through a different set of lenses—ones that reveal how the power of gender blinds us to the presence of women in international affairs—we begin to see what lies below the surface of the interstate power exchanges called international relations. Some women wield traditional international power as heads of state. There are also women in positions of less visible state and nonstate power, many of whom seek a more equal and just global order. And there are billions of women who bear, feed, clothe, and care for the world—whether as mothers, farmers, textile workers, electronics assemblers—yet have no formal political power.

Global Gender Issues connects the inequalities between women and men with the "world politics" of power, security, economy, and ecology. Through history, visual imagery, empirical data, theoretical analysis, and other narrative techniques, V. Spike Peterson and Anne Sisson Runyan alert us to gendered differences of power, violence, labor, and resources. In doing so, they suggest linkages between and among so-called women's issues and such world political matters as wars of secession, arms proliferation, global economic recession, and environmental degradation. At the same time, the authors hold out for us a clearly articulated, undogmatic hope for redefining and reorganizing gender relations and international relations as we begin to embrace difference, demand equality, and develop new standards of power and progress.

V. Spike Peterson is assistant professor of political science at the University of Arizona. **Anne Sisson Runyan** is associate professor of political science at the State University of New York–Potsdam.

Index